GET
STARTED IN
WRITING
HISTORICAL
FICTION

Get Started In Writing Historical Fiction

Emma Darwin

First published in Great Britain in 2016 by John Murray Learning. An Hachette UK company.

Copyright © Emma Darwin 2016

The right of Emma Darwin to be identified as the Author of the Work has been asserted by her in accordance with the Copyright, Designs and Patents Act 1988.

Database right Hodder & Stoughton (makers)

The Teach Yourself name is a registered trademark of Hachette UK.

British Library Cataloguing in Publication Data: a catalogue record for this title is available from the British Library.

Library of Congress Catalog Card Number: on file.

Paperback ISBN 978 1 473 60966 2

Ebook ISBN 978 1 473 60967 9

1

The publisher has used its best endeavours to ensure that any website addresses referred to in this book are correct and active at the time of going to press. However, the publisher and the author have no responsibility for the websites and can make no guarantee that a site will remain live or that the content will remain relevant, decent or appropriate.

The publisher has made every effort to mark as such all words which it believes to be trademarks. The publisher should also like to make it clear that the presence of a word in the book, whether marked or unmarked, in no way affects its legal status as a trademark.

Every reasonable effort has been made by the publisher to trace the copyright holders of material in this book. Any errors or omissions should be notified in writing to the publisher, who will endeavour to rectify the situation for any reprints and future editions.

Typeset by Cenveo® Publisher Services.

Printed and bound in Great Britain by CPI Group (UK) Ltd, Croydon, CR0 4YY.

John Murray Learning policy is to use papers that are natural, renewable and recyclable products and made from wood grown in sustainable forests. The logging and manufacturing processes are expected to conform to the environmental regulations of the country of origin.

John Murray Learning
Carmelite House
50 Victoria Embankment
London EC4Y 0DZ
www.hodder.co.uk

Also available in ebook

For Maura Dooley and Christopher Meredith,
who taught me how to write about writing.

Acknowledgements

This book has been much longer in the making than the months it has taken to write it, and just about every writer I have ever had a conversation with has unwittingly contributed to it. But very specific thanks go to:

All the writers I have taught or mentored, including commenters on my blog 'This Itch of Writing', and those at the back of the hall who simply asked a question which really made me think.

The authors with whom I've shared a seminar room, a platform or a pub table, most of all Debi Alper, in whose teacherly company so many of the ideas in this book got worked out, and also Jenn Ashworth, Linda Buckley-Archer, Annie Caulfield, Maura Dooley, Jerome de Groot, Suzannah Dunne, Essie Fox, Elizabeth Fremantle, Caroline Green, Philip Gross, Mary Hamer, Robert Low, Kellie Jackson, Pam Johnson, Maria McCann, Rose Melikan, Christopher Meredith, R. N. Morris, Sally Nicholls, Sally O'Reilly, Leila Rasheed, Susannah Rickards, Imogen Robertson, Manda Scott, M. L. Stedman and so many others.

My fellow members of the Historical Writers' Association, particularly those who contributed so many wonderful quotes: Martine Bailey, Christian Cameron, Robert Fabbri, Margaret George, Hilary Green, Caroline Rance, M. C. Scott, Sarah Sheridan, Deborah Swift and Robyn Young.

My editor, Victoria Roddam, and everyone else at John Murray Learning, and those who have worked with me on my own historical fiction: my agent Clare Alexander, and Charlotte Mendelson and Jennifer Brehl, from whom I have learned so much.

And, finally, many thanks to Jan Ryan for the alternative planning grid, and my daughter Violet-Finn Blackstaffe for compiling the Bibliography.

Thanks for permission to quote copyright material are due to: Fish Publishing for Michel Faber's Introduction in *All the King's Horses and Other Stories*; © Harry Bingham, 2010, *The Writers' and Artists' Yearbook Guide to Getting Published*, used by kind permission of A&C Black Academic and Professional, an imprint of Bloomsbury Publishing Plc. Nicola Morgan and Snowbooks for

Contents

	Introduction	xi
1	Why are you drawn to historical fiction?	1
2	Characters-in-action	17
3	Imagining the past	39
4	Researching the past	53
5	Hearing the voices: prose (i)	79
6	Story and plot: structure	101
7	How might you tell your story? prose (ii)	123
8	Different shapes of story: form	145
9	Different kinds of story: genre	167
10	Bringing it all together: process	187
11	What next?: going further, getting published	213
	Appendices	235
	Index	251

Introduction

Are you new to writing, or simply new to writing historical fiction? Have you always loved reading it, but only now feel brave enough to try writing it? Or have you only recently realized that stories can speak more powerfully when they're set at one remove from the contemporary world?

If you're new to writing of any kind, *Get Started In Writing Historical Fiction* will introduce you to the essential ideas and techniques for imagining and developing stories set in the past, and writing them vividly and expressively. If you've been writing for a while, this book should help you to understand the sideways shift your writerly self needs to make, in working with the past, in everything from how characters speak and travel to what they believe about the afterlife.

Wherever you are on the journey of becoming a writer, you will learn much about writing in general from trying historical fiction: it is, in a way, the ultimate challenge for a storyteller. You must evoke the otherness of a real Then and There for your readers, in ways that speak to our real Here and Now. Whatever your reason for picking up this book, I hope it gives you a start in understanding how historical fiction works, and in finding your own voice in this most exciting form and genre.

What counts as historical fiction?

The basic definition of historical fiction is that it is a story set in the past, but since neither history nor fiction is a solid, agreed concept, it's hardly surprising that their child isn't either. So, what counts as history, and what counts as fiction, for our purposes?

- **History for the writer?** A 25-year-old writer's 1950s-set novel is historical fiction to her, but not to her 80-year-old grandfather, who finds it odd to have it carefully explained how ration books or telegrams worked.
- **History for the reader?** If that grandfather wrote a novel set in the 1950s that he remembers so well, it's not historical to him, but it is to her. He'll need to make things more explicit for his granddaughter than he would for himself.

- **Fiction involving real historical characters?** If this were the definition of historical fiction, some of the great historical novels – William Golding's *Rites of Passage*, for example – would be excluded.

- **Fiction about some historical event?** Something that made the history books, in other words? History is all about change, and what people do when their world is changing fast *is* always particularly interesting. But what counts as 'historical' has been largely shaped by the educated, white men who did the counting. If fiction is in the business of evoking characters' lives 'as if' they were real lives, then it can be about anyone who is trying to survive in their own present, which is the past to us.

- **The book trade and the literary media** tend to think of historical fiction as fiction set in a time, and about a subject, which readers are already aware of and interested in, not least because that's what is easiest to sell.

- **The Historical Novel Society and the Historical Writers' Association** define historical fiction as, respectively, 30 and 50 years before our present time.

- **What 'history' and 'fiction' mean for the writer's job.** Unlike writers of contemporary-set fiction or speculative fiction, you're writing of times and places that you can't know directly but which were real and were recorded; unlike historians, you must write them 'as if' you were in fact there. So, for the purposes of this book, I'm working with Margaret Atwood's definition of historical fiction: '**Fiction set in a time before the writer came to consciousness**'.

- **Historical fiction is not life writing, biography or creative non-fiction.** Fascinating hybrid forms are emerging which use the techniques of fiction to tell real-life stories, so it's not always easy to draw the line between the two. But if you want to claim your narrative as a faithful representation of a life or events, then the narrative logic of cause and effect is pretty much prescribed for you, and the proportion of imagining and changing you can do is fairly small. If you want to imagine and shape things beyond what a biographer would allow themselves – re-create minds, write direct dialogue, evoke emotion and sensation, shape satisfying stories 'as if' we were there – then you're moving into the territory of biographical or historical fiction. That's fine, of course: call it a novel, make your own rules about what you must stick to and what you can invent, and get going.

How to use this book

I have built the book to work in an organized, cumulative way from your first steps, through first-drafting, completing and polishing stories, to thinking about a whole novel and how you might tackle it. The Workshop exercise in each chapter is particularly important, because taking the workshopping, editing stage seriously is the mark of someone who takes their writing seriously. However, there's nothing to stop you from dipping in to think about a specific issue, and many of the Snapshot and Write exercises included in each chapter also work as standalone writing prompts, warm-ups, planning tricks and confidence boosters.

Not all the writing exercises will result in a piece of writing which in itself is successful. In any craft, your first tries are likely to turn out a bit rough and awkward, and practising things in isolation may seem odd and unsatisfactory, but please don't let that dishearten you.

First, here is a quick key to the different types of exercise and features in the book:

 Write – exercises where you'll be asked to create your own piece of writing, perhaps 750–1,000 words long

 Snapshot – shorter activities about a particular aspect of creative writing: 200 words will usually be enough

 Workshop – a series of guided questions that will help you reflect on a piece of writing

 Edit – a chance to rework and strengthen a piece you've already created

 Key quote – words of wisdom from those who know

 Key idea – an important concept to grasp

 Focus point – advice to take forward

Next step – where we're going next.

If you want to develop as a writer, it's crucial to keep your writing mind ticking over by keeping a notebook: ideally, one nice enough to be encouraging, easily portable, not intimidatingly grand, which doesn't need a charged battery. Into your notebook go: little bits of history in buildings, landscapes, relics and notices; tiny pen-portraits of what you can see while you're waiting for a train, scraps of overheard conversation; sketch maps of the village in your current story; and mind maps of ideas or images which might make a future story.

Finally, much that I'm discussing here I first explored on my blog, 'This Itch of Writing'. Some of the posts go into more detail than is possible in print, so if you want to find out more, do go to thisitchofwriting.com and follow the links to the blog.

A note on pronouns

English has no gender-neutral singular pronoun, but *she or he* often renders a sentence very awkward, while the old-fashioned assumption that *he* includes both genders is sexist, and the modern academic practice of alternating paragraphs of *she* and *he* is logical but confusing in practice. So, generally speaking, when I need a pronoun to refer to a non-specific reader, writer or character, I have followed seven centuries of English usage in using *they*, *them*, *their* and the rest.

1

Why are you drawn to historical fiction?

Writers come to historical fiction for different reasons. This chapter explores what your reasons are, how you might therefore set about imagining and recreating places and times that you can't have experienced directly, and how to get started on an actual story.

Sara Sheridan

Sara Sheridan writes historical fiction based on real nineteenth-century explorers, and historical crime.

'The best historical stories capture the modern imagination because they are, in many senses, still current – part of a continuum. ... Writing historical fiction has many common traits with writing sci-fi or fantasy books. The past is another country – a very different world – and historical readers want to see, smell and touch what it was like living there.'

Why do you want to write fiction?

The most important thing about historical fiction is that it *is* fiction: a story of events that never happened, told 'as if' they did happen. Historians and biographers are bound by the constraints of what can be proved or assumed to have happened, but you have decided, already, that you don't want to be bound that way. Fiction escapes from the confines of real life so that the reader can 'come home' with a new, wider sense of what it is to be human: to fear, laugh, cook, have sex, clean teeth, fight, go shopping, worship or dream. Fiction writers deal in the riches of what we imagine *could* have happened – what's possible, or plausible, or even downright fantastical. So our job is to make our fiction so convincing that the reader 'agrees to forget' that none of this actually happened or, at least, we can't know if it did.

Key idea: write what you want, and make us *believe* you know it

Have you ever been told that you should 'write what you know'? That command has probably depressed you or made you cross. Many of us aren't interested in writing explicitly about our direct experience, but for a story to work on the reader it needs to have a similar smell of authenticity, a sense of 'reality'. In other words, if you want to write historical fiction, or, indeed, speculative, fantasy or science fiction, then the motto has to be, 'Write what you want, and make us *believe* – at least while we're reading – that you know it.'

Snapshot: all six senses

Settle yourself and, using a watch or a timer,
- spend one minute writing down everything that you can **see**
- then one minute writing down everything you can **hear**
- a minute of everything you can **feel**
- a minute of what you can **smell**
- a minute of **taste**
- and finally a minute of what's called **kinaesthesia**: how your shoulder knows that you've got your head cocked to one side, the pressure between your knees where you've crossed them, the way the table-edge presses into your wrist.

It's important that you do the senses in that order: sight – sound – touch – smell – taste – body sense, and that you don't let yourself give up before each minute is up: patiently *staying* with not-knowing-what-to-write is important because that's when the creative mind gets a chance to work.

Now, close your eyes and imagine your way back into the historical time and place of a story you want to write. Don't worry if you feel you don't know it very well yet, just let your imagination rip. Open your eyes and **do exactly the same exercise for that time and place.**

Focus point: we experience the world through our bodies, with all six senses

Cognitive science explains that when we're trying to decide whether something is true or not, we test it against our own physical and mental experience. So an important way of getting your reader to 'agree to forget' that this story isn't actually 'real' is to engage their own sense-experience and use it to serve your story. You may not know, or need to know, the precise name of that rope far overhead at the top of the mizzen mast: you *do* need to evoke the scrubbed, salt-soaked deck-planks under our bare feet, and the way the ship's movement keeps rolling us towards the side.

Why do you want to write *historical* fiction?

By definition you can't have experienced the world you want to write, which makes it harder to imagine and recreate the lives in it. So why do *you* want to write historical fiction? To help you to make writerly choices, ask yourself what your reasons are:

- **To explore lives that until recently weren't recorded at all,** or only by educated, white men: the lives of women, servants, children, immigrants, convicts, slaves, the marginal, the mad, the strange, the oppressed. (*The Long Song* by Andrea Levy)
- **To explore the inner life and subjective experience of people whose outer life *is* well recorded:** kings and queens, the rich and powerful, the famous and the infamous, men and women who shaped the worlds they knew, or discovered new ones. (*Wolf Hall* by Hilary Mantel)
- **To evoke a famous event in history,** and what it was like to live through it. (*The Siege* by Helen Dunmore)
- **To explore the past lives you sense** in old buildings and landscapes and bring them to full life. (*Stone Angel* by Barry Unsworth)

- **To evoke a particular time in history** which has a very strong atmosphere and dynamic which you want to capture. (*Pure* by Andrew Miller)
- **To explore fundamental human drives, desires and dilemmas,** by stepping away from the clutter and close-up familiarity of the modern world. (*Rites of Passage* by William Golding and its sequels in the 'To the Ends of the Earth' trilogy)
- **To explore modern drives, desires and dilemmas,** by stepping sideways from a specific modern world to look at how all humans are shaped by their circumstances. (*Restoration* by Rose Tremain)
- **To write about sex and love with more at stake:** with more barriers of law and custom before two people can get together; when there's no contraception and no divorce; when everyone knows that Hell is waiting for sinners. (*The Far Pavilions* by M. M. Kaye)
- **To write about violence and death when both are closer:** when death is only a sword's-length or witch's curse away; when small wounds can kill you; when honour is sometimes more important than life; when you need a priest before you can die without fear. (*Master and Commander* by Patrick O'Brian)
- **To work with gowns and breeches because they're more fun** than jeans and sweaters; to travel on horses or in chariots instead of cars and planes; to use unreliable human messengers instead of telephones or email. (*The Grand Sophy* by Georgette Heyer)
- **To exploit the comic or satirical potential** of casting what the reader knows of history into a modern tone: the Ancient Greek landlady who's stingy with the bathwater, the Aztec warrior worried about his drooping star-rating. (*The Walled Orchard* by Tom Holt)
- **To exploit the potential for magic and/or fantasy** if you move away from the literal depiction of the modern world. Who knows what could have happened in the dark forests and on the high seas when witches stalked the earth? (*Jonathan Strange & Mr Norrell* by Susannah Clarke)

Key idea: you can't write what you don't read and enjoy

We were all readers before we were writers and it's that reading which has trained your instincts for how stories work, and wired you as a storyteller. But if you want to write a form or genre of story that you don't already know, then you will need to acquire those instincts for it. If you don't learn to love the genre (however much you also see its limitations), then readers who *do* love it will sense that straight away. So head down to the library or the bookshop, or fire up your e-reader, and get reading. How does this kind of story work? What satisfactions does it offer the reader? What makes it lovable?

Write: evoke an historical place

Think about an historical place you've actually been to. Scribble down some notes, and perhaps dig out any souvenirs, to bring the memories up to the surface. *Set aside* your records, and start writing. Draw on your memory to write an evocation of the place: the physical, mental and emotional experience of being there, knowing that other lives were there before you. Remember to check in with all six senses, and if you find one of those lives coming alive, then let them on to the page.

Resist copying your notes straight into this piece: you're trying to evoke the experience of being there as you would in a story, not inform us about the place like a tour guide. First-draft your evocation and set it aside, without revising or editing it for now.

Here and Now, There and Then

You've just been working with the relationship between your Here and Now, and the There and Then of the past, but for the characters in your historical fiction, the world you're writing *is* their 'here and now'. Your challenge is to create them and their world for the reader with the same vividness and immediacy as you easily would if you were writing about the world inside and outside your own front door.

Snapshot: what fictional stories might come from the historical place you've just evoked?

Make a few notes about several possibilities, however vague. Notice which stories might address universals: perhaps love, birth, jealousy, greed. And which of them are all about embodying an actual historical moment, turning point or real historical character? Are any of them both?

How might you shape your story?

In reading any fiction, we've 'agreed to forget' that the lives in the story never happened, and want to read as if the characters are 'real people'. So in most fiction the narrative never steps outside the boundaries of the main characters' present moment, which is shaped by their immediate past and the future they hope for or fear. Even when novels such as A. S. Byatt's *Possession* play games with the novel in our hands being a constructed thing and not a 'real' story, the game only works while we're enjoying the tension between feeling that these people are real and knowing that they're not.

But fiction can't help drawing on our sense that the Now of the story is a chunk cut from a longer continuum of time and life. Some stories end with a strong sense of repercussions looming in the future, and not just because the writer has a sequel in mind. Some follow more than one generation of a family or society. Some fiction works with real events that the reader knows had a sequel in real life, even though the characters can't know. Some stories tell the story not in the normal order of time, but moving backwards as well as forwards, so that readers have to 'assemble' the actual order of events, and their connections, for themselves. Other novels again (although not so often short stories) weave together completely different strands of narrative, set perhaps in different centuries, to make a parallel narrative. Counterfactual stories work with 'What if?': for example, Robert Harris's *Fatherland*. We'll explore different structures for your story further in Chapter 8.

Starting to write

As children, we write something down to be as nearly 'right' as we can manage: our minds *try* to get the ideas right and the words as correct as we go. Later, we learn to check it, then we learn the value of a first draft, which we'll finally revise to be even more correct as a final draft. But 'right' and correctness are all about left-brain, logical, sequential orderliness and rules, and the creative self doesn't work that way, any more than a small child who wants to run and jump and throw should be expected to conform to the offside rule. The creative imagination uses both sides of the brain in an a-rational way: seeing connections where there were none, growing images which make metaphorical but not literal sense, following wherever the story-mind wants to go, and digging in its word-hoard to express what's being imagined. Even so, first drafts can be terribly depressing and therefore inhibiting, because they fall so short of the story that was in your head. Ernest Hemingway articulated that when he declared that every first draft, whatever the project, is terrible. Ann Lamott, in her classic guide for aspiring writers *Bird by Bird*, explains that this is simply an inevitable part of the process:

 ## Ann Lamott

Ann Lamott is a novelist and non-fiction writer.

'...*shitty first drafts. All good writers write them. This is how they end up with good second drafts and terrific third drafts … I know some very great writers, writers you love who write beautifully and have made a great deal of money, and not one of them sits down routinely feeling wildly enthusiastic and confident.*'

Key idea: crazy first drafts

Lamott's idea is very freeing for most writers. You don't have to get this 'right', she is implying, because that can come later: you only have to get it written. Nor do you have to wait until you're sure that you've got it all sorted out in your head, because you may never feel like that. Indeed, some writers prefer to think of their 'first draft' as what writing teacher Barbara Baig, in *How to Be a Writer*, calls a 'zero draft', which just gathers the material into a single document. Even more useful, I think, is to reckon that since this first draft doesn't have to be 'right', it's safe to let rip, as crazily as you like, without letting your 'Inner Editor' stop the imagining to check or correct things. Uncensored, your creative brain is free to discover the most exciting possibilities in the richest words. Only in second draft do you let your Inner Editor back in, to make sure this rich, crazy muddle becomes something rich and un-muddled for readers.

Snapshot: reading like a writer

Pick one of your favourite historical novels and open it at random. Read the pair of pages you can see, and stop. If you'd just been given a copy of these two pages and never read the whole book, what would make you know this story is set in the past? And what makes a connection with the present? Which of these have those effects?

- the characters' voices in dialogue or thoughts
- how the action, description, etc. are written, i.e. the 'voice' of the narrative
- any documents – letters, diaries, etc. – that are part of the story
- the setting: material things, clothes, food, technology, transport
- what the characters talk about: events and everyday life, beliefs and passions
- how characters behave towards one another

Do any of those elements feel 'wrong'? Too modern, too clunkily ancient, the wrong historical period, or just plain old awkward? Do you know the writer's got it wrong or does it challenge something you thought was historical fact? Might that be deliberate on the part of the writer? Why?

Take a few lines of the writing which feel most strongly historical. What's different from how they might be written in a novel set in modern times? The vocabulary? The grammar? The rhythm and syntax (word order)? The imagery? Maybe even the spellings? How much is the same as you'd find in a modern-set novel?

Focus point: we were all readers before we were writers

It's reading which creates, shapes and fuels your writing. Writers still read *immersively* as children and most adults do, plunging into the story, but we also read *analytically*, as in the Snapshot exercise: consciously noticing and learning how writing works. It's not just to help with future writing: we also go to good writers when the existing project has set us a challenge we don't know how to tackle. Gradually, you learn to do both kinds of reading at once, and alter the balance depending on whether you want a darned good read or writerly ideas and inspiration.

Key idea: reading fuels writing

Reading non-fiction and fiction shows you worlds and times that you *can't* experience directly, and so fills your hoard of voices, ideas, facts, images and emotions. What you read enters your creative stores and 'composts down', waiting for your own creative work to need it. But good writing also opens your eyes and ears and mind, ready for when you 'come home' to the real world. That extra awareness, that thinner skin, is something you have to cultivate as a writer. It's the key to experiencing the world fully, and that's the beginning of making the reader believe that you 'know it'. So reading isn't just training for writers, it's also our rocket fuel.

Write: objects hold stories

Think of an historical object which you've never seen, but know would have existed. It might be a toy your German grandfather left behind when he came to England on the Kindertransport, or the dagger that Brutus used to assassinate Julius Caesar. Don't look things up, and don't worry about being accurate for now.

Bring the object to the front of your imagination and make notes to evoke its *physical* presence. Make sure you've checked in with all six senses including kinaesthesia (what's it like to pick up, hold, throw, sit on?). Now start imagining outwards to one moment in its life, and keep jotting down notes. You probably first thought of the big moment – grandfather leaving the toy behind, Brutus holding the dagger – but our first thoughts are usually our default ideas: rather well worn or clichéd. So imagine further: where else might it have been? And where else again? Maybe your grandfather's toy had been *his* grandmother's. Maybe Brutus's dagger had been captured from a Phoenician slave trader. Again, this is crazy first-draft stuff: let your imagination run.

When you've found an atmospheric place, start making notes. Is the object here old, or new? What's around it? Again, go beyond your first thoughts to your second or third: are they more interesting? Who in this setting might have interacted with your object? Who else? Who loved it? Who hated it? Why? Pick one of those people: what did they do with this object? Hide it? Sell it? Buy another? Steal it? Destroy it? Give it away gladly? Give it away reluctantly? Who to?

Draft a story jumped off some of these ideas about how a character acts. Don't worry about it being historically accurate or polished. This is a crazy first draft: a rough-hewn story complete with a beginning, a middle and an end.

Writing what you don't (yet) know

Your early efforts at writing people and places that you know only from a book or two will inevitably be second-hand, and probably generalized and generic: you're imitating another writer's take on those worlds. That's why aspiring writers are told to 'write what you know', whether that's your high street or your dreams, because that will have the authenticity of direct experience. It feels *real* to the reader, so they willingly forget to disbelieve. You could say that 'what-you-know writing' is the gold standard for that kind of convincingness.

When you write historical fiction, imagination brings researched facts alive, and research digs up things you'd never have imagined existed: you *come to know* those times and places so that your story has the same quality of first-handness.

Historians and biographers want to bring the worlds they write about alive too, of course: try reading writers such as Simon Schama or Juliet Gardiner (*Wartime Britain, 1939–1945*) to get a sense of just how well some do so. But good historians distinguish carefully and clearly, in the text, between what facts they can prove, what was recorded as fact at the time (which may not be proved, or even true), and what is the historian's informed guesswork (which is another word for imaginative re-creation).

Historical novelists may do the same research and work with the same materials: compare Simon Schama's history *Citizens* and Hilary Mantel's novel *A Place of Greater Safety* and you'll see what I mean. But we're taking the different threads of knowledge, invention and research, and twisting and blending them together into a whole, single narrative. For that to happen, you must grant the researched material no special status, and no more importance, than anything else you already know or newly imagine: they must all 'compost down' together until your story starts needing them.

The other reason that aspiring writers are told to 'write what you know' is that beginner writers tend to start by writing versions of other writers' fictional worlds, drawing on Georgette Heyer's Regency or Ben Kane's Rome. Terrific though they are, there's a vast difference between researching a crime drama by watching cop shows, and by spending time in your local police station. Ben Kane's Rome has already gone through one writer's brain: not only do you not know what he's invented and what is factually true, but it will be third-hand when it reaches *your* reader. The scent of authenticity will have long gone.

Deborah Swift

Deborah Swift writes historical fiction for adults and young adults.

'The difference between a historical novel and historical non-fiction is the difference between show and tell. Historians tell us what happened. Historical novels show us what happened, and what's more, force us to live it moment by moment.'

Snapshot: what do you need to know that you don't know yet?

Almost any writing project needs some kind of research, even if it's only walking down your high street. In historical fiction, the research you need for accuracy does matter, but the real reason for research is to help you write this world and these people 'as if you know them'.

Go back to your (crazy) first draft of your story about an historical object. Jot down some of the things in the story that you 'don't know yet'. What might you need to imagine more fully, to develop this first draft into a story? What might you need to find out?

How might you get to know these things? Will the Internet or a book be enough? Who might be able to give you information or advice? Might you want to get hold of things written in the period of the story? Might you physically go somewhere to experience something directly?

Do some of the research. Did you find what you wanted? Did you find anything else that sparked ideas or was useful? Would a different research method have been more fruitful?

Showing and Evoking; Telling and Informing

'Showing and Telling' are the catch-all words for a very important idea in writing, and though you may have heard people say 'Show, don't tell', no statement about writing could be more wrong-headed: writers need to do both. There is more on this in Chapter 7, but the basic idea is very straightforward.

In many ways a better word for **Showing** is **Evoking**: making the reader feel they're in the imagined world. This is 'feel' as in smell, touch, see, hear, and so believe the actual physical, mental and emotional experience. As John Gardner says in *The Art of Fiction*, because humans test new things for truth by measuring them against their experience, writers get readers to read as if fiction were true by writing the immediate physical and emotional actions and experience of the characters: your rage beating in your ears, the wind whipping your cheeks, a beggar clutching at your enemy's coat.

Telling might better be called **Informing**: conveying information and understanding, and covering the narrative ground. The narrator may be a character or an external narrator who's telling the story in third person, and says things like, 'Once upon a time' to show where the story starts, relate how 'That was the year the peasants made themselves into an army', or 'The mountains were smothered in fine, volcanic ash'. Telling means working with the larger needs of the storytelling and sometimes stepping back from the direct physical and mental experience.

Workshop: what have you got in your (crazy) first draft?

Choose either your evocation of an historical place or your story based on an historical object. If you possibly can, set the document to double-spacing and print it out. If you can't print it out, set your word-processing program to 'Track Changes', so that you can see what changes you make.

Then read slowly and steadily through the piece, trying to experience the piece *as a reader* and recording your reactions: what feels good, and what doesn't? My image for this is pinging a wine glass with a fingernail: if it's whole, it rings sweetly and it gets a tick, if it's cracked there's a dull little clunk and I put a wiggly line underneath it. You might scribble a quick note about what's wrong if you know straight away, but don't let that divert you from reading steadily on. In other words, *don't try to change things yet*, because in doing so you lose touch with the readerly experience of the piece.

Then go back to the beginning and start trying to understand why the things which work do work, and what's going on with the bits that don't. And I do mean 'bits that don't work' because there's no 'wrong' at first-draft stage, only placeholder-words waiting for when you find better ones.

- Where have you Shown? Was that the right choice here? How could you make the Showing more vivid and immediate in evoking the mental and physical moment?

- Where have you Told? Was that the right choice here? How could you make the Telling more compelling in how it draws the reader onwards into the story?

- What sort of shape does the piece have? Is there a bit too much beginning stuff, as you wrote your way into the story? Would it work better if you thinned out or even cut it?

- How does it finish? With a satisfying, rounded-out end? With an intriguing sense that another story might be starting up? A bit hastily or feebly as you ran out of steam or time?

- What challenges did this piece set you? How might you meet them? Is there research which would help?

Key idea: storytelling has a rhythm of Telling and Showing

All storytelling has a rhythm of getting in close to the immediate physical and mental experience of characters – which for short we call Showing – and pulling out to narrate the overall ideas and events of the story, which for short we call Telling. A large part of the skill of storytelling is knowing which to do when, and how to move abruptly or smoothly to and fro between them.

Focus point: know what kind of work you're doing today

In the old days of typewriters and handwriting, writers knew at any moment whether they were making new words or revising existing ones. Now, with computers, everything always looks brand-new and perfect, you can fiddle with it for ever, and it's horribly easy to get side-tracked. You're trying to add new words or sort out a specific problem, but you keep seeing new things to change, re-changing things you changed yesterday, half-changing things, or forgetting to deal with the consequences elsewhere in the story. So it's crucial to know, when you sit down, what job you're doing today, and to stick to it until it's done.

Edit: revise your story to be as effective as possible

Take your marked-up first draft and start reworking it, taking into account your thinking from the Workshop. If you work on the computer, work on a duplicate of the original file, in case you decide that it's all gone horribly wrong. If you don't feel terribly confident of grammar, syntax or spelling, now's the moment to start taking that into account. As much as possible, look things up (for books to help you, see Appendix II), as that's how you learn things. If you use the computer to spell-check, make sure the dictionary is set appropriately to UK or US English. And switch off the grammar checker: it assumes you're writing business English, not creatively, and has a very narrow idea of good writing.

Next step

We've looked at what you want to do in writing historical fiction, and how writing fiction is, essentially, the business of telling stories through how individuals act. Historical characters were formed in a world you can't have known, so next we'll look at how you might set about imagining, finding and developing your characters.

2

Characters-in-action

Storytelling is rooted in people – characters – and how they act. So story emerges from character, and your job is to develop your characters so as to make their stories vivid and compelling. That involves creating them as 'characters-in-action', and getting them on to the page using basic techniques of storytelling.

Characters-in-action

Aristotle

From *Poetics*

'Tragedy is essentially an imitation not of persons but of action and life, of happiness and misery. All human happiness or misery takes the form of action; the end for which we live is a certain kind of activity, not a quality. Character gives us qualities, but it is in our actions – what we do – that we are happy or the reverse.'

That famous quote of Aristotle's is about the two narrative forms of his time, drama (i.e. tragedy and comedy) and epic poetry such as *The Odyssey*. Prose fiction, like film, is simply a newer form of the same human need to represent – Aristotle's 'imitate' – how we experience ourselves. If a piece of writing sets out a character's qualities but not their actions, then we call it a pen-portrait. Stories are about people *doing* things: talking, eating, fighting, sleeping, hating, laughing, racing, struggling: who they really are is embodied – literally, em-bodied – in their actions. But a novel isn't just a film script with the scenery described. Only in prose fiction can we take the reader inside our character's heads and explore their desires, fears, ideas and emotions: their *consciousness*. We can even write things which a character doesn't know they're thinking and feeling, and things which no character knows.

In working on major characters, you'll need to decide the basics: age, gender, sexual orientation, religion, ethnicity, language, job, class, family and work relationships and so on. You'll need a sense of their personality, too: do they fly off the handle easily, prefer animals to children, try to be optimistic but rarely succeed, find the other gender easier to get on with than their own? Basics and personality also shape what they look like, eat, wear, drive, read, sing, or do for fun. Exactly which and how much detail you need will depend on their role in your story: for example, if your main character is a servant, it might or might not be useful or important that his employer is of a different religion.

Some writers find it very helpful to think out these things before they start drafting, until the character is well formed and ready to act. Other writers just draft, finding the character developing as a *result* of the necessary micro-decisions: whether, say, it's more useful for a character to have a taste for racing her curricle or for doing petit-point embroidery. However, you can know vast amounts about all these things, but it's all no use unless you can create your characters as characters-in-*action*.

Snapshot: characters-in-action

Look back at the historical object you worked with in Chapter 1. Think of a character (real or imagined) who might have had possession of it, or known it well, at some time in its history. Jot down a few notes about who this person might have been, so that they're present in your imagination.

Now write down ten verbs for this character's characteristic physical actions. Last time I did this exercise I found I'd written: *jump, dash, crumple, push, snarl, nibble, taste, wolf, leap, flop.*

Write down ten verbs for their personality – their characteristic mental or emotional habits. For example: *spend, dither, hunger, dream, join in, crumple, flinch, rejoice, dread, argue.* Notice how *crumple* came up in both physical and mental actions? So often we describe more abstract, mental actions by using physical verbs as a metaphor.

Now pick another character from a different moment in your historical object's life, and do the same verb lists for this character. This is also a useful exercise for later in your work on a story, or just as a bit of writerly yoga.

Key idea: only characters, in action, make a story

Characters without action are merely portraits. Actions without character are merely a plot. What historians say about real historical people is merely data. Only fully imagined characters-in-action make a story.

The father of the modern short story, Edgar Allen Poe, defined the form as a story that can be read in a single sitting, but you still have to make them keep sitting. And if you're writing a novel you've got to make readers want to pick the book up again the next day. So, if a story is built from characters acting, then it's important that your characters act in ways which will make us want to discover what the consequences will be.

M. C. Scott

M. C. Scott is a novelist and first chair of the Historical Writers' Association.

'Every character is the hero of their own story.'

We'll concentrate first on your main character, but of course they're not the only one you need to think about. Secondary or minor characters present a similar challenge, because, as M. C. Scott's quote says, each of them is the hero of his or her own story. Although within **this** story not nearly so much of their story will show, we still need to sense it driving how they act and react. That means you probably need to work out at least some of your secondary characters' stories. In Joseph O'Connor's *Ghost Light*, for example, Molly and Synge's respective mothers are not on stage much, but how each child deals with his or her mother in adult life is a product of each mother's story too.

Snapshot: drama from characters interacting

Make a list of four different people, a mix of genders, who might have existed in the world of your current project. For example, a goldsmith, a teacher, a prostitute, an itinerant singer, a small child … For each, think of someone who would seem like an ally or friend, and another who would seem like a threat or an enemy. For example, the teacher might find the school cook an ally and the school inspector a threat, while the goldsmith might find a tramp a threat and the wife of a fellow goldsmith an ally.

Take one of these little trios, and think of a situation where the threat and the ally might both be present. Can you sense a scene emerging? If you want to, you could also consider what might happen if things turned out the other way round: the tramp turns out to be an ally and the wife of the fellow goldsmith a threat. Now try another trio.

WANTS AND NEEDS

People act when they want or need something. It needn't be material: wanting to be loved, needing to save your own or someone else's life, or their soul, are powerful drivers of human actions. But *wanting* is often a substitute for true *need*: finding a sugar daddy might seem the answer for a character whose real problem is that they don't feel strong and individual; someone seeking power over others might be compensating for having no one who gives them unconditional love. Indeed, before 'to want' meant to desire or to aspire to something, it meant to lack, as it does in Shakespeare. What someone *needs*, in other words, is usually about something they unconsciously *lack*: some incompleteness in themselves. Many books about story structure talk about this as a *flaw*.

Even the shortest short story, which apparently deals with the small and particular decisions and actions of an ordinary day in eighteenth-century New Orleans, embodies the essential drives and dilemmas of being human: food, work, family … or lack of them. The result may be comedy or tragedy, since they both deal in the same stuff, as do modern genres such as action-adventure, thriller, romance and drama: love, shame, allegiance, betrayal, hope, survival and triumph. But in historical fiction both wants and needs may be harder for us to understand. To a man in ancient Rome, wanting your wife to obey you in all things was not just a want, but also a need that deserved to be fulfilled. And some writers struggle to evoke what it's like to know, as unquestioningly as you know that the sun will rise in the morning, that Heaven, or maybe Purgatory, are waiting for you depending on your actions. Making wants and needs convincing to modern readers without just ignoring the historicalness of history – the Otherness – is one of our challenges.

In Chapter 6 we'll look at how the shift from *want* to *need* powers a story: for now, what's important is to start thinking of your characters in terms of:

- what they *want*, and why getting it sets them a problem
- how they might act in trying to get it
- what they actually *need*
- which parts of *need* they're conscious of.

 Key idea: characters in *inter*-action

A story starts when your main character is trying to get something or somewhere, and a person or a situation is in the way. But the other person has their own 'want' or 'need', which is driving their actions. Unless your character never meets another soul *and* never takes account of those back home or up ahead, their behaviour will be shaped by how other people think or act. Story is driven by characters in *inter*action.

LIKEABLE OR COMPELLING

Ultimately, what keeps readers reading is that we're so engaged with your main characters that, as the stakes in the story rise for both triumph and disaster, we keep on picking the book up again. We need to *want* to spend time with them, and experience the world through them, even if we know their truth isn't the whole truth. So your important characters don't have to be uniformly sweet and reasonable; indeed, we'd probably feel unconvinced, or irritated, if they were. We can love someone who behaves badly and hate someone who behaves well: the only real disaster is if we feel only mild liking, disliking or indifference, because then we won't keep reading. If you build your story round a central character with whom we can feel real human kinship, in both their good qualities and their flaws, we'll believe in how they act, and hope they end up getting what they need. What characters really need to be is *compelling*.

And wicked central characters? Mantel's Thomas Cromwell and some versions of Richard III are, like Shakespeare's Macbeth, classic heroes of a 'dark inversion' story: the good, honourable person whose drive to fulfil his wants leads him to ever-greater bad. Bret

Easton Ellis's American Psycho is bad from the beginning, and the book, in its attempt to pin down a very particular time in a very particular society, arguably counts as historical fiction; Ellis creates Patrick Bateman out of our own least admirable greeds and desires, and takes him to the logical limit. It's the horrible fascination of how that plays out in a very particular historical time and place which keeps the reader reading.

ENERGY AND ACTION

What any main character-in-action needs, then, isn't virtue, it's energy. In real life we're often stuck, powerless or peacefully happy, but the reader will only keep reading if they know that they *don't* know what will happen next, as the character chooses or is forced to change tack. *Wolf Hall* starts – literally and figuratively – when the young Thomas Cromwell's life with his bullying father becomes unbearable, and he runs away: the main story starts when Cromwell's master, Cardinal Wolsey, starts failing to deliver Henry VIII's divorce. Everything that follows is in one way or another a consequence of the failures of his father figures.

For a character to have to use their energy, you must put them into situations which make them *act*. That's why this chapter's first Snapshot exercise is about verbs, and it's why actors will do what they call 'actioning': working out a verb for each sentence and move: 'to defeat', they'll decide of one line, then 'to calm', 'to woo', 'to escape'. Even with a character who at the beginning is forced by circumstances or their own nature to be passive or merely reactive, we need to sense that there's latent energy which will emerge.

Of course, the response to the new and unexpected situations needs to be convincing, if only in retrospect. If your sensible, conformist, counting-house clerk Bill suddenly runs away to join the circus, we may be as surprised as his employer and his mother are, but that act needs to be consistent with the deepest aspects of his personality: the repressed inner Clown which frightens him and has caused him to reduce his life to columns of figures, a stovepipe hat, and being in bed alone by ten. Whether we sense or glimpse the Clown before that day, or only as we watch him feeling the fear and doing it anyway, is part of how you structure the story.

PROBLEMS, ACTIONS AND OBSTACLES

But what causes the crack in Bill's defences, so that he can't, or won't, go on keeping his chaotic inner craziness under lock and key? What is inside, or outside, your character, that will mean that they have to act? My shorthand for this is the character's **problem** – the thing they want which they don't have – and which they must act to resolve. But if they start to act and easily get what they want, the story will peter out, so something must get in the way. There is more on this in Chapter 6 but, put simply, the obstacles can be **external**: it's a day's walk for Isotta to find fresh water on the other side of the mountain; Johan's father won't let him go on crusade and thereby save his soul. Or they can be **internal** to the character: Paulina knows she must avenge her father's death, but it means killing her mother, whom she loves; the man Max loves never notices anyone as plain and poor as Max is, so how can Max become visible?

And to make the story compelling, those reasons to act need to be really strong, even if the actions themselves are quite modest. Riding into battle or going into labour are fairly universal problems, but in some ways the most interesting and revealing are those which put *this* character under a particular pressure. For example, crossing the deck of a ship at sea to chat up an heiress … when you only have one leg. Or finding out if your next-door neighbour has murdered his wife … when you are what these days would be diagnosed as agoraphobic.

The blurb of any novel is usually a very succinct summary of what the story is built of: character – pressure – obstacle. So shaping a main character you can build a story on is all about deciding:

- who they need to be
- what problem you might give them so that they *have* to act
- what obstacles are going to force them to draw on everything that they are, so that there's enough at stake for the reader keep reading.

It's probably more common to start from the character and then think about pressure and obstacles that you might put them under: you have a happy orphan, so what happens when the regime changes, the orphanage is closed and all the orphans are branded as untouchable heretics? But plenty of writers start with a pressured situation – a battle, say, or the birth of a baby or a change of religious regime. Then they start thinking, 'What character could I put into this situation which would set off something really, really powerful and exciting?'

Focus point: developing characters can start from the outside or the inside

Some writers find it very helpful to work on external things like appearance, possessions and tastes, as a way of focusing their imagination. Some prefer to think first about internal drives and desires, and wait to find out how they play out in external things. Some listen chiefly for the voices (see Chapter 5). Still others only know just enough to get started, and find out more as they write.

There is no one right way, no shortcut, no magic formula: you'll find your way by observing what works for you, but also trying other ways. It will always help, though, to spend time observing people in real life and noticing how you experience them as characters-in-action. And what might the equivalents of these modern people be like, in the period you want to write about?

Snapshot: put your characters under pressure

Take the two characters you made lists of verbs for. For each of those two characters, make a list of five situations – threats, opportunities, mysteries – which would put them under pressure. Try for a mixture of classic situations which would be major for anyone but elicit different reactions, and those which might seem small or minor, but which will dig into the particular personality of *this* character.

CHANGE AND GROWTH

Even if your first ideas are about the character's situation at the beginning, it's worth thinking about where your characters might end up. If the events of the story change them and their lives, where does it take them? Do they get what they wanted at the beginning, or does what they want change as they realize what they *need*? Do they get that? What is the change? Have they grown, established a new life, learned wisdom or rediscovered youth? In a good way? Or is their tragedy that they know they need to change, but are incapable of actually changing? Is the comedy that their topsy-turvy world is restored to order?

It's not unusual for a writer's imagination to start from the other end, of course: what need is fulfilled, what lack is finally made good? It's then a case of peering *backwards*, to see where the character comes from. Indeed, if your story fits a settled genre, what end the reader is hoping for and what they're dreading are among its defining qualities: the character gets their man or woman, or they don't; they save the city, or they don't; the murderer is discovered and justice is done, or it isn't. For more on genre, see Chapter 9, but it's worth remembering now that it's the novels which manage to deliver the pleasures of that genre while *also* being more original and satisfying as stories of rounded, convincing human beings, which stand out for readers.

Snapshot: developing a character from the outside inwards

Take one of your characters from the previous Snapshot exercise, and imagine him or her on the transport of the time: steam train, litter, trireme. Do some quick research if you like: no need for now to go further than Wikipedia. Write a pen-portrait of this character at this moment, following this order:

* What are they wearing and how are they wearing it? Is it too tight, too big, casual, smart, cheap, a scarf falling off unnoticed, a coat buttoned up to the throat, pockets bursting with … what?

- What are they carrying? An armful of legal documents that keep springing open? A black slate memorial tablet? A silk bag full of kittens?
- What are they doing? Eating a picnic spread out on their lap and reading a prayer book? Knitting dishcloths? Embroidering a wedding veil? Sneaking sugar plums out of a bag hidden in their pocket and spitting the stones out of the window? Carving a sex toy?
- Move inside, to how they feel inside their clothes, with the chicken-leg grease on their fingers or the thigh of the next passenger so close they can't move without seeming to be making a pass. Are they getting cramp from the lack of leg room or are they nice and cosy?
- Move deeper in, to their thoughts. Are they lonely in a crowd, or enjoying meeting strangers? Where are we, and when? What has this character left behind? Where are they going? How are they feeling about past and future? Are they thinking about something else? Why does it matter?

Working with real historical characters

There are few stronger motivations for writing an historical novel than to come across someone in history and find yourself thinking, 'What was it like to be them, at that moment, in that place?' It presents you with great opportunities, and if you want to sell your work it does no harm either.

But it also sets up significant challenges. You're writing fiction because you want to go beyond what non-fiction can do, but you need to stay connected to some of what these people and events were, otherwise why are you embarking on this project at all? You'll be researching voices, emotions and ideas, as well as clothes and weapons but also doing the more difficult but more exciting bit: imaginatively recreating this material into a story.

If you've come across a Canadian hermit, or a medieval Prince of Wales, and find yourself wondering what it was like when the railway came or the King died, then you need to be willing to do what it takes to create a *story*: a narrative built of character-in-action, of how wants and needs make people act, of energy and conflict, of growth and change. And it can be a challenge to make sure that a real historical character works in that way, while staying true to the facts and spirit of his time, *and* keeping the reader caring and turning the pages. (This, of course, never bothered Shakespeare: he cheerfully collapsed and expanded time, changed things round, and made characters meet each other who never did, to make a play work in dramatic terms.)

If you want to do this because stories are more fun in crinolines and togas, it's true – but not enough. If you can't be bothered to do the research-in-depth to discover the real souls and bodies inside those gorgeous clothes, then your story will be like one of those museum displays in which cheap shop mannequins with faces shaped for modern makeup are dressed in nylon velvet and machine-made lace.

If it's because you think real history is fascinating, that's true too, but check that you want to create an imaginative whole, not just sugar the pill of real history, or dodge the need for 'proper' scholarly research. If you don't let go of much that you know or find out, and change much else, then your story will read like those stilted TV docu-dramas whose only function is to provide more palatable gobbets of history.

But, like all challenges, writing historical fiction with real historical characters is particularly satisfying if you can make it work.

 Jane Austen

Henry Tilney, in *Northanger Abbey*:

'It is only a novel … or, in short, some work in which the greatest powers of the mind are displayed, in which the most thorough knowledge of human nature, the happiest delineation of its varieties, the liveliest effusions of wit and humour are conveyed to the world in the best chosen language.'

The first problem is that some things are a given, as they aren't with a wholly imaginary character. But what are the givens of a real historical character?

- **The actual historical facts which no one would argue with**: for example, that Queen Elizabeth I came to the throne in 1558. But how you handle even these varies: very few writers of fiction would feel they could move Elizabeth's accession, but many would feel they could shift the age, say, of that Canadian hermit.

- **What's recorded about your real historical character at the time.** The record is shaped by the writers, with all the biases of their personality, period and reasons for writing. For example, on the topic of Elizabeth I's proposed marriages, the secretaries of William the Silent and Robert Dudley would each have recorded very different facts, had different interpretations, and retailed different gossip. How much *you* conform to the records depends partly on what you read between the lines but also (as above) on how well known and significant both the recorder and the character are.

- **What later historians have done with those facts and records.** Each has made decisions about which sources they trust; which to reproduce in the book you're reading, and which to leave out for reasons of space or because it weakens their argument. They have professional boundaries and principles, but also their own biases of personality, culture and motivation, and all those form the story they shape about Elizabeth I's conscious and unconscious reasons for apparently seeking various marriages, while in fact avoiding them.

- **The spaces in the record between what is known.** Not only the character's thoughts and feelings, but many of the events, settings and actions, will not have survived to our time. This means your imagination has to create such things from scratch. For some writers that's daunting but for others it's easier, because their imagination can fly more freely and the story find its own drive and coherence.

- **The lack of space in very well-documented lives.** For some, this makes it easier: there is less to invent from scratch and therefore less to 'get wrong' in the historian's sense. But it can hamper you in building a good story if the known facts don't naturally make one, and some writers find having their imagination hemmed in by recorded things they don't feel they can ignore intensely frustrating and uncreative.

DECIDING YOUR OWN PRINCIPLES

When you're working closely with recorded facts, you're going to have to make lots of decisions about what you must stick to, what you will change, and what you can invent, and that's easier if you decide some kind of overall policy. It will also help you to avoid the crunching change of gear which I so often see in manuscripts, as the writer moves from anxiously animating a well-documented scene which they feel they're 'not allowed' to change, to a wholly invented scene where their imagination could flower. But this is your novel, and you get to make your own rules, so make rules that you'll feel able to keep.

Mind you, the highest rule of all is that *story is king*, as the book trade says: there's no point in being perfectly accurate to every last recorded fact if the result is so dull, so un-involving as a story, that no one reads past page ten anyway.

Point of view

We've talked about how your main characters are the people through whom we experience the events of the story, so how that 'through whom' operates is crucial, which is what the phrase 'point of view' really means. At the foundation of discussing point of view is the fact that any human being can perceive certain things through their senses, and not perceive others. As visual animals, we talk about 'view', but it encompasses all the senses: we can feel the pillow behind our own head but not see it; we can smell the bakery next door to us and hear church bells half a mile away; we can't hear a song being sung in China or taste the chocolate that we haven't bought yet ... except in our imagination.

But in writing (as in the rest of life), this idea of what a particular human perceives in a given situation gets widened to include *how* they experience these things, and so how you write them. Have a look at this little example:

> *I unsheathed my rapier, made a feint in* tierce, *and ran the coward Eichner through before he could cry for help. If it turned out to be murder, I had no doubt that the Lord would forgive me.*

The narrator of the story is also an act-or in the story: he is an 'internal narrator', he refers to himself as 'I', and the story we get has been filtered through his consciousness. Now look at another version:

> *Delapierre unsheathed his rapier, made a feint in* tierce, *and ran the coward Eichner through before he could cry for help. If it turned out to be murder, Delapierre had no doubt that the Lord would forgive him.*

Here, the narrative has what we call an 'external narrator', who is not a character, and the narrative is therefore in third person. But *it is still in Delapierre's point of view*: he's referred to as 'he', but we see the action from his place in the scene and the narrator has access to his thoughts and expectations: 'Delapierre had no doubt' and 'before he could cry for help'. More subtly, we pick up Delapierre's take on things because some of the phrases sound like his voice: 'the coward Eichner'. This last technique is most often called *free indirect style*, and we'll be looking at it more in Chapter 5.

Now think about what exactly the same moment would be like if it was in Eichner's point of view, and with Eichner as the internal narrator:

> *Delapierre dragged out his rapier and thrust it clumsily towards me; it caught my ribs on my sword-hand side, but I would never, not even were it Doomsday, show that I was frightened. Besides, I truly felt no fear, for I knew him of old.*

And if it had an external narrator, telling the story in third person but still through Eichner's point of view?

> *Delapierre dragged out his rapier and thrust it clumsily towards Eichner; it caught Eichner's ribs on his sword-hand side, but he would never, not even were it Doomsday, show himself frightened. Besides, he truly felt no fear, for he knew Delapierre of old.*

So point of view controls how we experience a scene, but it also makes a difference to structure. If you imagine the whole scene, the story might be told in a different order, depending on point of view. Perhaps in Delapierre's point of view the swordplay would be evoked in precise detail, and Eichner would be described in ways which justify Delapierre's trying to kill him. If we're in Eichner point of view we might only know as much about the fight as is needed to explain (or even laugh at) Delapierre's failure to kill him.

Key idea: point of view is much more than just physical seeing

When we're in a character's point of view, one of the things that draws the reader, intuitively, into experiencing the story through that character's consciousness, is if you allow the character's nature and take on what's happening to colour both *what* is narrated, and *how* it's narrated. Voice, in the sense of the voice of the narrative, and including the use of free indirect style, is one of the subtlest but most important ways the writer can control the reader's experience.

Write: character-in-action

Look back at the historical object you explored in Chapter 1. Imagine a character, A, from *one* of the times your object has known and jot down a few notes to focus your imagination. A has this object, but she/he must give it to character B. Why does A hand it over? Does A *want* to hand over the object, or not? Does B want to have it, or not?

Jot down a few notes about the circumstances and the setting, so as to give your imagination some anchors. Then write the scene from A's point of view, in first person (i.e. A saying 'I') and past tense, and start at the moment when A and B meet, not before.

For now, just guess any historical facts or details that you don't know, and keep writing; don't worry about getting the scene 'right' – this is a first draft and you can go with the flow of the interaction.

Key idea: research serves character-in-action, not the other way round

Research *is* enormously important, because it's with 'the reality and detail', as John Gardner puts it, of the world and people of your story that you persuade the reader to buy into this world. But the researched materials of your story are only worth working with if the story and people they're being used to create are worth reading. The fact that something is historically accurate is not a good enough reason on its own for it to get into your story.

Write: the other point of view

Take the little scene you've just written, where Character A was giving Character B your historical object. Then, Character A was saying 'I', and telling the story from their own point of view. Now rewrite the scene, *as experienced and narrated by B*, in first person, with B saying 'I' and past tense.

Stick as closely as you can to the same actions: dialogue, and what actually happens in terms of physical action and gesture. These are your givens, so what makes this version different is in B's *experience*. For A, this handing-over might have been really serious, for B it's trivial. B might have had all sorts of childhood memories conjured up, while A is only interested in the object's value on the open market.

So, as with Eichner and Delapierre further up, not only will B experience the scene physically from a slightly different angle, but his or her emotional and logical understanding may affect how much gets told, about what. B might linger over the nostalgia of how the object smells, A might look at its glitter across the room and think, 'gold leaf is very easy to sell'.

Focus point: understanding and controlling point of view is crucial

The business of point of view interacts with character-in-action, and it's fundamental to how you control your reader's experience of your story. When you're reading, notice how the author handles point of view. Does it serve the story well? What would the story be like if they handled it differently?

Workshop: comparing points of view

Look at the *first* version of the scene, in A's viewpoint. Read over what you've just written. Did the object get handed over? Was that the outcome you expected? Are you happy with the outcome? How does your idea of your Character A come across? Do they think, feel and behave in ways which are characteristic of them: ways which seem right for their age, gender, job, class, personality, relationship to the object, relationship to the world? Humans are always a mixture of what we think of as typical for that kind of person, and un-typical: is the mix convincing? Or are they so typical they're clichéd, or do they at least seem a bit off-the-peg and standard issue? Look at:

- physical actions, and interactions with B, the object and the setting
- voice in dialogue
- their thoughts, and the voice of their thoughts in the narrative. Is what they think about convincing, but also the *way* they think about it?
- their appearance
- any surprises in how they behave, think or feel. Do we believe that they could have surprised us in this way?

Look at Character B, as seen in A's viewpoint. How vividly and characteristically do they come across, given we experience them only from the outside and given that you've done less, so far, to develop them? Go through the bullet points again: is B convincing in those ways?

Now look at the second version of this scene, from B's viewpoint. What did you learn from doing this? Did writing B's version make you change your mind about this scene in some way? Look particularly at the places where being in B's voice and point of view means the words are different. Does either B or A come over more vividly in this second version? Do you feel that one version is more satisfactory in itself than the other? Or are they simply different?

Finally, if you were going to develop this scene, what other work might you need to do? What more imaginative work? Developing the characters? Imagining their backstory or the world they inhabit? What research work? More about the object? The material or social world of the time? The psychology and world view?

Focus point: we can understand what non-viewpoint characters are thinking and feeling

Just because you've locked the narrative into a particular character's point of view doesn't mean you can't convey what's going on inside other characters, and get the reader to care about those others. After all, in real life, and in plays and films, we can't go inside other people's heads, but we still care about them, and have a sense of them as autonomous people with their own inner life. Through what we experience of a non-viewpoint character, we sense or deduce their thoughts and feelings, and we can care about them too. We can even disagree with the viewpoint character's view of them.

Hilary Green

Hilary Green's fiction is set during the First and Second World Wars.

'If your imagined situation is sufficiently vivid, sometimes a character will walk into the story unbidden and fully formed.'

 Edit: working on point of view

Look at your two versions of the scene. You're now going to use them as the basis for a new story, drawing on what you discovered in both versions to make the characters-in-action as vivid and distinct as possible. If you're really hampered by not knowing something, do that research, but don't let the research-tail wag the story-dog. Use *third* person and past tense, and handle point of view as seems best for the story. Roughly speaking, your options are:

1. Lock close into either A's or B's point of view for the whole story, letting their voice colour the narrative and using free indirect style.

2. Stick with A or B, but also pull out a little, to use the external narrator's voice to set the scene or convey things more neutrally wherever it seems right.

3. Start with either A or B, but change point of view at some moment to the other viewpoint.

Two hints to help with moving point of view:

- Use that pulled-out, narrator's point of view to make the switch gradual, rather than teleporting the reader straight from inside A's thoughts and feelings to inside B's thoughts and feelings.

- In 750 words it's hard to do more than one switch without things getting messy, so think hard about exactly where the switch should happen, for maximum effect on the storytelling.

You've already done lots of imagining of characters, and thought about some of the issues involved in your characters coming from history. We're now going to explore more widely the business of how to imagine past worlds and evoke what you've imagined on the page.

3

Imagining the past

The fiction writer's primary task is to imagine the past, inventing things which, by definition, never happened and people who never existed. There are different ways to get your imagination creating these things, but they all mean by-passing the censor which tests what you think for likelihood and reasonableness. Historical material you find and draw on needs to go through this re-creative process before it can work as storytelling.

When you write fiction, you are creating something which didn't exist until you imagined it. So the business of making your story convincing is fundamentally about imagining: dreaming a narrative chain of cause and effect in an imaginatively recreated past, transferring it on to the page and thence to the reader's mind.

Of course, at its best there's a rich, mutual fuelling going on between what we imagine and what we find out, and holding the two apart, as this and the next chapter do, is in a sense artificial. But it *is* important to recognize the difference.

 # W. H. Auden

Auden here is advising the teenage poet and communist John Cornford.

'Real poetry originates in the guts and only flowers in the head. But one is always trying to reverse the process and work one's guts from one's head. Just when the Daemon is going to speak the Prig claps his hand over his mouth and edits it.'

By 'the Daemon' Auden means the stuff in the writer's psyche and imagination – his or her 'guts'. By 'the Prig', he means the organizing, controlling, correcting part of the writer's mind: the 'inner editor' which is in charge of making sure that what we write will work on the reader as we want it to. The Prig worries about accurate research and reliable facts; good techniques of writing (the tools, guidelines and rules of thumb about how best to affect the reader); grammar, syntax and spelling conventions, so readers read as you want them to; ideas, and ethical and moral standards that you care about; what readers will like and want more of. Of course, these are all good things, and Auden *isn't* saying that conscious, deliberate reworking and editing shouldn't happen: as he says, a creative piece 'only flowers in the head'. But he *is* saying that the Daemonic experience and passion can't be put to work to produce exactly what the Prig wants, and if you let the Prig in too early, that experience and passion will never get on to the page at all.

Unfortunately, we get a great deal of practice at ignoring the Daemon and keeping things logical, commonsensical and reasonable (and, while we're at it, also polite, provable and likely to get a good grade in the exams). So you need ways to let your imagination run outwards, and inwards, into those unknown, uncensored, uncontrolled, unedited places where the wild things are. And the simplest way of all is to practise writing without doing any editing or censoring.

Snapshot: freewriting

Find paper, pen and a clock or kitchen timer. Choose an anchor phrase: something neutral like *today is* or *my home town is*, or the name of the month. Start with that, and write non-stop for 15 minutes – don't worry if it's not very legible. There are only two rules: your pen must not stop moving, and you must not cross out, correct or otherwise change a single word. In other words, don't try to shape, control or censor what words get on to the page. If your brain stops serving up words, just write the anchor phrase, over and over again; more words will arrive *as long as you keep going*. If your brain is protesting that this is a waste of time, trust me – and all the other writers for whom this is a fundamental exercise – and keep going. Besides, it's only 15 minutes.

If you must use a computer, then you'll have to discipline yourself not to start fiddling with the words, or even reading back over what you've already written. Some writers turn the screen off; others just close their eyes.

When you've done your 15 minutes, read it through like a reader, circling any words or phrases that you like, which have some extra energy, or some sort of glow or strength. Don't edit or even ask yourself why they do: just register their presence as nuggets of something rich in the dust.

What use is freewriting?

The basic technique of freewriting is useful at any stage of a project, and it's definitely something that you get better at. Around ten minutes in seems to be a common moment to hit a wall of no words coming, and it's usually *after* you've written through that wall that the really interesting stuff begins to emerge. Some writers do freewriting at the start of every writing session, as a form of mind-clearing and focusing: novelist Jenn Ashworth likens it to the washing machine starting by pumping out the last dribbles of the old, dirty water from last time. Many do it as writerly yoga, others find that flipping the off-switch on their censor circuits also helps a first draft pour out, particularly for passages where a character is in an altered mental state such as sex, violence or dreams.

Some writers use freewriting as a developmental tool with a suitable anchor phrase: *Emperor Claudius is…* or *The brothel is…* or *Jealousy is…* to see what comes out of their pen, either because the narrative voice is evoking a direct, physical experience of things, or when it's deep inside a point of view and so a particular character's moment. It's also very useful if you have a commission, and have to make a story happen whether it wants to or not.

Clustering

Having found these nuggets of rich stuff, what do you do with them? Clustering is a different, more focused way of working with your mental free-association muscles. It's a bit like a mind map, but instead of connections of logic, you write whatever is prompted by the previous word. Again, there's no right or wrong and, like freewriting, this is a technique you get better at with practice.

Snapshot: clustering

Take a piece of paper and a pen – or a felt pen plus a huge wall or whiteboard can be great fun. Write one of the potent words from the freewrite in the middle of the page and circle it. Then start free-associating outwards, in chains of words and phrases so that you get a spider-diagram, until the page is full. Try to open your mind to whatever turns up in it: the next word might be connected by sound – rhyme and rhythm – rather than meaning, or references, connotations, patterns or oppositions.

Above all, don't try to *force* the logic, or censor anything just because it doesn't seem to make sense. If you go blank, just stay with the blankness – with what poet and novelist Philip Gross calls the *not-knowing* – or switch to another chain, or start a new one. For an example of a cluster I did on the word *Gold*, see Appendix IV.

When the page is full, look it over. Are there any other connections you can spot, in sense or sound? Draw a line between them. Are

Sometimes it's emerged from the sound or rhythm (the *prosody*), sometimes from the direct meaning (the *denotation*), sometimes from the wider ideas it carries with it (the *connotation*).

It will improve your writing immeasurably if you develop the habit of being aware of all these three aspects of a word. In historical fiction we're trying to create a sense of the otherness of the past, without actually confusing the reader or making the story awkward to read. So usually we have to stick to the denotation of a word that the modern reader will understand, although that may be different from its meaning in the past. And with connotations, too, there may be a gap between, for example, what your medieval yeoman farmer would think of when someone said 'bank' (a working goldsmith who happens to have a strong vault, or a Lombardy merchant with a nice line in promissory notes) and what your reader would think of (a vast glass building full of corporate ants). So, very often it's the prosody – the sound and rhythm, the music of the sentence, the way it would be said aloud – that does much of the work in getting the reader feeling that the past is speaking to them. For more on this, see Chapter 5.

Focus point: warm-up exercises are also good for unsticking you

Exercises and techniques which seem to be about warming up or getting started are often very useful when you get stuck or feel blocked, or when you want develop specific things in your story. Freewriting, clustering, all-six-senses and other Snapshot exercises are not just useful for the *What is this about?* of the story, but the *How should it be told?*: not just plot, but also voice, not just objects but also feelings, not just characters but also themes and abstract ideas. If you're using one of these techniques for a specific purpose, keep an eye and ear out nonetheless for anything else it throws up which has some potency about it, and make a note of those as well.

Write: imagining the past from nothing

Choose a combination of place and time which you know very little about, except that it must have existed. Twelfth-century Japan or post-First World War Idaho, say; Sparta – or Patagonia – when Homer was around; Madagascar in the time of Mohammed; Moscow or Melbourne in the time of Genghis Khan, or in the Cold War. Don't worry about researching the genuine history and geography, but instead work with your best guesses and make up what you need, rather as you might if you were writing speculative fiction set on another planet or in some alternative universe. What's important is to work at imagining this little world in enough specificity that it becomes concrete and believable for the reader.

Pick one of these opening lines as a starter, and write a 750-word story. Feel free to change voice, tense, names, details – anything, really – if it suits your setting and story:

- *Johanna the Mad stormed through the gate and up to the meeting-hall. She put a hand to the great double doors, and gently, quietly, pushed one open an inch. She stooped, and pressed her ear to the crack.*

- *What else could I have done? The snows were on their way, and there wasn't enough corn in the village to feed everyone, not all winter. But no one was willing to recognize it, and no one was willing to hear me say it.*

- *Petrus is one of those men who won't take no for an answer, but Andrei decides he's going to say no nonetheless. No, he practises in his head. Then he opens his mouth, and says, 'Yes.'*

- *The letter arrived on a Tuesday in the hottest August even Grandmamma could recall. It came out of the messenger's bag as clean as the messenger himself was dusty from the roads. Everyone watched as I turned it over and over. Then I slid my fingernail under the edge of the seal and prised it open.*

Focus point: writing down your imagining doesn't have to mean planning

Many writers recoil from the idea of 'planning', in the sense of constraining what they will write in the draft. But with longer projects, especially, if you don't work out some of the larger, structuring story ideas first, there's a huge risk that you end up with a great many thousand lovely words which go nowhere very much.

And there are many ways of imagining-on-paper (or on screen), which are explored more in Chapter 10: sketch maps, family trees, mind maps, index cards … Even a crazy first draft is really just one more way of making what your mind is forming into something solid and communicable.

Obviously, your imagination will be helped by research, not just into the material culture of this world, but – arguably even more importantly – into the society of the time. If the 'I' in the prompt about snow in the village is old, then is this a society that ignores old people? Or does it honour them, but he or she is the 'wrong' gender, class, colour or creed for anyone to take notice? And are there wider social or political forces at work in the history of this time and place, which might give depth and urgency to your story? How might you explore those?

Writing a story set in a place and time you know nothing about is a tall order. And there is always a risk, when writers work with the unknown, that they just use their own default settings, their sense of people and places in their own time, not what's real to *that* time and place. Or you may try to move away from your modern default settings but, from fear of getting the 'history stuff' spectacularly wrong, stick to vague, generic, all-purpose landscapes, things and behaviour which are little more convincing.

Of course, mostly writers choose a time and place that they *do* know something about, but this is why it's not a given that you should research before you imagine, let alone write.

Snapshot: what do you do with a crazy first draft?

Reread your story like a reader. Mark the places where the story isn't yet fully imagined, convincing, and grounded in believable things. Looking at where you've marked, make a list of what you must 'come to know', to make those things work. For each, think about different developmental techniques which might help you to do that: brainstorming, freewriting, clustering, sketch maps, all-six-senses, and so on.

Snapshot: researching what the story asks for

Look again at the story you've just written, and make a list of the things that you really *must* find out for the story to come alive in your imagination. Then make a list of the research that you would like to do, or feel you 'ought' to do.

Between what you imagine and what you research is what you already know. It *is* worth checking things, because we do all misremember what you think you know. More interestingly, except for trained historians of the period, much of what we *think* we know about history – the well-worn 'everyone knows…' level of knowledge – is usually very limited, one-sided or just plain wrong. So, checking what you think you know against proper, up-to-date historical knowledge doesn't only protect you from making mistakes the reader will spot, it helps you to avoid clichés, stereotypes, hackneyed images and situations, and well-worn, predictable ideas.

Write: a story developed from your choice of starting point

Choose a place and period that you know more about than the deliberately strange place of the last exercise. Think about how you might find a starting place for your imagination. You may already have something, but if not, go looking in books or online for this kind of thing:

- an historical place or object
- a letter or diary entry from that time
- a garment: try a museum of costume, pictures of the time or a search for images online with a term like *sixteenth-century costume*
- a picture or photograph of a place or people which looks as if there's a story there. If you're drawn to a portrait of a known historical figure, you're going to have resist researching just yet
- an opening sentence of the sort we used in the last exercise
- a closing sentence which makes you want to know how we got there
- a phrase of dialogue.

Once you've got something which feels as if there's a story latent in it, decide how best to make that latent story a little more solid and present. For example:

- Give the person a name, and do a freewrite to find out more about them: *Giorgio is...*
- Start a cluster from the name of your historical object, and find out more both about the object and what connotations it has.
- Name the people in the picture, and draw a mind map of their different relationships with each other: not stopping at 'brothers', 'boss' or 'step-uncle' but including the emotional dynamics: 'is jealous of', 'is in love with' 'despises for being effeminate'...
- Sketch a map or write a quick pen-portrait of the historical place (don't worry that it's not accurate to the actual place) to make it vivid and present to you.

When you feel that this imagining-on-paper is bringing at least some aspects of the story out of latency, start writing.

Workshop: thinking about how research and the story interact

Choose one of the two stories you've written in this chapter, print it out double-spaced (or turn on Track Changes), and read it like a reader, marking it up as we did before. What sings and what clunks? What is vivid and particular, what is bland and generic? Is there anything which is plain, simple and strong?

What research does it really need, without which the story won't work? Think about not just material things, but manners, beliefs, ethics, social customs, politics, practicalities of things like transport and cooking, and so on.

What are you fairly sure you got right, but would like to check? What do you suspect is just your default idea or assumption, which might well not be true to the past and to this place? How might research challenge your own defaults and assumptions? What could the story do without, but will be enriched and developed more excitingly if you find out more?

Where might you find these things? If you can't physically get to the place – as you can't physically get to the time, of course – what could you do instead? Ask people who were there? Browse the library? For what kind of book? Look online?

Pick one topic or piece of research that the story really needs, and do what you can to find out about it. At the same time, try to notice the relationship between your imaginative work and your researching work: where were your imagination and instincts right about this place and time? Can research nonetheless make things more vivid? What clashes with what you invented, what challenges your default assumptions, what was right for the present but wrong for the past? Does it matter? What might you do about it, if it does matter? Did you find things that you weren't looking for? Do they change the story? Do you want that to happen?

Rose Tremain

As well as being a distinguished writer of short and long fiction, Rose Tremain taught writing for many years.

'...all the research done for a novel – all the studying and reading, all the social fieldwork, all the location visiting, all the garnering of what is or what has been – must be reimagined before it can find a place in the text. It must rise into the orbit of the anarchic, gift-conjuring, unknowing part of the novelist's mind before it can acquire its own truth for the work in question...

'Graham Greene, when asked by a journalist how he would make use of an important experience he'd had in South-East Asia, replied: "It's yours to remember and mine to forget." He was talking about the novelist's task of reimagining reality. Reimagining implies some measure of forgetting. The *actual or factual has to lose definition, become fluid, before the imagination can begin its task of reconstruction. Data transferred straight from the research area to the book will simply remain data. It will be imaginatively inert.'*

In Tremain's 'anarchic, gift-conjuring, unknowing' space, the normal rules of logic and common sense and reasonableness don't apply. No conjuror ever learned their trade by never throwing anything in the air in case she dropped it; no exploring infant or adult ever found anything new, except by first imagining unknown things out there waiting to be found, and then setting off to find them. Nothing new was ever created, in other words, by censoring one's first steps outwards into the unknown.

What Tremain is really saying is that the researched material must have no special status for the fiction writer. It must become no more (though also no less) important than all the other things that we 'know' in the writerly sense, and which we draw on instinctively or deliberately to weave our stories. Treating researched material as in some way special and sacred is a particular trap for the writer of historical fiction, because both writers and readers are so often drawn to it for what I call the 'non-fiction appeal': to get a fix of history in an easy, tasty form. Our medium – prose on the page – is so close to the historians' medium, it's hard to escape the sense that we are writing history and must play by its rules, but escape we must. Playwrights, scriptwriters, sculptors and other visual artists find it much easier to use history not as a set of shackles but a springboard for storytelling, and it's important that we do the same.

 ## Edit: what kind of development is needed?

Take one of the stories you've worked on in this chapter, and decide what developing and revising it needs next. You might want to do any or all of the following:

- Developing characters, settings, themes, voices or plot: which techniques might be best for each of these?
- Researching essential things. This may be easier for the story that's set somewhere you're familiar with, but if you would like to explore the unfamiliar setting, then go for it!
- Researching to take the story further, make it richer, or challenge your default assumptions and the things you suspect are historical stereotypes and clichés.

Revise the story to integrate your imagined and your researched material. When you've got it into shape, do a final pass to pick up the fine detail and spot the slips and missing bits that always happen when you're reworking things.

 ## Deborah Swift

'With today's media, we are so used to a constant stream of images that we sometimes forget to convey the first freshness of the vision itself. The seventeenth century was a time when everything was seen for the first time directly with the eyes, and the first encounter with something could indeed be a wonder.'

We've been discussing imagining, knowing/remembering and researching as different processes which prompt each other and fuel each other, in the cause of integrating everything into a single story which is told as if it were all real. So your goal in handling your materials is for the reader *not to be aware*, as they read, whether something is imagined, remembered or researched.

The only exception to this is if your story 'breaks the frame' of fiction, as postmodern fiction often does, and acknowledges in some way that it's a constructed thing, made by a writer who can change it at will. John Fowles's *The French Lieutenant's Woman* is a good example of this kind of novel. Even so, such a project only works if, *within* the frame, things are conjured up as vividly and believably as in more conventional fiction. If we don't believe in that picture, then there is no thought-provoking shock in being reminded that this is, in fact, all made up.

Next step

We've been looking at the primary process of writing a story, which is imagining the characters and events and gradually working out where and how researched material might come in. In the next chapter, we'll look in detail at how to do research and how to handle what you discover.

4

Researching the past

Research can help you find stories, as well as helping you write stories you've already found. Learning where and when to look for research material, how to collect what you find, and how to handle it, is a basic part of understanding how to write historical fiction. Working with real historical characters and events is particularly challenging, though for some writers it's also particularly exciting.

There are many different ways in which 'real history stuff' relates to the process of writing fiction. So let's start by thinking about the different role researched material might have in your story.

- **Imagining a story based on general historical material** about places and times that you know something about, and letting the story tell you what you need to check, and what you need to find out from scratch.

- **Imagining the outlines of a story and then looking for an historical context** which will enable you to develop your idea most fully and dramatically. Kazuo Ishiguro, for example, says that the essence of a novel, for him, isn't in the setting. He wanted to write about a man who realizes he's wasted his working life, and his emotional life, and then went 'location hunting' to write what became *The Remains of the Day*.

- **Taking specific historical places, people or events**, and

  ▷ using the biography and history as the centre of the story (*Schindler's Ark* by Thomas Kenneally; *Alias Grace* by Margaret Atwood)

  ▷ using the biography or historical events as the spine of the story, but developing and embroidering on and around it (*Music and Silence* by Rose Tremain; *Pompeii* by Robert Harris; *An Instance of the Fingerpost* by Iain Pears)

  ▷ using the biography or historical events as the basis for a largely fictional story: jumping your storytelling off them and going as far as you like into fiction (*The Devil in the Marshalsea* by Antonia Hodgson; *Cold Mountain* by Charles Frazier)

  ▷ giving biography or history new names and imagining onwards from there (*Beloved* by Toni Morrison; *The Leopard* by Giuseppe Tomasi de Lampedusa).

- **Taking places, people or events from the fiction of the past** and jumping a story off them (George Macdonald Fraser's *Flashman* books; *March* by Geraldine Brooks).

- **Developing a story in any of these ways, and then weaving it together with** a parallel story set in a different time, so that the contrasts and correspondences illuminate both stories more strongly (*The Hours* by Michael Cunningham; my own *A Secret Alchemy*).

Which of these ways comes naturally to you? Which might you find challenging but exciting? Even if you aren't planning to write a parallel narrative, it's worth thinking about what the parallels with other times, including ours, might be, and maybe doing some research so you can bring them out more strongly. As Jill Paton Walsh says in her Author's Note to her novel *Knowledge of Angels*, a novel is always also about the world in which it was written.

Key idea: research to 'make the strange familiar and the familiar strange'

The eighteenth-century writer Novalis (who is, not coincidentally, the central character of Penelope Fitzgerald's novel *The Blue Flower*) proposed that the artist's job is 'making the strange familiar and the familiar strange'. Writers, in other words, are trying to evoke new and strange things in ways which make them present and fully imagined for the reader. But the writer is also working with things that readers already know, and those must be written in ways which make us experience them afresh: as something new and strange.

One reason for trying to dig deeper and imagine further than the general-knowledge, everybody-knows-that level of historical understanding is that readers sense when your material is recycled from ordinary, off-the-peg, second-hand sources: the general websites, school textbooks and folk memory. It takes digging through those to find, first-hand, what's new and strange about it all.

Margaret Atwood

From Atwood's essay 'In search of *Alias Grace*':

'The past is made of paper ... There is – as I increasingly came to discover – no more reason to trust something written down on paper then than there is now. After all, the writers-down

> *were human beings, and are subject to error, intentional or not, and to the very human desire to magnify a scandal, and to their own biases ... History is more than willing to tell you who won the Battle of Trafalgar and which world leader signed this or that treaty, but it is frequently reluctant about the now-obscure details of daily life ... If you're after the truth, the whole and detailed truth, and nothing but the truth, you're going to have a thin time of it if you trust to paper; but, with the past, it's almost all you've got.'*

What Atwood is saying is that research matters, but we must look *through* the record, imagining what to the writers of the time was invisible. For them, details of daily life drop away, but so do other trivia, like the role of women. In her biography of Eleanor of Aquitaine, Alison Weir sets out a classic example: Eleanor acted as regent for Henry II, issuing official documents and writs under her own name and seal, supervising accounts and presiding over law courts. That was the historical fact. It was the *chroniclers* who, blind to the presence of women, wrote her out of their accounts of the governance of England, and of course it was their accounts on which later historians based their research. It took feminism to alert historians to the way that women who are recognized and instrumental in their own time get written out of the history that we read.

What is historical material?

There's more in Chapter 10 about *when* in the process of writing a story you should do research, but *where* do you find this 'historical material' that we all know you need? Historians divide it into **primary sources** and **secondary sources**. For our purposes, a primary source is information from someone who has first-hand or nearly first-hand knowledge of what they're recording. Secondary sources collect, select, compare, analyse and interpret those primary sources.

PRIMARY SOURCES OF INFORMATION

Primary sources will be quoted in secondary sources – books about the period or topic – but the historian's or editor's choice may not be the things which are useful to you, for example the essential texture and dynamics of life: the constant background presence of servants, the fact that everyone wears a hat outdoors, that women don't travel on the top of a stagecoach. Luckily, the Internet has made it much easier to track down original documents and to see them digitized if you feel it would help.

- **Letters, diaries, chronicles and other first-hand and immediate accounts** have two uses to you: they convey information about the people concerned and life at the time, and they give you the voices of the period. Of course, a letter of the time telling the story of a battle where the writer wasn't present isn't quite the same as if they had been there, but it is still an authentic record.

- **Memoirs and autobiographies** are also rich sources: the writer's greater distance from the events gives context and perspective, but of course the writer is also creating a story which is perhaps different from how they experienced it at the time.

- **Other sources written at the time** include journalism, reportage and essays; travel writing and guidebooks; biographies of contemporaries; textbooks about medicine, dancing, religion, farming and so on; and accounts of contemporary events written for posterity.

- **Legal documents and other records include** wills, account books, contracts, servants' indentures (job contracts), parliamentary records, royal and government service records, law court records and so on. These give us a picture of what people owned and bought, what they argued over and sued each other for, what landed them in prison or hung them on Tyburn Tree. A good specialist history book can be a very good way in; the records themselves are more challenging to dig into directly but many are accessible on the Internet, including the entire archive up to 1913 of the Old Bailey.

- **Pictures, photographs and material objects.** The actions of your characters-in-action are shaped by the material world they operate in: furniture; cooking equipment; weapons; horses, dogs, hawks and hunting kit; equipment and machines for crafts and industries, and so on. Trying on authentic versions of historical costume shows you how difficult it is to breathe, or even raise your arms, in the clothes of a great Elizabethan lady. I always think togas must have got dreadfully in the way if you were a senator trying to murder Caesar: Roman slaves had it much easier in their less glamorous tunics.

- **Physical places.** Your characters act in a physical space: mountains, staircases, rivers, knot-gardens. Some battlefields are incredibly evocative; others have been built over. When it comes to buildings, if you can't get to the one you really need then go to a near-equivalent, and map what you find on to what you know of the real place. Antique maps are lovely as well as useful, as are panoramas and engravings of cities. Google Earth and Street View are a boon, but it does really help to go there for the sounds, echoes and dead spots; the smells and textures; what it feels like to climb the path up into the castle or look down on to a torrent; to discover what you can see from the tower or what creatures live in the brook.

- **Modern, first-hand accounts of things which will be useful to you.** A seventeenth-century medical treatise will show you how seventeenth-century doctors (and so eighteenth-century ordinary people) thought about and treated disease. But a modern nursing textbook is better for the actual symptoms and progression of septicaemia, so you can get your deathbed scene really vivid. Similarly, a modern memoir about childbirth, or modern travel writing about crossing the Caucasus, might tell you more than a medieval poem or a Victorian picture. Just make sure that you also create the real, unquestioning faith that a saint's girdle will bring a woman safely through both Caucasus and childbirth.

- **Film, TV and sound recordings made at the time.** These include newsreels, archive and documentary footage, oral history recordings, and broadcast programmes as well as transcripts.

- **Fiction, drama and poetry written at the time** (but not things written later, *about* that time), can also be vital primary sources. Mind you, until the novel came along as a form, in the late seventeenth century, literature was very rarely trying to reproduce everyday, conversational speech and writing. Plays, epics, romances and poems all dealt in *heightened* language of one sort or another, whether comic, heroic or tragic, which may not be the effect you want.

- **Films and radio plays** *made at the time* can also be rich sources for the practical details of life, and how that world saw and described itself. However, do remember that, until recently, the technology and also the aesthetic of film were derived from theatre: the picture it presents may be stylized as well as selective. Just think about what films made in the Second World War make it look like, compared with the reality.

SECONDARY SOURCES OF INFORMATION

- **History books and articles.** Most important are social history topics – clothes, food, housing, transport, armies – and psychological topics: sex and love, families, violence, religion, superstitions. You will also need to know something about the historical events going on: how much depends on how central they are to your story. Books written by specialists for fellow specialists can be a goldmine but they can also be rather daunting, and articles, maddeningly, can turn out to be merely a survey of previous research. So don't be afraid to be ruthless in choosing what to read: the abstract, contents page and introduction are a map of what the book contains, and you may find you only need the broad picture in the introductory paragraphs of each chapter, not the close detail that follows. On the other hand, if the general picture at the beginning is the 'familiar' you're trying to go beyond, then the specific evidence may be where those riches lie.

- Be careful about the dates, and the geographical and social context, of the material you find. Mealtimes, for example, move around at different periods, and both vocabulary and times vary widely between classes and areas. It can also be difficult to discover when things came into *general* use. The first gas lighting in the world was installed in Pall Mall in 1807, but when might a lower-middle class apartment in Albany NY get gas lighting in the parlour? And when would it convert to electricity? The fiction of the time can really help with this, and of course a few years or miles either way might not matter. But if you're way off, the reader will feel uneasy even if they don't know that you're definitely wrong.

- **Websites and blogs about your period, topics, themes, subjects or geographical area.** Websites for the general reader may tell you very little you haven't found in three other websites, but you may strike lucky and find an wonderful, individual enthusiast's or group blog. Wikipedia, though a word which fills scholars with horror, is, with care, very useful. On a topic that has a large following of specialists or enthusiasts there should be plenty of detail, and you can be reasonably sure that any real inaccuracies will have been picked up, while the references and links will lead to more specialist information. If it's a very controversial topic, bear in mind that one or other side may have got a stranglehold on the entry, so approach the interpretations offered with caution. If you're researching a non-English-speaking country that has its own Wikipedia, that version may have more detailed entries and images.

- **Historical magazines and journals.** Journals are usually the first place where new historical research shows up, which is exciting, and even those aimed at a general readership may still be scholarly: *History Today* is one of the great magazines of the world, and its archive is possible the richest goldmine of all. Academic journals can also be very useful as well as interesting and the academic databases make them easy enough to track down: a specialist journal on textile history might have just the silk for your Spitalfields weaver or battledress for your Mayan warrior.

- **Biographies.** Even if you're not building or basing your novel on a real historical life, these are still very useful for personal and private details, letters, photographs, diaries and so on, to help you (re)create the mind, spirit, feelings and practicalities of a real life. They can also be handy when you need a secondary or minor character, and want to conjure up someone with a bit of interest and originality to them.

- **Radio, film and TV documentaries about historical topics.** Modern programmes can be a wonderful way to experience material objects, places and recordings (or reconstructions of them) which you can't get at yourself. Seeing a modern historian standing on the remains of Uruk brings the terrain and scale home as few other things can, and Neil MacGregor's *A History of the World in 100 Objects*, which began as 15-minute programmes on BBC Radio 4, is an object lesson – literally – in drawing stories out of things. However, many such programmes will be aimed at a general audience and tend to focus on the best-known and perhaps clichéd topics. They will also be filtered through the programme-makers' idea of what's story-worthy, which may not be yours. Even the sort of compiled programmes of clips – news bulletins, music, reminiscences – which have no commentary or apparent editorializing will, of course, have been selected and presented to form a certain story arc.

Don't rely on other historical fiction for your facts, however rich a source of writerly inspiration, education and pleasure it is for you as a reader. Some writers get facts just plain wrong (my pet hate is when titles such as 'Reverend' and 'Lady' are wrongly used), others have selected, changed or invented things for perfectly good creative reasons but it's still second-hand to you. Either way, your creative reasons are not the same as theirs, so always check what you find in historical fiction against actual history books, and then look a bit further, for proper, first-hand fuel.

A similar warning applies to fictional stories in film and broadcasting. Don't assume that they are first-hand, accurate historical material. The clothes, cars and settings in *Downton Abbey* are for the most part beautifully and carefully accurate. The dialogue, on the other hand, is excruciatingly inauthentic, and the social stuff of manners, morals and habits is wildly wrong. Please don't take such programmes as a source of historical fact, however much you enjoy them, admire the storytelling, and would like to emulate their popularity.

Christian Cameron

Christian Cameron is a Canadian writer, re-enactor and military historian.

'They always tell you to write what you know. To me, the only way to know history is to experience it – to wear the clothes and eat the food and ride the animals and shoot the bows. To experience it until it is comfortable, not merely survivable, so that you can tell the reader that people really lived back then, and not tell them how hard it all was.'

WHERE TO FIND PRIMARY AND SECONDARY SOURCES

This is just a brief list but it should be enough to start you off. Don't feel you *must* spend weeks in obscure archives to write a good story: you'd be amazed how many fantastic novels have been written without the writer going further than his or her branch library. But do be brave and explore widely, because it can be fun, and you will find wonderful riches you'd no idea were there. If you think you're likely to go on writing historical fiction, consider buying some of the books you find most consistently useful: whether you refer to a wartime memoir twice a week for the year it takes you to write the novel, or go back to a big (and expensive) illustrated history of costume every three months for the rest of your writing life, it may be money well spent to have your own copy sitting on your desk, not least in saving library fines.

- **Your local library** is a good place to start: librarians are hugely knowledgeable and trained to help you search, and the library computers should give you access to the major online reference databases, encyclopedias and dictionaries which you would otherwise have to pay for; you may even be able to get a login to use at home. In the UK the central county or borough library will be the biggest, and hold the main collection of books, while branches will have the basics and will order books in for you. Central libraries also hold the area's local history collection, and branch libraries may have pamphlets and other material for the parish. If you're travelling to an area for research, check when the library will be open beforehand, and take some photocopying money, or learn to use your phone or camera to take readable pictures of texts.

- **University libraries** mostly have a system for admitting non-members, although you may have to pay and/or demonstrate why you want to join. The collections of specialist books, journals and theses can be enormously useful, not just for history but other topics (social, medical, artistic, psychological) that the magpie nature of research for fiction sends you to.

- **Records offices and archives:** these can include personal and public letters, documents, photographs, legislation, minutes of meetings, newspapers and anything else which holds a society's collective history. Companies, local councils, stately homes, universities, charities, schools and professional and benevolent associations all have archives, which may be held on site or elsewhere. archiveshub.ac.uk is a wonderful searchable database of the archives held by several hundred institutions in the UK. All countries have a national archive where legal, royal and government records are kept and can be read; records of births, marriages and deaths may be held in parishes or counties, or at national level. Some records for colonial Canada and Australia, for example, may also be held in the British National Archive at Kew.

- **National libraries:** the British Library, the Scottish, Welsh, Irish, Canadian, Australian and New Zealand equivalents, and the US Library of Congress, are the ultimate source of physical books, newspapers and other publications, since publishers are legally obliged to deposit copies of everything they produce. You will only be able to read the books there, not borrow them, and you probably can't browse the shelves but only search the catalogue and order up what you want. The catalogues are searchable online (very useful even if you're not planning to go there) and you should be able to order the books in advance so they're ready for you; most libraries are lovely places to work as well. In the UK, British Library books may well be available – for a fee and a longish wait – through inter-library loan at your local library.

- **Sound archives:** The glorious National Sound Archive includes most of the BBC Sound Archive and is held by the British Library: it goes back to the earliest days of recorded sound. Most countries have some kind of equivalent, and many archives have at least transcriptions of oral history recordings, so online searching should turn up some useful links.

- **Local and national museums, galleries and historic buildings** are full of social history and material culture: costumes and hairstyles, carriages and agricultural machinery, crafts and early industrial technology, domestic artefacts of every kind, room sets, pictures, maps... They are often happy to answer questions by email, too, so don't be shy, just polite and grateful but also persistent: they may be able to advise you where else to look. Their websites may have information, images and fact-sheets, and they will often have research collections not on display which you can book a time to see. Be patient if they're understaffed, and take their conservators' rules seriously about photography, handling and copyright.

Conservators hate flash with good reason, so learn to set your camera to take an adequate picture without it.

- **Online sources** are richer than ever before but they can be bewildering. The trick is to get clever with searching: generally speaking, the more *specific* words you add to your search terms the closer the search engine will be able to get to what you're looking for, and if you use 'advanced search' you can include or exclude specific things. Be prepared to scroll through a couple of pages of results to find the little local archive, obscure journal or enthusiasts' blog which has *exactly* what you need. As you browse, make a folder in your browser's Favourites/Bookmarks to keep links to things which might be useful later. The National Archive databases and collections are searchable online and include archives held elsewhere, while all sorts of things have been digitized.

- **Project Gutenberg** has digitized, downloadable versions of vast numbers of out-of-copyright books, including some extremely ancient texts. Translations are usually Victorian or other out-of-copyright versions, but that may be an advantage in capturing the written voice of other eras. You can always get a more modern version from the library if you need to, though be careful of copyright issues. Project Gutenberg is particularly useful for the more obscure fiction, drama and poetry of your period, which may never have been produced in a modern edition.

- **Google Books** is another online goldmine and includes in-copyright books. How much of them you can read without buying the book will vary, but if you're canny with the search terms you may well be able to find the pages you need. **Google Scholar** is the equivalent search engine for scholarly writing: it only sends you to academically respectable, peer-reviewed sources. For a minor point the abstract or first page may tell you what you need to know, although to read the whole paper you may need **access to the JSTOR database or similar**, for example through your library. **Google Maps, Google Earth** and **Google Street View** are also very useful for getting the lie of the land, though it's surprisingly difficult to tell how steep things like hills are, and what you can and can't see from where. Googling 'old map of [your novel's setting]' should find the websites of dealers with good enough images for your purposes.

- **Online booksellers** will give you access to both new and second-hand books. Sometimes, again, you will only need what you can see from their Look Inside facility, while the good second-hand booksellers (most easily found through abebooks.co.uk) should be happy to answer an email question about a book. You don't need me to tell you that pirate websites offering downloads of books for free without the author's and publishers' agreement are a) illegal and b) cheating your fellow writers out of the payment they deserve for their professional work.

- **Online dictionaries.** Writers need more detail than the free, quick-reference online sources supply, and historical fiction writers need more detail still. Your local library should give you online access to the great scholarly dictionaries such as the *Oxford English Dictionary* and the US *Merriam-Webster*: they are easy to search, will give dates for when words come into common use and, very usefully, give examples of their changing meaning and usage in different periods. A different and equally useful approach is **Google NGram Viewer**: you can put in any word or name (or even several, to compare them), and it will search across the whole Google Books corpus to draw a graph of its frequency over the centuries, so you don't accidently call your medieval French peasant Wayne and make him eat chilli.

- *History Today* **magazine** has a goldmine of a searchable, downloadable database of individual articles: you can buy one at a time, or packages, and other magazines will also have searchable indexes of back numbers. Long reviews of history and other non-fiction books in booky publications such as the *Times Literary Supplement*, the *New York Review of Books* and the like are often really solid articles about that topic, as well as assessing the book itself; again, the archives can be searched.

- **YouTube** can be a good source of clips, images and archive footage and, like **Google Image, Pinterest, Wikipedia** and all such first-dip sites, can lead you onwards to sites with deeper information: not just in the references on the Wikipedia page, for example, but links to historical re-enactment societies, outdoor museums and living history events and exhibitions.

- **Genealogical websites** are the obvious place to start if you're researching real historical characters, and they can also be an excellent way of getting a feel for the lives that people lived in the place and period you're working on. The big sites are paid-for, and do draw on sites that you can get at for free in the National Archive. But a taster trial may be all you need, and they do allow you to search lots of sources at once: registers of births, marriages, deaths, military service, census records, passenger lists and shipping records, criminal records and so on.

Key idea: 'reimagining is partly a process of forgetting'

Rose Tremain's reminder is important. When you come to write your own story, it can be difficult to go against the apparently authoritative versions, but for your imaginative processes to work properly, you *do* need to 'leave the research behind', as Tremain says elsewhere. So don't feel you must obsessively note down everything you read, or be paralysed by the fear of not remembering the 'right' facts. Make the notes by all means, as a way of lodging the material in your memory (and writing notes has been proved to be much more effective for that than highlighting or cut-and-pasting) but then let your memory sieve out what your story needs.

Snapshot: connecting Then and Now

We all have ideas and themes that we find particularly interesting in real life, and which tend to keep cropping up in our writing: for example adultery, political betrayal, adopted sons, mothers and daughters, love versus family or religious loyalty. Or maybe there's a theme that you've always wanted to explore but have never got round to.

Pick one such theme, and use the techniques we've explored – freewriting, clustering, drawing – or any others, to explore in and around this theme a little bit further: the real-life examples, the human dynamics, and the images, associations and metaphors.

Now go looking for a place and a period which would enable you to develop a strong story, full of urgent, important conflicts for the characters, where there will be a lot at stake. For example, if your theme is betrayal, then a time of religious tensions would be a fruitful setting: a man hoping to survive by switching sides might not only be betraying his community, but end up dying in battle and then burning in Hell. If your theme is adopted sons, then a farming family in a time of famine would have plenty at stake as the parents age, and the farm is too small to support all the adult children.

Do a bit of digging into the period, looking for possible ways your story might fit but also staying open to other possible stories.

Focus point: read and browse non-fiction widely

It's important for your development as a writer of fiction to explore times and places that you know little about, or thought had no interest for you. All the sources I've mentioned for research are also good for browsing, to widen and enrich the possibilities for current and future projects. It will also keep reminding you that your assumptions about the past may be well off-beam for other societies in other times.

Don't feel you have to remember everything, but if you make any notes, do record where you found this material in full detail: the magazine, issue and page number, the author and publisher of the book, the website name and the URL, which library or friend the book came from. It's desperately frustrating to be unable to track it down when, three years later, you suddenly realize that it *is* the next novel.

Snapshot: working with your new historical location and research

Take two people, from this just-beginning idea you have for a story, who you think are likely to be important to it. Use any techniques you like to develop them a bit further: freewriting, pen-portraits, sketching if you like drawing, finding portraits online, clustering and so on. Do any bits of research along the way that would be useful, but don't get too sidetracked: research is crucial, but it's also a terrible time-suck if you let it be one. And you can always check things later, when you know what it is that the story actually needs.

Write: working with a theme and the location you've found for it

Take the theme-based research you did in the Snapshot exercise, the point in space and time where you chose to locate it, and the two characters you tentatively thought would be the important ones. Think of a crucial moment in the story which will bring them into conflict with each other, or with a third character. Jot down a few notes about what led up to this crisis, and then write a first draft of that scene.

If you're working with a setting in time and place that's very new to you, then don't worry if you come across things you don't know about the period: relax and call this a zero draft. It will tell you what research it would need if you developed this story.

Focus point: don't let research become procrastination

Research is exciting, fruitful, essential and often huge fun. It can also, insidiously, become a form of procrastination: it *feels* like virtuous and creative work, and you're not on Facebook, after all (although sometimes Twitter is the quickest way to get a simple question answered). The thing is, forming your own real, new words on the paper is hard work and opens you to being judged, which is daunting. By contrast, grappling with facts and books which lead naturally on to the next, and reading and enjoying other writers' words, can be much easier and more comfortable. But research is not writing. As a friend of mine said, Melville could have spent a whole lifetime researching whales and whaling, but that wouldn't have resulted in *Moby Dick*. To stop research becoming procrastination, remind yourself of these points:

- Research doesn't get the story written; only writing does.
- Browsing people's blogs and the easy sites may feel like researching but it's often more about avoiding writing. Good historical fiction imagines deep below the bland, basic information that such sites offer. Does the site you're looking at have real substance to fuel that deep-diving?
- You are not a historian, and your job is not to chase down historical facts and records to their *ultimate* truth. Your job is to use as much as you need to write a vivid and compelling story.
- You need to stop some time, and get on with writing.
- Trying is enough: do your reasonable best, then forgive yourself for the facts and records which you chose not to track down, and for anything which you might have got 'wrong' which you would prefer to have got right, and get on with it.

When the real history comes first

That Write exercise started with the idea and theme, and then researched a location for them. But much more often, for most writers, it's the other way round: a real historical character or event demands that the story be written, and this immediately sets up fixed factual points that you will need to work with or work around. As we discussed in the context of real historical characters in Chapter 2, there is always a tension between the need for imaginative freedom and the need to keep your story anchored in some kind of historical reality. How should you decide to deal with it, in your projects?

Thomas Kenneally asserts in his author's note to *Schindler's Ark* that 'I have attempted to avoid all fiction, though, since fiction would debase the record, and to distinguish between reality and the myths ... most exchanges and conversations, and all events, are based on the detailed recollections of other *Schindlerjuden* (Schindler Jews), Schindler himself, and other witnesses'.

Jill Paton Walsh sets out the layers of time and story (re)telling in *Knowledge of Angels* thus: 'This story is based very remotely on the true story of the Maid of Châlons – vide Rousseau, *Epître II sur l'homme*. It is set on an island somewhat like Mallorca, but not Mallorca, at a time somewhat like 1450, but not 1450. A fiction is always, however obliquely, about the time and place in which it is written.'

Toni Morrison explains in her foreword to the 2007 edition of *Beloved* that the true story of Margaret Garner 'is fascinating, but, to a novelist, confining. Too little imaginative space there for my purposes'. Her decision to recreate Garner as Sethe, however, has an ethical as well as a creative dimension: some years earlier, in interview, she explained how she felt that, 'Making a little life for oneself by scavenging other people's lives is a big question, and it does have moral and ethical implications. In fiction I feel the most intelligent, and the most free, and the most excited, when my characters are fully invented people. If they're based on somebody else, in a funny way it's an infringement of a copyright. That person owns his life, has a patent on it.'

Margaret Atwood describes in her essay 'In Search of *Alias Grace*' how her novel of real-life Grace Marks, the servant who was imprisoned for murdering her employer, had plenty of records to draw on, and she had to work out her own rules: 'When there was a solid fact, I could not alter it… Also, every major element in the book had to be suggested by something in the writing about Grace and her times, however dubious such writing might be; but, in the parts left unexplained – the gaps left unfilled – I was free to invent … The past is made of paper… there is no more reason to trust something written down on paper then than there is now'.

And although both names and places in Peter Ackroyd's *Hawksmoor* are real, he uses his Author's Note to fend off the idea that he is trying to animate real history: 'Any relation to real people, either living or dead, is entirely coincidental. I have employed many sources in the preparation of *Hawksmoor*, but this version of history is my own invention.'

Robert Fabbri

Robert Fabbri's Vespasian series of novels has reached Number VI.

'I always work from the basis that if a historical fact doesn't fit the plot it's not an inconvenient fact, it's the wrong plot.'

CENTRING STORIES ON REAL HISTORICAL CHARACTERS

It can be incredibly exciting to give yourself permission to inhabit a real historical character and write them as they tell their own story: novels like Margaret George's *The Autobiography of Henry VIII* or Marguerite Yourcenar's *Memoirs of Hadrian* do just that. Some of these novels explicitly 'ventriloquize' historical characters, as A. S. Byatt puts it: the story is formed as letters, diary entries, confessions or memoirs, where the fact that the narrator is writing them is in some way part of the story; Robert Nye's *The Voyage of the Destiny* is a brilliant example.

On the other hand, sometimes it's imaginatively easier to approach a real character obliquely, through someone else's eyes, as Margaret Forster does with the poet Elizabeth Barrett Browning in *Lady's Maid* and, more eccentrically, as Andrew O'Hagan does in *The Life and Opinions of Maf the Dog, and of His Friend Marilyn Monroe.* Servants, friends, siblings and even pets can all be fruitful narrators: they may be wholly fictional or, like Forster's maid-narrator, have existed but only be documented from the outside.

Or you might choose to adopt the voice of a storyteller, a chronicler, looking back to tell events. They may have strong opinions which you want the reader to read 'through' to a different truth, as Mary Renault does with her eunuch Bagoas, telling the story of Alexander in *The Persian Boy*. Thomas Keneally's solution in *Schindler's Ark* is the exact opposite: the narrative voice is cool and impersonal, perhaps from his anxiety not to 'debase the record'.

Snapshot: finding the 'white spaces' between the facts which you can write on

Think of a real historical character who you might want to write about. Do some research, specifically looking for a gap where your imagination might have free play *and* where your characters-in-action will have plenty at stake and lots of reasons to act. The gaps might be:

- gaps in time, where we have no information about what they were doing
- gaps in space, where we have no information about where they were
- gaps in understanding, where we know how they acted but have no insight into the chain of logical and emotional cause and effect.

Make some notes about what scene or scenes you might write in this white space which is so full of potential. If you've spotted several gaps, use these notes to work out which seems most promising.

When to research

There is more on this in Chapter 10; for now, I'd say it's worth developing ways not to interrupt your drafting for research. For small, specific things I just put [square brackets] in, with a description inside them of what I haven't yet found out. That way, the piece reads fairly naturally as I'm working, and later when I search for the [ ]s I know exactly what I need to sort them out. For example, my first draft might have things like this:

> *He groped inside his [warm thick outer garment] and brought out a [scroll of parchment or paper? Wax tablet notebook?]; I took it gingerly – because who knew what this knowledge might lead to? – and stuffed it into my scrip.*

However, if the scene turns on the scroll or tablet being destroyed, or being used as a weapon, I would probably stop and look up which it should be, because the physicality of that is going to make a big difference to the scene.

Write: a real historical character

Take the character you've just been researching, the 'white space' you've spotted in their story which you can write on, and the approach you've decided, and write that scene. As you go, make a note of anything you might want to research, but try not to divert from the main flow of writing your first draft.

If you come across the sort of dilemma we've been discussing, about whether you're free to invent or change something, or whether instead you must find out and stick to what historians have said, again make a note, but for now go with the option that would be best for the story.

Key idea: lack of research, or lack of confidence, leads to blurring

Yes, you are not a historian, and your job is not to chase down historical facts and records to their *ultimate* truth. And where you can't find out something and you don't feel free to invent, it's surprising what you can get away with just avoiding altogether. If the texture of the gangway under the reader's feet is vivid enough, we'll never notice that you haven't said a word about the rigging: the shape of a gown doesn't matter if we're too busy catching our breath from running.

But the 'reality and detail' of your world *is* what, overall, makes the reader willing to enter into and stay in their side of the contract. So the more often you blur, dodge, brush over or just stick to safe, generic, off-the-peg stuff which can't be wrong but which the reader's mind skids over, the blander and less vivid the world and the characters will be. The reader may 'believe' in it in the sense that they don't trip up on something obviously wrong or anachronistic. But intuitively they won't feel so deeply involved, and instead will grow bored and restless.

Workshop: how is the story working?

Take the story that you've just written based on a real historical character, print it out double-spaced, and read it like a reader, recording your reactions but not worrying about the solutions yet. Some of the things you should have your ears pricked for are:

- What sings? What sounds 'just right', in the instinctive sense?
- What clunks?
- Are there places where you've blurred over a lack of research or something that isn't yet fully imagined?

- Are there places where something feels too modern – whether it's language, material detail or how your characters act?

- Are there places where something feels too self-consciously olde-worlde – again, whether it's language, material detail or how your characters act?

- Do the characters feel as if they sit and move and act naturally in their place and time? Or do some feel like modern actors stuffed into off-the-peg period costumes?

- Are there lumps of information – of explaining or back-story – which feel undigested, rather than emerging as a natural part of the storytelling?

Now go back over what you've marked up, and think about how you might set about solving the problems. What needs more imagining, and how might you do that? What needs more research and where could you find what you need? Could you cut the info-lumps and explaining, or slide them in as a natural part of the characters and what they do say and think?

Snapshot: what if this character were fictional?

If you decided to create a Queen Henrietta VIII of England who had eight husbands, then you're into Alternative History (more on that and other historical genres in Chapter 9). But, as Toni Morrison did with *Beloved*, with less well-known figures you do always have the option of giving at least some of them different names, settings or experiences and changing the timeline or events, or doing anything else that makes a story work better.

Look at your real historical character, and consider their real life as the raw material for a wholly fictional story. Brainstorm on paper: where could you branch off from the original towards new and exciting possibilities? Which aspects of their real life – their real personality and experiences – would you keep? What other people in their life might you also make fictional? Which might you keep as 'real'? What sort of principles might you make for yourself about sticking to the historical facts, versus invention?

Edit: tackling what your problem-finding found

Take whichever you like of the two stories you've written in this chapter, and revise it fully, first doing a problem-finding read if you didn't before. Then do any more research and further imagining that you now know the story needs. Finally, work your way through the story, revising as you go – i.e. solving the problems – to end up with a second draft.

Convincing readers that you are right

Sometimes you will be spot-on with the material culture, voices, beliefs and facts, yet some readers won't believe you. You need to be aware of things that your 'average' reader might not believe, and it helps to ask anyone giving you feedback to highlight anything like this. That doesn't mean conforming to what readers believe if they're wrong, but it does mean you'll need to work a bit harder to persuade them that you are right.

For example, because writers in the past rarely wrote contractions such as *didn't* or *can't*, many readers will feel it's 'modern' when you make your characters speak like that, even though we know from evidence, as well as common sense, that *speakers* have always contracted or elided words. Besides, not contracting words in your prose or dialogue can so easily sound stilted or self-consciously olde-worlde. You may need to be a bit tactful about it: I'd suggest you read your work aloud as relaxedly and naturally as you can, listening for the rhythms of the speech to see (and mark) where the contractions feel most natural, and where something more formal or sounds more 'right'.

Similarly, it is a fact that medieval women often rode horses astride, because the only side-saddles available gave the rider no control and so the horse had to be led by someone else on the ground. But some readers may know only that 'in the old days women rode side-saddle because of their long skirts', and baulk when you make your medieval heroine, authentically, ride astride. Here, you might decide to meet the reader's possible reaction head on. You could make one prissy old man disapprove and the woman think, 'He's no right to despise me. My mother always rode this way, and no man ever called her wanton. Grand ladies too, and all who'd rather take their fate in their own hands than be at the mercy of some shuffling groom.' Or maybe a nervous young groom asks rather doubtfully if she's willing to ride astride, because there's no lady's saddle in the tack room. Such tricks do risk being a bit info-lumpy, for the experienced reader at least, but it helps if you can tuck the point about the side-saddle into a moment which is apparently about something else. You might make the stuffy old man have another function in the scene, or the groom be embarrassed, or embarrassingly forward, as he has to give her a leg-up.

Next step

We've been thinking about how research both feeds and supports your imagination, and putting some of that into words, and we've already touched on voice. Now we move on to think more closely about what's going on when we try to conjure up historical worlds in a voice that works for the modern reader.

5

Hearing the voices: prose (i)

Voice is what draws the reader into a story from the first page, and all fiction has a narrative voice as well as dialogue. Voice in historical fiction presents particular opportunities and challenges, because it's both your medium and part of your 'message' of the otherness of this story-world. Voices speak from the texts of the period, and you need to draw on them, not to pastiche or imitate, but to strengthen and control the reader's experience of your story.

What is 'voice'?

When writers talk about the 'voice' or 'voices' of a story, we don't just mean the dialogue that characters speak aloud, or even the 'silent speech' of characters' thoughts written out directly. We also mean the *narrative* voice, and even if the narrator never directly addresses the reader, and doesn't have a personality as a character has a personality, it still has a voice. It's this which draws the reader in long before we can get to know the characters or care about what happens to them. It's also the main thing that controls the 'tone' of your story: the way that you want the reader to take it. For example, if the story is about illegitimate and legitimate children, it's the voice that leads us to read it as comedy (*Wise Children*, Angela Carter), drama (*Fire from Heaven*, Mary Renault; *Fingersmith*, Sarah Waters) or tragedy (*Les Misérables*, Victor Hugo).

Key idea: voice is what draws the reader in

The voice of a narrative is the medium through which the story will be transmitted: it is a synthesis of how people speak and write now with how they spoke and wrote in the era of your story. It's what makes the reader feel connected to the human consciousness through which the story is being conveyed, and thus to the characters of the story. Because of that, a compelling voice is the thing above all that editors, publishers and agents are looking for.

Narrators

The basic choice you have to make, right at the beginning, is whether this story is being told by someone who takes part in at least some of the events of the story, or by some kind of entity outside those events. Often, these are talked of as 'first person' versus 'third person' narratives, but what's at issue isn't pronouns, but *where the narrator stands in relation to the events of the narrative*. So thinking of your narrator as **external** or **internal** is much more accurate and useful.

EXTERNAL NARRATORS

An external narrator is outside the events of the story. All the actors in the story are referred to as *he* and *she*, so these narrators are sometimes called 'third person' narrators because there is no *I* present in the action of any scene. They may be a fairly neutral voice transmitting the story entirely through the thoughts and perceptions of the characters (*Wolf Hall*, Hilary Mantel), or they may comment directly on things, or transmit information that no character inside the story can know (*The Blue Flower*, Penelope Fitzgerald).

Here are some openings:

- *Some years ago there was in the city of York a society of magicians. They met upon the third Wednesday of every month and read each other long, dull papers upon the history of English magic.* (Susannah Clarke, *Jonathan Strange & Mr Norrell*)

- *Lilias Papagay was of imagination all compact. In her profession this was a suspect, if necessary, quality, and had to be watched, had to be curbed.* (A. S. Byatt, *The Conjugial Angel*)

- *A young man, young but not very young, sits in an anteroom somewhere, some wing or other, in the Palace of Versailles. He is waiting. He has been waiting a long time.* (Andrew Miller, *Pure*)

- *Sebastos Abdes Pantera was twelve years old and nearly a man on the night he discovered that his father was a traitor.*
  It was spring, the time of bright flowers, and Passover, the time of celebration, sacrifice and riots. (M. C. Scott, *The Emperor's Spy*)

- *At the first gesture of morning, flies began stirring. Inman's eyes and the long wound at his neck drew them, and the sound of their wings and the touch of their feet were soon more potent than a yardful of roosters in rousing a man to wake.* (Charles Frazier, *Cold Mountain*)

- *'So now get up.'*
  Felled, dazed, silent, he has fallen; knocked full length on the cobbles of the yard. His head turns sideways; his eyes are turned towards the gate, as if someone might arrive to help him out. (Hilary Mantel, *Wolf Hall*)

Notice how each has a very different tone, language and historical feel. Some are 'wide-angle' and full of context; others are close in to the immediate moment and perceptions of the character. The order I've put them in is not accidental, but connects to this idea, which writers call *psychic distance*, of which more in Chapter 7.

In fact, the narrator of *Jonathan Strange* does say *I*, occasionally, but as a narrator, not as a character: *I doubt if it will surprize anyone to know that, of the two, London preferred Mr Strange.* Literary criticism sometimes talks of this kind of narrator as 'the author', but it isn't really: this is not Susannah Clarke speaking, but a storyteller-narrator.

INTERNAL NARRATORS

An internal narrator participates in the events of the story. Maybe it was years ago; maybe it's happening now, but they refer to themselves as *I,* with the other characters referred to as *he* and *she*. Here are some openings:

- *You must and will suppose (fair or foul reader, but where's the difference?) that I suppose a heap of happenings that I had no eye to eye knowledge of or concerning. What though a man supposes is oft (often if you will) of the right and very substance of his seeing.* (Anthony Burgess, *A Dead Man in Deptford*)

- *My father, Giovanni da Cola, was a merchant, and for the last years of his life was occupied in the importation of luxury goods into England which, though an unsophisticated country, was nonetheless beginning to rouse itself from the effects of revolution.* (Iain Pears, *An Instance of the Fingerpost*)

- *I am a witch for the modern age. I keep my spells small, and price them high. What they ask for is the same as always. The common spells deal in love, or what love is meant to make, or else hate, and what that might accomplish.* (Sally O'Reilly, *Dark Aemilia*)

- *Q: Why is London like Budapest?*
  A: Because it is two cities divided by a river.
  Good morning! Let me introduce myself. My name is Dora Chance. Welcome to the wrong side of the tracks. (Angela Carter, *Wise Children*)

- *Beyond the Indian hamlet, upon a forlorn strand, I happened on a trail of recent footprints … the tracks led me to their maker, a white man, his trowzers & Pea-jacket rolled up, sporting a kempt beard & an outsized Beaver, shovelling & sifting the cinder sand with a tea-spoon so intently that he noticed me only after I had hailed him from ten yards away.* (David Mitchell, *Cloud Atlas*)

- *Chip told us not to go out. Said, don't you boys tempt the devil. But it been one brawl of a night, I tell you, all of us still reeling from the rot – rot was cheap, see, the drink of French peasants, but it stayed like nails in you gut.* (Esi Edugyan, *Half Blood Blues*)

Again, notice how different the feel is, even though they all start with *I*, *me*, *my*, or *myself*. These are all characters who are in some way part of the story, but while some address the reader/listener directly, others don't. What they narrate may be their story (*Wise Children*) or it may be someone else's story (*Dead Man in Deptford* is about Christopher Marlowe). And it's worth remembering that a character-narrator *is still a narrator*: this is the story they choose to tell, and if they want to evoke events at which they were not present, there's no reason they shouldn't. However, since the narrowly conventional modern approach to point of view dictates that a character-narrator can't write events at which they were not present, if you want your narrator to do that, you may decide that you need to 'educate' the reader early on about how this narrative works, as Burgess does here with such panache.

Focus point: choosing an internal or external narrator

The choice of an internal or an external narrator is the one of the earliest choices you have to make in writing a story. With an internal character-narrator, their voice will dominate the whole narrative, which can be either a huge pleasure or annoyingly restrictive, especially if you decide your character-narrator should only narrate events at which they were present. With an external narrator, and a narrative voice which doesn't belong to one single character, you are free of that problem. You also have the possibility of allowing the narrative, not just the dialogue, to be coloured by the voices of different characters, in free indirect style. It is possible to change from one to the other type of narrator later in your work on the book, but it does involve more than merely switching the pronouns and tidying up the verbs.

Narratives in second person – *you* – are rare, but they do exist. Some narrators address the reader as *you*, although this audience may not ever be named or identified. The *you* in *Dead Man in Deptford* is of this kind.

But in a true second-person narrative, the *you* is the actor in the narrative. This 'generic you' is somewhere between the impersonal, third-person 'one', and 'you' as in the reader. Few historical novels seem to do it consistently but it's a technique worth knowing about, as there may be moments when it's just what you need. In Joseph O'Connor's *Ghost Light*, the 'you' here is the main character of the story who elsewhere is *she*: a famous actress, now old and fallen on hard times:

> *In the top floor room of the dilapidated townhouse across the Terrace, a light has been on all night. From your bed it was visible whenever you turned towards the window, which you had to do in order to fetch your bottle from the floor. ... You are sixty-five now, perhaps the age of that house, perhaps even a little older – what a thought. You approach your only window; it is shockingly cold to the touch.*

Snapshot: look for different narrators

Study the examples of different kinds of narrator that you've just read, and maybe find a variety of examples in other historical fiction.

Which really draw you, personally, in? Which make you feel that this might be a story you'd read? Ignore whether it's a period you fancy, or a genre you enjoy: try to listen for which voices your mental cogs want to engage with or just enjoy.

Now look at all the extracts objectively. First, what, if anything, makes the reader feel that these stories are set in history? Are there material things or names? Spellings? Unfamiliar or old-fashioned words? Familiar words arranged in unfamiliar ways? Read some aloud and listen for rhythm and sound. How dense are the elements which make the voice feel historical?

> Finally, think about how each narrator has some kind of quality or personality, a 'feel': urgent, reflective, immediate, considered, close-in to the character and the moment, or further out. Who might they be? Are they telling the reader something which has just happened to them, or a story from a while ago and some distance away? What actual words, phrases and sentences create that feel?

Paul Kingsnorth

From the 'Note on Language' in Paul Kingsnorth's *The Wake*:

'The way we speak is specific to our time and place. Our assumptions, our politics, our worldview, our attitudes – all are implicit in our words, and what we do with them. To put twenty-first-century sentences into the mouths of eleventh-century characters would be the equivalent of giving them iPads and cappuccinos: just wrong.'

How 'historical' might your voices be?

Imagine the 'historicalness' of narrative voices as a spectrum. At one end are novels like *The Wake*, set in an Anglo-Saxon village just after the Norman invasion and conquest. Kingsnorth describes the voice of the novel as a 'shadow tongue': it uses only Anglo-Saxon words and syntax, as much as possible using the spellings and forms of words that were used then. He has had to make some changes for the reader to understand it at all, but reading aloud helps, especially when you know that before Norman French began to infiltrate English, *c* was always pronounced like *k*:

> *the night was clere though i slept i seen it. though i slept i seen the calm hierde naht only the still. when i gan down to sleep all was clere in the land and my dreams was full of stillness but my dreams did not cepe me still.*

At the other end of the spectrum are novels like Christopher Meredith's *Griffri*, whose narrator – or, rather, a real historical bard – would have been speaking medieval Welsh:

> *Listen, Idnerth. I've been called a paid arselicker and I'm proud enough of my job to consider that a kind of compliment. After all, who with any sense would do such a thing if they weren't getting paid?*

Most of the examples we've seen so far are somewhere in between those two poles. In each extract, the sense that this voice is coming from history is created by different means; the writer has chosen which aspects of language they draw from history and which from our language.

In some ways, it's easier to make those choices when your characters wouldn't have been speaking English at all; when you have historical English as a reference point, the question is how much of it to let on to your pages. But this doesn't mean it's impossible to represent – as opposed to reproducing – the voices of the past.

 Julian Barnes

On his novel *Arthur and George*:

> *'I wanted to write a page-turner, but not a historical novel, rather a contemporary novel which happens to happen a hundred years ago … It depends what your path is to the reader. A historical novel is trying to put the reader back in that time, with all the furniture and fittings of the time. I wanted the reader to be in the twenty-first century.'*

But, even if you agree with Kingsnorth more than Barnes, how can that work out in practice? For example, the mid- to late fifteenth-century Paston letters are perfectly readable – certainly so with modernized spelling – but their *shrewd* translates as *hurtful*, *child* as *servant*, and *take* as *give*. It's just not possible to use those words 'authentically', and convey your meaning: if you try (I speak from experience, here!) at best you will achieve an uneasy pastiche, at worst it will be unreadable. And even if your novel is set in the 1930s, the rhythms of the written language have changed since then, the sentence structures have evolved, and the default vocabulary too (just read fiction written in the 1940s if you don't believe me). Do you try to reproduce it, which will be evocative for some readers but 'old-fashioned' or pastiche for others? Or do you acknowledge that this is a modern novel, as Julian Barnes does, and risk some readers finding it inauthentic?

Many writers will use shorter sections of documents such as letters and diaries, which are more strongly voiced than the narrative. In real life such records carry the real historical voices that we're trying to evoke in our narratives, and it's an opportunity to channel those more strongly, for a short time, with voices that many readers would tire of if they formed a whole novel. Where novels (William Golding's *Rites of Passage*, for example) are wholly formed as a diary or confession, the voice usually evokes, rather than mimics, real historical texts.

Focus point: let go of trying to reproduce 'genuine' or 'authentic' historical voices

Historical fiction is usually trying to evoke a sense of the voices of the past, but the point is not to fool modern readers into thinking this is an actual historical document. On the other hand, you probably want to avoid words and usages which break the frame for the reader, as a digital watch would on the wrist of an actor in a period drama.

But even musicians obsessed with early music know that there's no such thing as being historically authentic in the strict and narrow sense, because we are all trying to perform for an audience of modern ears and minds: the closest anyone can get is an 'historically informed' performance. So creating this intuitive sense of 'historical-ness' is a very subjective business: judging what will sound 'too modern' or 'too difficult' to different readers, and finding the right 'feel' and 'impression'. This doesn't mean giving up: voice is one of the most powerful ways to draw your reader into this historical world, and you are making your job more difficult if you don't exploit the possibilities.

WHAT ABOUT WORDS THE READER DOESN'T KNOW?

Using words which aren't in common, modern use can really help to 'make the familiar strange', *provided* the reader understands what you're trying to convey: it's a rare reader who wants to go in search of a dictionary. If the well-known historical words and references are believable in how you write them into the story, your reader will come to trust how you've used one they don't know. They may even be *more* convinced by things which are strange: after all, the past is a foreign country.

The real mistake is to lob in an explicit definition, unless you can make the explanation the natural action of a convincing character. Even then, making her or him say, 'They called those funny round boats *coracles*' is horribly clunky, and trebly so for readers who already knew. The trick is not to explain, but to tuck the clue into the words. 'My combinations were a bit damp but I got dressed anyway,' doesn't give much help to the reader. 'My combinations were damp and clingy, but they warmed up once I'd put my dress and coat on over the top,' does: we're talking about underwear. But subtlety is the key: readers of historical fiction love learning, but they much prefer to feel that they're doing so by osmosis, not being instructed by a teacher.

Unfortunately, one technique is easy and obvious, and so has become something of a cliché, as with using foreign words to get the reader to 'hear' that the characters are not speaking English. The words tends to be greetings, swear-words and other 'extra' bits of speech: 'Bonjour, madame! *Can I give you a lift into town?* ... Zut alors! *That's one heavy suitcase!*'. The historical equivalent could be something like this: '*Good day to you, madam! Would you like a ride to market? I'm going that way myself ... By the Mass! What's in this basket? It weighs a ton.*'

Yes, 'Good day to you' and 'By the Mass!' get us hearing the speech and the character well flavoured with the setting, without cluttering up the meaning. But, like certain physical gestures, these tricks tend to become a sort of lazy shorthand, 'signalling' to the reader what this is about without actually evoking the individuality and immediacy of the moment. If you want the voice of your narrative to feel authentic rather than second-hand, then you're going to have to dig a little deeper and work harder to integrate your historical models and your own writerly voice in a way which is fresh and vivid. Suzannah Dunne's *The May Queen* is a lovely example of how to do this: there's scarcely a word or phrase that is deliberately 'period language', but the overall effect is beautifully evocative.

Focus point: what determines a voice?

How a narrative comes out is the product of two things: what needs telling, and why it needs to be told. So when you're thinking about a story and how you might write it, ask yourself these questions:

- **What** happened?
- **Who** is telling the story?
- **Why** are they telling it?
- **To whom** are they telling it?
- **How** will they therefore tell it?

Write: the voice of a character-narrator

Imagine a character, A, now old. Something happened when A was young: a small or brief incident which had big repercussions. Scribble notes to pin down what it was.

Now A is old, or older, and needs urgently, even desperately, to tell the story, *either* to justify things to themselves, *or* to make confession to their priest or their God, *or* to set things right with an enemy or a friend. They may be writing this account or they may be dictating it to someone, but paper and time are short. They must cut straight to the heart of what happened, and tell this little story in a way which will get them what they want: to make peace with themselves, to make peace with someone else, or to win absolution. So this account will be in first person, but the Now of its telling matters, as well as the Then of the past.

Characters' voices

Of course, each character has a voice too, in dialogue in any directly quoted thought, and as reported speech or 'reported thought' – i.e. free indirect style. Their voice is one of your strongest tools in making a character who is vivid to you also vivid to us, because it's shaped by their personality. It's also important to make the most of the *contrasts* between voices: just as red is redder and green is greener when they're put against each other, the more you can make different characters speak, move, think and act differently, the more they will stand out as individuals. And it can be feeling your way towards good dialogue that helps your sense of a character develop.

You may be one of the lucky writers who just has to think 'gentle, impatient teenaged Outback girl' or 'clever, cynical Royalist old man', and that voice pours out of your fingers. (Most of us have some writerly things which come naturally, after all, while we struggle with others.) But we also sometimes need to step back and think, 'How can I make this character's personality come across?' So try asking yourself some questions about how each character sounds:

- Do they use long, clever words or short ones?
- Do they use long sentences or short ones?
- Do they use very exact, vivid words for things or bland, off-the-peg, clichéd ones?
- Do they finish their sentences, or tail off from lack of confidence? Do they keep interrupting their own thoughts? Do they jump in on other people's speeches and interrupt them?
- Do they use good, formally constructed sentences, or long, lollopy *and – and – and –* ones? Do they use correct formal grammar, normal informal grammar, a specific regional dialect, or strange constructions unique to them?
- Do they express ideas fully, or make simple statements?
- What are their references? Do they quote proverbs or famous authors, popular songs or political slogans, religious books or things their mother always says?
- Are they speaking in their native language? Is how they speak influenced by some other language or patois? Do they use words wrongly?
- Do they use similes, or metaphors, or both? Do be careful not to use figurative language drawn from a period later than the story, unless anachronisms are all part of the game you're playing. Generally speaking, no helicopter parents in 1750s Harvard, in other words, or potato-shaped faces in medieval Athens.
- Are they friendly, condescending, sycophantic, or cool? Do they change how they speak according to who they're talking to?

If their speech does change, does it match the other's speech, perhaps unconsciously, or emphasize the differences?

Caroline Rance

Caroline Rance writes fiction and non-fiction rooted in medical history.

'In the early drafts, I like to have fun with archaic or regional words and slang, and then tone it right down. If I'm lucky, the authentic-sounding speech rhythms remain – it's a bit like excavating them from a rock of unnecessary detail. For me, the aim is to keep the dialogue inconspicuous; it should do its job quietly, without hitting the reader on the head with forsooths and do-not-yous.'

So how might your characters speak? Have a look at these extracts, then pull some of your favourite books off the shelf and see how those authors do dialogue. What draws you in, what puts you off? What feels authentic and convincing, and what doesn't? What it is about the words *and how they're put together* which is having that effect on you? What choices has the writer made? What would you have done differently? There are no rights and wrongs, but there are more successful and less successful ways of doing things.

- *'In the meantime, perhaps you would condescend to speak the actual text as it appears on the page rather than the superior one which appears to exist in your head.'*
  'If it doesn't exist in my head, Mr Synge, then it doesn't exist at all.'
  'I see we have a philosopher as well as a playwright.'
  'And I see you'd prefer a parrot.' (Joseph O'Conner, *Ghost Light*)
- *'Might as well do another take,' he said. 'The disc ain't all bad. And my damn visas ain't come yet. What else I got to do?' ... Then he gave me a long, clear look. 'We goin to get it right. Just be patient, buck.'*
  'Sure,' I said. 'Sure we will. But wasn't that last one any good, kid? Good good? Would it make us?' (Esi Edugyan, *Half Blood Blues*)

- *'But what about the public baths,'* persisted Antius.
  'Closed until further notice.'
  They won't like that, admiral.'
  *'Well, it can't be helped. We've all grown far too soft in any case
  ... The Empire wasn't built by men who lazed around the baths
  all day.'* (Robert Harris, *Pompeii*)

Snapshot: dialogue

Take your character-narrator A from the Write exercise, and
imagine another person in the room, B. Some minor problem
arises: A needs more ink, B has spilt the wine, or A needs to ask if
B knows something to help with the account A is writing.

Write this little bit of the scene, *but all in dialogue*, as if it were
a radio play. Whatever A sounds like, try to make B's voice as
different as possible, in some of the ways we've been discussing.
If you need to put in a bare minimum of stage directions just to
anchor your imagination, then do. It's better than getting tangled
in things like, 'Oh dear, I've knocked over my expensive wine-cup
with my left elbow.' But this is all about the conversation and the
contrast between the characters.

FREE INDIRECT STYLE

This may well be something you do quite naturally, although you
may not know it has a name or know it as 'free indirect discourse'.
Whatever the name, it's a crucial technique, and not difficult to grasp.

First, think about directly quoted speech: *Josef shrugged his cloak on
and said to Magda, 'I don't believe you, and I'm going to prove it.'*
If we want to report what was said in the speech, as we often do in
real life, we use the tense of the narrative and the pronouns that the
narrator uses: *Josef shrugged his cloak on and said to Magda that he
didn't believe her, and he was going to prove it.*

Free indirect style does the same but with thoughts (it is, in effect,
'reported thought'):

> *Sorcha poured the coffee. Hugh will kill me if I can't pay the
> rent, she thought. I'll just have to hope Fergus will cough up.*

becomes:

> *Sorcha poured the coffee. Hugh would kill her if she couldn't pay the rent. She'd just have to hope Fergus would cough up.*

Again, the words stay the same, but the tense changes from the tense the character would speak or think in to the tense of the narrative, and the pronouns change from the *I* the character would think or say to the *he* or *she* of the narrative. So with free indirect style, the thoughts and the narrative are integrated: the reader can move smoothly in and out of the character's head without a change of gear. What's more because we have two hundred years of experience, readers often don't need help like a *she thought* after *if she couldn't pay the rent.*

It works just as well if you have a character-narrator narrating in first person. Here, both speech and thought are all given directly:

> *I gave Eloise the scroll. 'Can I offer you a drink?' she asked, putting it aside. 'Sorry, I haven't got any wine.'*
>
> *When did you become an abstainer, I wondered. Who's persuaded you that pomegranate juice is a good drink for a Friday evening? But what I said was, 'Juice, how delicious. Thank you.'*

But they could all be given indirectly:

> *I gave Eloise the scroll; she put it aside and asked if she could offer me a drink. She was sorry but she didn't have any wine.*
>
> *When had she become an abstainer, I wondered. Who'd persuaded her that pomegranate juice was a good drink for a Friday evening? But I only said that juice would be delicious, and thanked her.*

Key idea: free indirect style

Because free indirect style and reported speech can cover narrative ground without stopping the narrative voice to slot in the 'real time' voice of actual dialogue and thought, it keeps the narrative profluent – forward-flowing – while still vividly evoking the individual, subjective voices of the characters.

Snapshot: using free indirect style (reported thought) and reported speech

Look at the little passages with Eloise, and mark each of the verbs. Notice how, in the move from directly quoted to indirectly reported speech and thoughts, the tense shifts one step backwards into the past.

Take a couple of historical novels from your shelves, find some dialogue and scribble down what each line would be in reported speech, to get a feel for how it works. Then look at how that author deals with thoughts: are they directly quoted, conveyed in free indirect style, or a mixture?

REPORTED SPEECH

Many writers rarely bother with directly quoted thought, but almost invariably use free indirect style. On the other hand, very few writers would willingly work without directly quoted speech. But reported speech, too, is useful when you want to slot something in without disturbing the flow of the narrative. The real skill is to develop a sense of when to give speech or thought directly and when to report it. In that last version of the Eloise clip, we still need the *I wondered*, to shift us from Eloise's speech reported as *she didn't have any wine*, to the character-narrator's thought reported as *When did she become*. That's a little clue that there might be a more fluent way to do things.

There are several possible versions, and it's worth trying a few out, perhaps when you're revising a first draft. You need to think about which are the important, significant thoughts and speeches, and which are necessary for the scene to make sense, but less important in the grander scheme of things. These are my choices:

> *I gave Eloise the scroll and, putting it aside, she asked if she could offer me a drink.* 'Sorry, I haven't got any wine.'

> *When had she become an abstainer? Who'd persuaded her that pomegranate juice was a good drink for a Friday evening?* 'Juice, how delicious,' *I said, and thanked her.*

As I see it (you might disagree), the important thing is the narrator's indignant realization that someone else might be influencing Eloise, the well-known drinker, in a fairly dramatic way. *'I haven't got any wine'* sets this up, and then we get the narrator's thought as part of the forward-flow of his narrative. Giving *'Juice, how delicious'* as direct speech points up the important contrast between his indignant thought and his bland speech. The automatic thanks is not important to the story, but it is revealing that he bothers to tell us, as if he wants us to know his suspicions of Eloise didn't override his good manners. As a result, we will read the rest of the scene waiting for the indignation to spill out.

Write: working with voice

Imagine another small but very significant moment in a particular person's life – the same person as in the Write exercise earlier in this chapter, or a different one. Choose an event which will need dialogue (so there will need to be at least one other character in it), but also thought and physical action. Write that scene with an external narrator, i.e. in third person. Make your own decisions about:

- what sort of voice the narrative has
- how historical the voice is, in both narrative and dialogue
- what the narrator's tone is (comic? tragic? etc.), and how it colours the tone and effect of the narrative
- what the characters' voices are like, and how different they are from the narrator's
- when to give the characters' speech and thought directly, and when to use reported speech and free indirect style.

Researching for voice

Voice is a slippery business, and many wonderful writers have trouble explaining what, exactly, is going on between what they read and what comes out of their own pen. But you do need to go back to the voices of your period, even if that means translations. There are two main ways of doing this kind of reading: immersively, to train your intuition, and analytically, to teach your conscious understanding.

- **Training your intuition:**
  - ▷ Just read, the way you read as a child: letting the words soak into you. Go slowly, but don't be afraid to slide over a word that you don't know.
  - ▷ Read aloud. Don't be shy about it: in throwing yourself into expressing the meaning, you'll find out a lot about how the sentence structures work and how words and the rhythms feel.
  - ▷ Copy out passages: like reading aloud, your brain has to do more processing, so your intuition absorbs more.
  - ▷ Listen to audio books. This isn't a substitute for reading aloud, but it is a bit like shining a light on to the text from a different angle.

- **Analysing:**
  - ▷ Look at a particular sentence and work out how the same thing would be said in an equivalent text written nowadays.
  - ▷ Look a page, and ask yourself first what effect it has, then dig in to work out *which* words and phrases are making that effect happen, and why it works.
  - ▷ If there are any words you don't know, or which seem to be being used very differently, look them up in a good dictionary that provides information about changing meanings over time.

Snapshot: imitating historical voices

Pretend you're in training to be a forger of historical documents, and write some paragraphs out in the style of a historical document that you've read. Go on, have some fun: no one's looking. Build the sentences differently from your normal style, enjoy different words and their order, play with the different meanings. Then do the same with another document, preferably of another kind. Try out letters, play dialogue, chronicles, poetry. Have some more fun.

Compare them to some of the originals which inspired them. What matches and what doesn't? Could you make your versions more convincing?

Workshop: strengthening voice

Look at your second Write exercise, where you were writing in third person, and print it out if possible. *Read it aloud.* (It's much easier to keep reading aloud and holding the overall shape and rhythm of a sentence while you make quick ticks or wiggly lines with a pen, than if you're faffing around on a keyboard.) Then go over it, looking for issues of voice in particular. Remember, you're not solving the problems, only finding them. Ask yourself these questions:

- Would a reader know it was set in the past? How? How much of that is the voices? Do they feel right?

- Is the narrative voice consistent? Does it have some kind of character, however faint, of its own? When you were writing, did it seem to settle into itself, or did you struggle to find a consistent, fluent voice? Would you like the narrative to be more 'voice-y', or are you happy with it as it is? If you're not happy, how could you make the voice stronger and clearer?

- Do the characters' personalities come across in the voice of their speech, and in any thoughts that we have access to? Are they as well differentiated as they can be, given who they are? What more could you do to characterize their voices more strongly?

- Is the historical flavour too strong in places? Does it sound stilted? How could you make things sound more natural? Or are you just over-egging the pudding? Which strongly flavoured things should be cut, so that the things that stay can work better?

- Is the historical flavour too faint in places? Are there things which feel too definitely modern? Can you find more effective replacements? Or is it just a bit flat and bland, because you were trying not to be too specific in either direction? What might you do about that?

Were there places where research would help make a voice work better? How might you do that research?

Key idea: evoking historical voices matters, exact years don't

In *The Wake*, Paul Kingsnorth had a clear boundary in 1066, but in most of history how words evolve is a less exact business. So obsessing about when, exactly, a word came into use, is unlikely to be useful. For one thing, words are usually in use before anyone writes them down, and for another, as your attempt at forgery will show, when it comes to creating a narrative that can sustain a whole novel and keep the reader reading, you will be using dozens of words in ways that are not strictly authentic to the period. But readers vary, and many will have a vague sense of unease if your language is well off-beam, even if they're not sure why. So although you may want to check the origins and dates of words when you suspect that they may not be right for the date, that can only ever be to help you decide which word is right, in the context of your novel, for a modern reader.

Edit: editing for voice

Take the story you've just workshopped, and do any research you want or need to do, whether that's looking up words or trying to find examples of voices. Then revise the story, concentrating on the voices of both narrative and dialogue, so that they come across more clearly and strongly. Think about how deliberately, consciously historical you want them both to seem – how evocative of voices of the past – and make sure they're consistent.

In this chapter we've been working with voice, as the 'human interface' between the reader and the story, but also as a crucial way that characters are evoked. Now we are moving on to look at how stories work, and the techniques which will make yours irresistible.

6

Story and plot: structure

If story is 'the journey your characters make', then plot is 'the route your characters take'. Together, they form the structure of your story. Mystery and suspense have a part to play, too, at both the macro- and the micro-scale, while thinking in terms of act-structure will help you to keep the reader reading.

Martine Bailey

Martine Bailey's debut, *An Appetite for Violets*, is set in the eighteenth century

'Having the story idea is only a start. It is the unspooling plot that keeps the reader turning the page. I use the classic Three Act movie format, hopefully building to a gripping climax.'

Story comes from character

The dictionary definition of 'story' is 'a causally related chain of events', and in fiction those events are centred on the characters-in-action. Each action is caused by something, and has consequences, which cause new actions – and so the chain of physical, mental and emotional consequences grows. For anything other than the shortest of stories, it's wondering what the consequences will be, and what they will then cause – what will happen next?, in other words – which keeps us reading.

The changes may be external or internal to the characters. In *Wolf Hall* Thomas Cromwell is given the problem of engineering Henry VIII's divorce from Katharine of Aragon: externally, he becomes richer and more powerful than he could ever have dreamed of, and England divorces itself from the Church of Rome. Or the change may be internal: in *Bring Up the Bodies* Cromwell is given the problem of engineering the fall of Anne Boleyn, and has to act in ways which change him from a shrewd but relatively honest lawyer and faithful quasi-son of Cardinal Wolsey into a manipulator, perjurer and ultimately a monster. But in the most satisfying stories change is both internal and external: in *Wolf Hall* Cromwell also grows up and gains internal self-confidence in the face of snobbery and political suspicion, and in *Bring Up The Bodies* his internal change is paralleled by an ever-greater external dependence on Henry VIII in the face of danger from rivals, and more monstrous deeds.

Of course, not all novels or even short stories have only one main character. (Marge Piercy's panoramic *Gone to Soldiers*, about the Second World War, has no fewer than ten main characters, but that's a hard trick to pull off.) And, of course, each secondary character is also the hero of his or her own story: they act in accordance with their own story, not necessarily the main character's.

> # Key idea: change is the motor of fiction
>
> As John Yorke puts it in *Into the Woods*, at its heart, storytelling is the telling of a process: thesis – antithesis – synthesis. A character-in-action, in acting to survive or achieve something (thesis), encounters obstacles outside or inside themselves (antithesis). They have to change how they act in order to cope with those obstacles, and in doing so either they, or the world, or both, become someone or something new (synthesis).

PLOT COMES FROM STORY

This chapter is going to assume that you have one main character, and that the overall shape of the story is formed by what one might think of as the 'big change', or arc, that occurs for that character on the journey from the first page to the last. If *story* is the journey of change that a character makes from their original nature and situation, to a new nature and situation at the end, then *plot* is the route of the journey that the character takes. In other words, story is about who your character is at the beginning, why and how they act, how they react to obstacles, how they change, and who they will be at the end. Plot is about the chain of events: what will make your character have to act and what obstacles will give rise to a convincing series of changes. To change the metaphor, plotting is the engineering of the changes that form the story.

Sometimes a story will arrive as one very vivid, specific scene which hands you a piece of plot on a plate: you then have to work out the story-journey that it belongs in. Often, a story will come along in the form of a main character, whose journey you need to find so you can then engineer the plot. Sometimes a story arrives as the sense of the journey itself – from grief to healing, say, or from cynicism to openness – and you then need to find the character who will embody that journey in the most rich and dynamic way. Sometimes it's the world which comes first: then you need to go looking for the character and story which will exploit the most fascinating things about it.

But whatever comes first, it's pretty much impossible to write a compelling story unless you know what your character wants or thinks they want – what their problem is – and what they actually need, if it's different. And stories are invariably more interesting if they *are* different, because that's a change right at the character's heart. If you tend to use your first draft as a way of finding out these essential drivers of the story, rather than knowing them before you start, be prepared to rewrite *radically* in second draft, cutting away what doesn't contribute to this overall story of wants, needs and change.

 Key idea: what's at stake?

For a reader to stay involved with your characters enough to keep reading, we need to feel that the outcome matters: that it's enormously important that the characters we care about survive and win, rather than lose and die – whether 'survive and win' is physical survival (as in a thriller or action-adventure story), emotional survival (as in family drama or romance), or mental survival (psychological or political thriller), or a mixture. So what's at stake tends to come in pairs: reaching Heaven versus going to Hell; winning the holiday camp's Beautiful Baby competition versus your un-divorceable mother-in-law forever calling you a failure; catching the murderer versus the evil staying unpunished and on the loose.

'What's at stake?' is writerly and editorial shorthand for this important idea: what does the character want and need badly enough to do *anything* to achieve? And what's the worst that could happen if they *don't* succeed?

HOW WILL YOUR STORY RELATE TO THE HISTORICAL RECORD?

It can be difficult to work out what writers mean when they talk about 'accuracy' versus 'imagination', unless it's in a long, searching literary interview such as those for the *Paris Review*. One author saying, 'I have taken liberties with X' might mean she's moved a real historical gunsmith's workshop from one real street in seventeenth-century Padua to the next real street along; another author might say much the same about having slotted an extra President in between James Monroe and John Quincy Adams and an extra battle into the Civil War.

What's more, because so much of the time historical fiction is publicized and sold in terms of its non-fiction interest and accuracy, much is made, in interviews, of how the author spent the weeks in dusty archives and was thrilled by historical sites. It's a brave author who sits on a platform and declares, as Graham Swift has, that research is unimportant, he scarcely researches at all, and only after he's written the book. And yet if the book works, does it matter?

Snapshot: working out your principles

Grab a stack of your favourite historical novels: try for a mixture of fiction built round purely invented characters and round real historical characters. You're looking for authors' notes, prefaces, afterwords and historical notes, where authors talk about the relationship of their novel to the historical material they drew on. But you're also looking for how their principles work out in practice, which is why it's best to do this with novels that you've read. How has each author chosen to integrate imagined and invented things with researched facts and the historical record? Which approaches make sense to you, and what 'rules' might you make for yourself? For example:

- What principles feel too restrictive, too stultifying? Which feel too loose and unhistorical? Do they vary, depending on the project?

- Which type of material facts would you feel you should stick to? Which type might you change in small ways, or in big ones to build a better, stronger story? Large-scale geography? Local geography? Clothes? Food? Travel times?

- Which beliefs, behaviours and ethics would you feel must be authentic, and which would have an unwanted effect on how your modern reader felt about the story? Violence towards women, children and other inferiors? Racism? Sexism? Anti-Semitism? Religious belief? Religious bigotry? What if characters you want your reader to like and empathize with would, to be authentic, have shared these bad beliefs and behaviours?

- How much would you mind if one super-expert knew the story was 'wrong' about something, as long as everyone else didn't know or didn't care?

- How much would you mind if some of your readers blamed the story for being 'wrong', when in fact it's their idea of the facts which is wrong?

WHERE DO YOU START AND FINISH?

Many of us, beginning to think about a story, start with the idea of where the characters are coming from: who they are, what their situation is, what the continuum of their life is before their problem comes along. This is the reason that all teachers, editors and mentors keep finding themselves saying, 'The story really starts in Chapter Three.' The stuff of what life is like before the problem comes along has no inherent narrative tension; it's the problem, jolting the characters out of their existing tracks, which sets us wondering *what will happen next*. We only need to know enough of the existing tracks for us to feel and understand the jolt. And we certainly may not need be told about those tracks in the narrative before the jolt: you always have the option of them leaking out (sorry, mixed metaphor!) in retrospect.

Similarly, many manuscripts go on for a couple of chapters after the climactic crisis and its immediate resolution. In real life things do go on, and as a writer you want to sort everything out for your characters and your readers. A friend may say, 'I wanted to know what happened afterwards,' but that's simply a tribute to how alive your characters seemed. Poets, on the other hand, understand that a poem, as often as not, is transformed by having the last two lines cut. Those lines tied up and made clear what the poem was about, but in fiction, too, it works much more richly on the reader if you supply all the material but leave the reader, *after* the end, to decide what the story was about: to write those lines for themselves.

Focus point: 'Get in late, and get out early'

This is the thriller-writers' motto. Short-story writers often say, 'Start as near the end as possible,' which is much the same idea. If what you tell us is vivid and convincing and consistent with the characters' actions, you'll be surprised how little the reader needs backstory, 'side-story', the wider context, or tidying up at the end.

Snapshot: a whole life in slices

Think of a character you'd like to explore: either invented or real, but with a life which leaves you imaginative space. Assume they lived to a ripe old age. Do a little research if you need to, and jot down an imagined skeleton of the whole of their life: babyhood (sickly? precocious?), small childhood (jealous of baby sister? pet of father?), older childhood (a bully at school? an oblate to a monastery?), early adolescence (apprenticed? orphaned?) … onwards through marriage (children? infertility?) to middle age (widowed in poverty? finds fame as a soothsayer?) … extreme old age (serenely waiting for death? manipulative?).

Having thought about what would be typical, remember that everyone's life is a mixture of things that are typical of our gender/class/ethnicity and things which don't fit the stereotype. In what ways is your character's life typical and in what ways *convincingly* atypical? What changes would make this person more fruitful as someone to build a story on?

Write: the skeleton of a novel

Look at the list you've just made: where might you take a slice of this long life, and make a novel-length story out of it? What might be the start-and-finish points? Now write a synopsis – say 500 words – telling the story as a 'causally related chain of events'. Don't worry if you've never written anything at novel scale, just give it a go. It will help to read the blurbs (US = 'cover copy') of a few of your favourite novels, then flip through and get a rough idea of their big skeleton. Also, don't worry about the quality of the prose for now: what's important here is the *structure* of the story: how one thing leads to the next.

Margaret George

Margaret George is the author of *The Autobiography of Henry VIII* and other epic historical novels.

'Historical writing must follow the same rules as any other fiction in order to hold the reader's interest. The hero/ protagonist has to have something he must do, and somehow cannot do: is prevented from doing. The more urgent it is to achieve the Must, and the harder the barrier of the Cannot, the more the tension and drama. Simple formula but it works. Scenery and props alone can't carry a historical novel; there has to be a compelling drama as well.'

Narrative drive

We saw in Chapter 2 that a character who's carrying your story needs to be compelling for us to be willing to spend time with them. However, that's necessary, but not sufficient: to *keep* reading we need not just to enjoy their company but to care about what happens to them – to fear the worst and hope for the best. So their problem needs to be urgent and important for them, psychologically and practically, and what's at stake needs to be serious. The writerly shorthand for this is 'narrative drive', and it needs sustaining all the way along that 'causally related chain of events'. A short story might be the working-out of a single problem, but at novel length, even though there may be one overall problem, there will need to be a whole chain of cause and effect within it.

When you're thinking about 'urgent and important', it's not that every plot has to be about taking Vienna for Allah and civilization before the infidel's plague wipes out your army. Even if a tiny little short story is about an old granny who needs to get her grandson back from the other side of the river before the bad airs of night get him, it matters to her, and can therefore be made to matter to us. In other words, a plot needs a reason for the character to have to act *now*, and a reason why what happens next really matters.

SUSPENSE VERSUS MYSTERY

Suspense, or narrative tension, is about 'What will happen next?', whether it's 'Will Juan manage to get Anita alone and propose?' or 'Will Corinna get the boat through the storm without sinking?' Creating suspense involves setting up situations which can't go on as they are, so that we know that *something* is going to happen. But it's only really compelling when we know something about what we might hope for, and what we fear, which may or may not be the same as what the character hopes and fears. Juan must propose to Anita the heiress because the debt-collectors are after him, so do we want him to succeed? Corinna must sail to find her child in the town across the bay, but do we, perhaps, know that the child is already dead, so she's risking drowning to no purpose?

Mystery, on the other hand, is all about '*Why* is this happening?': why Anita keeps avoiding Juan even though she obviously loves him, or why Corinna's brother didn't tell her, before she left, that the storm-warning flag was flying from the castle. Creating mystery means showing that there *is* an answer but delaying our finding it out, by giving us bits of the answer but not all of it: we need scraps of Anita's hesitation before she leaves the room, hints of the brother's duplicity. These hints and clues intrigue us and lead us onwards, but only if they carry the scent of something that matters: we have to *need* the mystery to be solved, just as the characters do, and solving it has to be part of what drives the characters, and causes them to change.

Key idea: withholding doesn't work, tempting onwards does

Hints and clues – information partly revealed – are crucial to creating suspense and mystery, but it's a mistake to think in terms of 'withholding'. If you focus your writerly mind on what's *not* being shown, the reader senses when information is being artificially withheld and feels cheated. Even if the withholding happens fairly naturally as part of the action, you can't assume we'll care enough to keep reading if we know you're withholding the interesting stuff.

Instead, you need to think of hints and clues as sweets: deliciously potent morsels which you write so that the story appears to drop them in front of us quite naturally, to tempt us into following the trail into the forest.

FORTUNATELY–UNFORTUNATELY

If a character starts a story by trying to achieve something, and achieves it immediately or immediately gives up, the story will be very dull and very soon over. One of your jobs is to *delay* either triumph or disaster in convincing ways, so that we keep reading. You do that by throwing obstacles in your character's way. As ever, those obstacles can be external – other people, weather, wars, geography – or internal and psychological, and a mixture of the two is even better, so your character-in-action has to cope mentally and emotionally as well as practically. And the basic game is a very simple one that drama students play to practise improvising scenes. For example:

- *Unfortunately*, every time Juan nearly gets Anita to listen to his proposal, her chaperone wakes up and demands to know what they're talking about. *Fortunately*, there's a storm and the chaperone suggests he stays the night. *Unfortunately*, Anita says she has a headache and goes to bed. *Fortunately*, as Juan is trying to get the drunken chaperone safely upstairs, Anita emerges to help him. *Unfortunately*...

- *Fortunately*, Corinna's brother warns her there's a terrifying current just outside the harbour. *Unfortunately*, as the weather worsens, the current changes direction. *Fortunately*, Corinna manages to cope with that. *Unfortunately*, the boat starts to leak. *Fortunately*, the storm eases and she has a chance to bail out the boat. *Unfortunately*, she sees the storm flag, realizes her brother could have warned her and didn't, and drops the bailing bucket. *Fortunately*...

'JEOPARDY MUST INCREASE'

Of course, even when the immediate suspense is resolved – Anita accepts Juan's proposal, Corinna finds her child – the mystery will fuel the next part of the story. What secret has Anita still not admitted to, and what might it do to the marriage? Why did Corinna's brother not tell her about the storm warning? Does that mean he'll try to get rid of her in some other way when she gets home?

In a short story you might choose to stop there. But in a novel, even if the overall problem still exists (or it's been solved but in doing so created a new one) the longer the reader has been reading, the more likely they are to have had to put the book down. Your task is to *make us want to pick the book up again.* That's why it's important that your characters' problems get bigger and harder to cope with: as the thriller-writers say, 'Jeopardy must increase'. A novel which starts with scalding your hand on the range and having no butter to treat it with might end with your being trapped on the top floor as the San Francisco fire buckles and melts your fire escape. The other way round would be rather less compelling.

Sometimes the goal is constant, sometimes it will change, but either way we need to feel that failure is both more likely and more serious, and success less likely but even more longed-for. In *Pompeii*, the grief-numbed engineer Attilius starts by struggling to persuade others that the volcano is up to no good; by the end he understands the true danger but finds himself alone with the man who wants him dead, just as he has begun to feel the possibility of a new love. In Elizabeth Fremantle's *Sisters of Treason*, Katherine Grey's secret defiance of Queen Elizabeth's rules for her imprisonment helps to sustain her, until she gets pregnant. Not only does she have the primal fear of a parent for her child, but her fear for herself is increased, since now her own claim to the throne is strengthened by having produced a male heir, as jealous, ruthless Elizabeth herself has not.

Snapshot: play fortunately–unfortunately

Just start with a Fortunately, or an Unfortunately, and see how far you can go. Try for at least four stages (as in my examples above), but it's worth pursuing at least one for longer, to get a feel for just how long it's possible to keep going. Try one of these starters, or experiment with something of your own:

- *Fortunately, Rosemarie Mae had learned years ago how to fire up a steam engine. Unfortunately...*
- *Unfortunately, Aleksey finds me, his landlady, irresistible. Fortunately...*
- *Fortunately, between them the enlisted men had all the necessary tools to build the fort. Unfortunately, I...*
- *Unfortunately, that week the quilting bee was moved to the Señora's house, three miles away. Fortunately...*

As a final bit of fun, you could also try working backwards from that opening. Who is Aleksey, that finding his landlady irresistible is an Unfortunately? Why must it be Rosemarie Mae who fires up the steam engine?

Thinking in acts

We are temporal creatures: we are born, live and die in time. And as John Yorke explains, it's not coincidental that human storytelling takes the same shape: beginning, middle, and end: thesis – antithesis – synthesis. Or, as many of us would put it: beginning, muddle and end.

So how might this three-act structure work out? Here are some examples:

1 The character has a problem to deal with:
   - Anna discovers that a usurper is about to invade.
   - Boris is weak and vulnerable in a violent feudal society.
   - Cristoforo is lonely and without sex or love.

2 They act to solve their problem by trying to get what they want:

- Anna goes into the forest to murder the invader.
- Boris plots and acts to take over the dukedom.
- Cristoforo seeks out beautiful people to find someone to marry.

3 What they want becomes what they actually need, and everything changes:

- Anna decides the usurper is the right ruler, and helps him win.
- Boris wins the dukedom but only by forcing the woman he loves to be married to someone else.
- Cristoforo finds real love in someone who isn't beautiful and who can't marry him.

Of course, writers vary widely in whether they think as baldly as this. And literary writers, in particular, stretch, twist, bend and break this very basic human mental structure in interesting ways. But bending and breaking works only because our sense of the underlying form is so hardwired. For example, cutting the last act before the synthesis can be worked out (as Chekhov almost always does in his fiction, as well as his plays) may leave some readers 'writing' the 'real' ending for themselves and thinking about how real life can't ever be tidied into satisfying endings; other readers may just feel baffled, unsatisfied or annoyed.

THINKING IN FIVE ACTS

Three-act structure is a very useful way to think about structure in what you might call one-sitting narratives: short stories, movies, and the modern two-hour play. But novels are long-form (as are TV series and classic plays such as Shakespeare's) and this gives the writer two problems. First, the much greater amount of story material that's needed means that the middle-muddle is going to be very long indeed, and the writer, too, can get in a muddle. And second, there's the business of renewing your hold on the reader after a break.

So it helps to separate out that middle muddle into separate phases. Rows of books have been written, mostly by screenwriters, about act-structure, and it can all get very rigid and even silly. Each book is only putting a particular slant on the human need to shape the randomness of life into a chain of cause and effect. Yorke also points out that some brilliant writers deny furiously that act structure is any use at all, although their writing in fact works in precisely that way: their sense of story works in act structure, even though their creative process and consciousness doesn't.

So, how does thinking in a five-act structure help us build a story so it keeps the reader reading? Taking the series of questions about your character-in-action which we explored in Chapter 2, we get something that looks suspiciously like a map of the journey. The stages that I've set out may not correspond exactly to the divisions between the acts, but they are a way of thinking, as an artist's lay figure is for thinking about skeletons and structures before the real work on a picture starts. (Having said that, these days I plan novels in acts, and often leave traces of that, as 'Parts' in the finished book.)

- At the beginning, the character has a problem: they want something that they (and maybe their family or community) don't have. **'Act One'** sets this problem out:

  ▷ Anna wants safety for her people.

  ▷ Boris wants power and autonomy.

  ▷ Cristoforo longs for the perfect physical and mental love.

  ▷ Damaris is determined to become a great artist.

- They act to solve their problem by trying to get what they want: round about **the end of 'Act One' and the beginning of 'Act Two'** they set out:

  ▷ Anna swears to kill the invading usurper, and sets off into the forest.

  ▷ Boris plots and works to take over the dukedom.

  ▷ Cristoforo finds a beautiful person to marry.

  ▷ Damaris gives up everything to train as an artist.

- They're committed to their action, and maybe things go well for a while, but then obstacles arise. As **'Act Two' develops into 'Act Three'**, they must cope with (for example):

  ▷ Anna: the dark forest; the threat of the invading army

  ▷ Boris: the back-stabbing lords; the suspicions of the woman he loves

- ▷ Cristoforo: the inhibitions caused by his own fears of being rejected; problems caused by trying to win love
- ▷ Damaris: loneliness; starvation while she can't sell her art; a tempting offer of marriage and financial stability.
- Bit by bit (or suddenly), in coping with the obstacles, they learn or realize that what they thought they *wanted* may not be *what they really need*. After this middle point of the story, often round about **the middle of 'Act Three'**, nothing can be the same again:
  - ▷ Anna sees that the usurper has wisdom and skill: he'd be a better ruler than the legitimate king.
  - ▷ Boris can win the dukedom, but only by forcing the woman he loves to marry someone else.
  - ▷ Cristoforo realizes that he and his beautiful fiancée are only prizes and status symbols for each other: can he give her up and look for real love elsewhere?
  - ▷ Damaris recognizes that marrying will mean children and a household to run; independence and art mean, effectively, celibacy and loneliness.
- After the midpoint, **the rest of 'Act Three', and then 'Act Four'**, are driven by a huge choice: to stay where they are, or revert to their original life? Or to move forward? Recognizing the new insight and acting on it is frightening:
  - ▷ Anna should go home: supporting the usurper is a mortal sin and a crime.
  - ▷ Boris could give up on the dukedom and persuade his love to run away with him.
  - ▷ Cristoforo could make a shallow, unsatisfying marriage with his beautiful lover.
  - ▷ Damaris could give up her art in accepting marriage.
- Or will they choose to act on that new insight? The climax in **'Act Five'** brings them to the point of the final battle to resolve the crisis:
  - ▷ Anna switches sides to help the usurper to the throne.
  - ▷ Boris wins his dukedom but has lost his humanity (the 'dark inversion' plot).

- Cristoforo leaves his lover and sets out to find love even in un-beautiful or difficult places.
- Damaris applies to join a religious order; she can accept the restrictions in return for the support for her art.

Key idea: storytelling is a crude business

If you were reading those skeleton-stories with horror at how clichéd they sound, then in a sense you're right: all stories at the skeletal level have the same structure because that's how we humans understand our existence as temporal creatures. Since the beginning of spoken language, storytellers have won dinner and a place by the fire by satisfying the human need to have experience shaped to fit our sense of narrative.

But painters don't often exclaim how clichéd it is that their model has two arms, or ten toes. The fascination of figure painting is in finding ways to work with the givens of the human skeleton, but work with it, as Cubism did, to open the viewer's perceptions in new ways.

Besides, as soon as you start thinking about a particular, bare little skeleton, it gets more interesting, because it gets more individual. We might have wanted Boris to give up his ambitions and regain his love – and yet there's a glory in him have achieved his dukedom. Will Damaris *always* feel that art was worth more than love and sex and the hope of children? What if we think Anna is deluded and the usurper is going to be a disaster? And so on.

Deborah Swift

'The history is not the real plot. The real plot is in the changing priorities and desires of the characters as they grapple with the historical events. If the history is the spine of the book, the plot is the tendons that hold the story to that central core. Like the tendons of the body, the story events are tied to the history yet constantly exerting pressure on it. The reader must feel that tension, and have a sense that historical events were fragile and could so easily have been different.'

OPENINGS

We've talked about 'get in late and get out early', and how voice draws the reader in, but what does that mean for what gets on to page one? The old crime writing dictum that you should have a body on page one is a clue, because death *always* has consequences and so the situation is unstable: things are guaranteed to happen. But that doesn't mean, necessarily, that your opening must be full of violence. In a TED talk, 'Story Telling is Joke Telling', Pixar's Andrew Stanton describes how the opening of a story must make a promise: this story is going to be urgent and important, and so worth your while. The instability might be more a matter of dropped sweets than dead bodies, but those sweets need to be promises of more vivid, intriguing, moving, hilarious, exciting or life-changing things to come. If you flip back to those openings in Chapter 5, you can see how that promise is made:

Sebastos Abdes Pantera was twelve years old and nearly a man on the night he discovered that his father was a traitor.

It was spring, the time of bright flowers, and Passover, the time of celebration, sacrifice and riots. (M. C. Scott, *The Emperor's Spy*)

Father – traitor – riots. The situation is unstable in both private and public life.

Chip told us not to go out. Said, don't you boys tempt the devil. ... we locked up real quiet, gone our separate routes back to Delilah's flat. Curfew was on and Paris was grim ... dreading the sound of footsteps. (Esi Edugyan, *Half Blood Blues*)

See how it builds: 'Told not to go out' might be just bossy, but curfews don't happen in peaceful places. And then 'dreading footsteps': what do *they* fear?

When feedback says that you need to cut the first two chapters, it's almost always either because the situation is too stable, with no sign of cracks, or that they are full of background material. The real story starts at the point were things start to change. On the other hand, a zingy page one full of both sweets and bodies is no good if we then have to plough through ten pages of backstory and explanations.

Focus point

The problem that powers a story must seem urgent and important, and that sense is created by:

- the urgency and importance of the problem to the character
- the degree to which readers care about the character
- the inherent interest of the problem for the reader
- the strength of the chain of causally related events
- the vividness and freshness with which the writing conveys the urgency and importance.

Most of us find some of those elements come more naturally than others, but you can work consciously at the others. Which are your strengths? Which are your weaknesses? How might you work on the latter?

ENDINGS

We've discussed getting out early, but that's different from deciding how *resolved* the ending needs to be. Classic, all-sorted-out endings – the monster dead, the wedding bells ringing – may feel too over-determined to the modern reader: we know that, actually, life goes on and throws up marriage problems and new monsters. So most 'satisfactory' endings will leave some things unresolved or unsatisfying, as in real life.

Indeed, the writer may be more interested in the process of change than the outcome. Such stories may take the reader to the point where the character realizes the choice they must make, and then leave them there. *Wolf Hall* ends at the point where Cromwell gives up his support for the out-of-favour Queen Anne Boleyn, and decides to join the King where he's courting Jane Seymour: a beginning, as much as an end – although of course we know the end. Yes, the writer risks some readers finding that unsatisfactory, and it's perhaps more characteristic of fiction at the more literary end of the spectrum, which is happier with endings which are equivocal, unresolved or open.

Snapshot: thinking in acts

Take an example from the Fortunately–Unfortunately Snapshot exercise, or some other situation with two or three characters. How might you shape it into a five-act story? It will need:

1. an opening which promises that reading on will be worth the reader's while
2. a problem worth reading about
3. obstacles and successes
4. leading to a midpoint, after which things can never be the same
5. more obstacles and successes, which lead to an unavoidable choice to revert or to move forward
6. an 'Act Five', where the choice to change causes the climax.

Write: a five-act story

Take this five-stage plan and write the story. If it's far too big – which it may well be – look at one part of it, work out the five-part structure for that scene or mini-group of scenes, and write that. Don't worry if it looks a bit crude and bony: this is about getting used to thinking in this way.

Key idea: act structure is fractal

Act structure (three or five) doesn't apply only to a whole story but also to the units that make it up: act, chapter, scene, page, even paragraph. A page is a unit of moving the story along: thesis – antithesis – synthesis. Whenever a unit of a story has lost its way and is saggy or dull, have a look at the structure, and whether you need to bring out more clearly the sense of the journey, from beginning, through middle-muddle, to the end. This is particularly helpful when your character has to do some thinking, or when there's some uninspiring action which is necessary to the plot: look for the mini-journey latent in those paragraphs.

Workshop: looking for structure

Print out your story double-spaced, and go through it, registering your reactions. Then reread it, thinking specifically about structure. How do the first few lines, and the first page, make the promise that it will be worth the reader's while? If not, is it because you've started the narrative at the wrong point of the story? Or have you started in the right place but not dropped enough sweets to lure the reader along?

Where does the character's problem start to show? Is it interesting enough? Is its importance and urgency coming over? If not, why not? Do we not believe that it matters to the character and is what drives them to act? Or does the prose lack energy and vividness?

Where would you say the 'middle-muddle' starts? Do we believe in what gets in the way? Is what the character then does convincing? Are their actions and reactions proportionate, or do they overreact or underreact to what's happened? What makes us hope that things will end up right? What makes us fear that things will go horribly wrong?

Does it end in the right place? How sorted out and tidied up is everything? Too much? Not enough? Where could you leave space for the reader to do the imaginative work?

Edit: using a synopsis for thinking in acts

Look back at the synopsis-writing exercise you did. Look at how much the skeleton does or doesn't fit the ideas about structure that we've been thinking about: the promise of the opening, the five acts, narrative tension, the resolution. Think about what would be right for this story, and revise it in those terms.

We've looked at how stories are built on a chain of cause and effect which results in change for the characters, and then what that means for the structure of a story which will keep the reader reading. Next, we'll be looking at the business of how you might tell your story.

7

How might you tell your story? prose (ii)

How you write your story is the outcome of the story you want to tell, and why you want to tell it. So there are big, basic decisions you have to make at the beginning about the 'how': narrators, viewpoints and narrative tense. But there are also page-by-page decisions about things which change, such as point of view, showing and telling, and psychic distance. Together, they add up to the main ways you control your reader's experience of the story.

Mark Twain

Mark Twain broke new ground in fiction in using vernacular, uneducated, demotic narrators.

'Don't tell us the old lady screamed. Bring her on and let her scream.'

'The difference between the right word and the almost right word is the difference between lightning and a lightning bug.'

Choices that need to be made at the start

You know *what* the story is and *why* you want to tell it. The next decisions are the ones about your overall handling of the story: narrators, point of view and tense.

TELLING THE STORY THROUGH AN INTERNAL NARRATOR

If your main character – let's call her Sigrid – tells her own story, in first person, then in many ways your life is made easy. The reader is 'inside Sigrid's head' throughout: the events we experience are the events she experiences, and her voice and consciousness are the filter through which everything reaches the reader. So a lot of your decisions are made for you: voice (it's Sigrid's); what to show (what Sigrid can see and feel); what you can hide (what Sigrid can't know); what's important in the story (what Sigrid thinks is important); what mood and tone the story has (the mood and tone that Sigrid's personality and experience dictate).

Don't forget, though, that it's perfectly possible for your reader to read between the lines of Sigrid's narration, and come to different conclusions. *She* might have total faith in her NKVD handler, but what he actually does and says might make *us* think, 'Hm, don't trust him,' and read what follows with that scepticism.

But having an internal character-narrator telling their own story does have its limitations. First of all, the usual advice is that an internal narrator *can't narrate directly any event at which they were not present*. Anything the reader needs to know about events where Sigrid wasn't present will have to be conveyed by some other means. And there's a perennial problem with female character-narrators in historical fiction: they would not have been present at so many of the important events which changed the world they lived in. Even if you think of a way to convey what happened off-stage – messengers, letters – it will always be second-hand compared to the story being able to take us right into that cabinet meeting or on to that ship. Besides, how many accidental overhearings and deliberate eavesdroppings can one story stand?

Another limitation is that you may not want the reader to know something important about Sigrid till later, but we'll feel cheated if we sense that the character *would* have been conscious of it. You may plan a surprise 'twist' at the end when we discover that the NKVD handler who betrays her is her brother. But if we've been inside Sigrid's head all along, then it will feel unnatural and therefore unconvincing if, in all this time, she's never transmitted a flicker of that knowledge.

If your narrator is telling *someone else's* story then it can, paradoxically, be more freeing: you can shed a fascinating sidelight on a known historical character, perhaps quite different from the usual view of a character that popular perception holds or historians project. Your medieval duchess would not have been at the battle of Crécy, but the page or jester telling her story might have been. Having the main character not be the narrator can also make it easier to hold back information about the main character: just engineer things so the *narrator* wouldn't know it, or wouldn't tell it.

Snapshot: point of view in an 'I'm leaving' scene

Imagine a little scene between two characters who either work or live together – or work *and* live, if you're feeling brave. Decide what the work or the relationship is: 'work together' could mean colleagues, or boss and underling, and 'live together' could mean a family relationship or friendship rather than a sexual one.

Character A has decided to leave for good, and has, just this minute, told Character B. Bear in mind that better drama often comes from the scene taking place *not* in the obvious place, but somewhere wholly unsuitable for such a conversation. If you want to, write what A actually says to convey, 'I'm leaving.' Have a quick think about what B's reaction might be.

Now make a list of:
- what A is thinking
- what A is feeling
- what A is aware of in this setting.

Then do the same for B:
- what B is thinking
- what B is feeling
- what B is aware of in this setting.

What are the differences? Could you make them stronger? How might that create drama and narrative drive?

Internal narrators are both actor and storyteller

If Sigrid is narrating events which have already happened, then it's perfectly possible for narrator-Sigrid, as the teller of the story, to narrate stuff that character-Sigrid, as an actor *in* the story, had no knowledge of: the obvious example is an adult narrator telling the story of their own childhood. That's why the question *Where is the narrator standing, relative to the events of the story?* is so useful. Then you can think about what narrator-Sigrid knows and you can use her to tell things that character-Sigrid didn't know. Laurence Sterne's adult Tristram Shandy sets out to tell his life story but with so many digressions and flashes forwards and backwards that it never gets beyond the age of five; Charlotte Brontë's Jane Eyre, by contrast, sits down to write her life story from childhood, and writes it straight through, up to a couple of years before she is writing.

That's why having a character tell their own story *in present tense* can be restrictive, and the prose you tell it in can seem simple-minded. It's difficult to find ways for the character, experiencing the story *now – now –, now –* to convincingly step aside from the present moment to bring in context and understanding. An external narrator can bring that wider perspective, and so can an internal narrator, if they're looking back from later and telling the story in past tense.

Indeed, as we saw with *Dead Man in Deptford* in Chapter 5, your narrator might even explain that they will be imagining and narrating scenes which they couldn't know much about. If you are doing something like this, you probably need to build in, early in the novel, ways for the reader to learn how this story works and how it needs to be read.

Key idea: what internal narrators can know

Most writers choose to restrict a character-narrator to narrating only those scenes at which they were present, but (assuming you're not working in present tense) you can still have them telling us about things in their role as *narrator* which, as a *character*, they didn't know at the time of the events they're narrating. You will need to decide how to handle that so that it's convincing to the reader that the narrator is able to say such things. You don't necessarily need to explain how they came to know things like what was going on simultaneously on the other side of town, but we need to feel, intuitively, that they could have.

TELLING THE STORY THROUGH AN EXTERNAL NARRATOR

If you decide to use an external narrator, narrating in third person, your life is made easier in different ways. Your external narrator can work through as many characters' viewpoints as you decide to grant it access to, and can also tell things no character knows. The traditional label for this kind of narrator is 'omniscient', although 'knowledgeable' is arguably a more accurate term and 'privileged' is a useful idea too: it is you who grants your narrator privileged access to certain information and particular characters' consciousness. But when a scene can be told from any point of view, when an external narrator, potentially, knows everything about the story and things beyond it, how do you choose what gets into the story and how to write it? The key is to decide how this story will work best, and then be consistent, so let's think about the options.

- **Staying close in to a single character's point of view for the whole story.** This is very like having an internal character-narrator, except that the external narrator has its own point of view: it can convey things which the character might not know (e.g. that this will be the year of the famine), or wouldn't be specially conscious of (e.g. the weather, while the character is still asleep in bed). It's up to you how far beyond the viewpoint character's point of view you choose to go, of course, which is why this kind of narrator is sometimes, confusingly, said to have 'limited omniscience'. (The 'limit' is that such a narrator can't go inside any *other* character's head or convey things from that point of view.) This has some of the practical disadvantages of a character-narrator and few of the advantages of the reader feeling immediate, personal contact with a character-narrator's personality.

- **More than one viewpoint, staying close in to a single character's point of view for each chapter.** This operates by the same rules, except that obviously it makes conveying the plot easier. You don't get stuck with having no access to key scenes, and yet you can avoid conveying information you don't want the reader to know yet, by simply moving away from that character and their viewpoint to another character and/or another part of town.

- **More than one viewpoint, moving only between scenes.** It's easy to move viewpoint between scenes in short or long fiction by exploiting psychic distance (more on that in a moment). As we leave one viewpoint, the narrator is in charge, narrating us towards the new scene, getting us close to the new character and then leading us into that viewpoint.

- **More than one viewpoint, moving during scenes if you choose to.** The mid-scene move needs more careful handling if you're to avoid ending up 'head-hopping' – moving too often and too abruptly – but it's still essentially the same. Again, the simplest way is to move outwards in psychic distance until we're not deeply in any character's head but in the space that they share, and then inwards from there into the new viewpoint.

However, convenience isn't enough of a reason to change point of view: what matters most is the reader's involvement with the main character/s and what happens to them, and if you change too often you risk weakening that involvement. So you need to think very hard and carefully about which characters' viewpoints to work through across the whole story, and which to use in any given scene. There are no rules in these things but, in my experience, one rarely turns out to need as many viewpoints as at first seemed essential. And when you switch – especially the first few times, when the reader's still working out how this novel operates – you need to make sure the reader is clued-in immediately to where we now are.

WHICH VIEWPOINTS TO USE?

As a start, it's rarely a bad idea to use the viewpoint of whichever character has the most at stake in the scene. For example, Wilf has decided to ask Ermine to marry him (or join him in a rebellion?). The beginning of the scene, while he's trying to decide how to put the question, working up his courage, and watching for a moment when the shop is empty, is likely to be strongest if it's from his point of view.

That might well do for the whole scene but it's worth considering that, once he's asked the question, the real interest for the reader may be in Ermine. In a world without divorce or contraception, marriage is a huge decision (as joining the rebels would be in a world where rebels are hung, drawn and quartered). And she's been happy at the orphanage. So a switch to her point of view at some point after he's asked her might make the scene even stronger, so that we get her *inner* turmoil as she tries to decide what to say.

However, if you want the proposal to come as a shock to the reader as well as to Ermine, it's safest to keep us out of Wilf's viewpoint completely, rather than taking us inside his consciousness but artificially withholding those thoughts from us.

And don't forget that it can also be very revealing of *both* personalities to show us an important character through another character's eyes. Perhaps Ermine suffers from painfully low self-esteem, so she assumes Wilf's stumbling greeting and trembling hands herald his announcement that he's marrying someone else (or has betrayed her rebel sympathies to the authorities). If we've been in her viewpoint, then, as he blurts out his true question, we are surprised not just that he's asking an important question which we didn't see coming, but because his question is the reverse of what we and Ermine had expected. In other words, it's an opportunity to set up a little Fortunately-Unfortunately reversal.

And remember that observers, too, can have a great deal at stake: the scene where Sir Walter Raleigh lays his cloak over a puddle for Queen Elizabeth to walk on could have very different flavours if we saw it from the point of view of the lady-in-waiting who embroidered his cloak with coded symbols of her own love for him, or from the point of view of Raleigh's rival for Elizabeth's favour and Cecil's naval contracts.

Moving point of view

If you will be making scene-by-scene decisions about viewpoint, it's worth being aware of the things that can go wrong in moving point of view. They are:

- changing too often
- jumping straight from deep inside one head to deep inside another ('head-hopping')
- changing at the wrong point in the scene, so as to weaken, not increase, our involvement
- changing between too many viewpoints (we don't need access to someone's consciousness to engage emotionally with them: their thoughts and feelings will come across in their actions)
- changing *purely* to hide something that would otherwise be revealed (the reader will sense that you're 'cheating').

The first two are easily avoided once you understand psychic distance, and the others can be dealt with if you look at what problem you were trying to solve, and tackle that problem another way.

Write: thinking about viewpoint and story structure

Take the situation from the previous Snapshot (A leaving the life or work they have with B) or something similar. Add a third person, C, into the same 'I'm leaving' scenario. Give them names, and do anything else you find useful to make the scene, setting and points in the Snapshot for C; make a sketch map of the setting; look up some basic facts or places online. You're going to write this in third person, but locked into a single point of view, so you'll need to make some decisions:

- **Point of view:** which character's point of view is likely to make the scene strongest
- **Wants and changes:** what each character wants at the beginning of the scene, and whether and how that changes
- **Start and finish:** where to start narrating the scene and where to end it, to make the most of any change that each character experiences. Does the bombshell of A's announcement come at the beginning, in the middle or at the end?

Write the scene from the single, most fruitful viewpoint. Do what you can to help the reader know what the *non*-viewpoint characters are thinking and feeling. Does the viewpoint character notice that too, or do they ignore or misunderstand?

PAST AND PRESENT TENSE

This is another of the fundamental decisions that you need to make: will your main narrative tense be past tense (*I went*, *they fought*, *she died*) or present tense (*I go*, *they fight*, *she dies*). Until well into the twentieth century there wouldn't have been any question: stories were told in past tense, as a storyteller tells them, and present tense was used – by the likes of Dickens – for specific, special effects. Then Modernist writers such as Faulkner (in *As I Lay Dying*) realized that present tense was really rather effective if you were trying to conjure the deep-inside of human consciousness, which is always experiencing the present moment and has no real Before and After. Before long, a strange, special effect had become perfectly normal.

However, it's not as simple as that. And present tense has a very different effect, depending on whether the narrator is internal (first person) or external (third person). So your choices will depend on what you're trying to do with your story.

Past tense – the advantages

- The events of the story have a context beyond its boundaries because narrator and character are separated by time.
- Free indirect style works fluently.
- You have huge flexibility in the speed and order of how things are told; there are more forms of past tense than present tense to work with.
- The future is a mystery, not a blank, so the narrator can create suspense by dropping hints.
- It suits themes beloved of historical fiction, such as the way past, present and future are layered together; there is scope for dramatic irony.
- The focus of the narrative is on *understanding*: making sense of what happened.

Past tense – the drawbacks

- The story is over and the reader knows it; we guess that an internal narrator didn't die. (Though novels have been narrated by ghosts before now!)
- Especially *in third person*, it's easy to slip into a distant, bland narrative with the bad kind of Telling: informing the reader, where you should be Showing/Evoking the minute-by-minute tension of action.
- The *had had* problem with flashbacks needs a bit of thought, and some writers who aren't confident with grammar find handling the more complex forms of past tense tricky.

Present tense – the advantages

- Immediacy and realism in time: the story is projected into the reader's 'now'; the action is continuous and proceeds at real-life pace; *in first person* there's no clear gap between character-narrator and character-actor.
- Disorientation: the stream of one-thing-after-another-after-another suits characters who are in an altered mental state (drunk, mad, having sex).
- It suits themes of forgetting or repressing that past and future, and how the human condition is evanescent.

- It simplifies tenses: there's only simple and continuous present tense to grapple with.
- The focus of the narrative is on *perception*: what is happening.

Present tense – the drawbacks

- Immediacy is also inflexibility: there's not much scope for expanding and compressing the pace of the narrative to get rid of trivial actions and details.
- Free indirect style is much more awkward to handle and less effective.
- The 'special effect' of present tense on modern readers is negligible; the eternal present weakens the sense of the story happening in time, and the relationship of past and future.
- *In first person* it's tricky to pause the action while the character actually stops and conveys to the reader their wider understanding and the context. Explaining and flashbacks tend to feel dumped into the flow like a stone.
- *In first person* the fact that a character is both narrator and actor can create a sense of detachment from the events: they must be observing at the same time as experiencing.

Another possibility is to use both tenses, taking into account the proportions of different elements in your storytelling: past tense for the main narrative, for example, and present for separate sections of extreme experience: memories, flashbacks, visions, nightmares. Alternatively, there's an obvious logic to using present tense for the 'now' of the main narrative and past for important memories.

Key idea: present tense may make things *less* urgent and immediate

It's often assumed that present tense makes a narrative more urgent and immediate, and past tense makes it slower and more contemplative, but that isn't necessarily true. As we've seen, having the story told eternally in the present can actually reduce the sense of the pressure of time, while having the story told in past tense gives you the opportunity to expand and compress the action to the strongest effect, as well as giving more scope for irony and pressures from the wider context.

Choices along the way

Up to now we've been looking at the decisions you need to make at the beginning of working on your story, but there are also decisions that you need to keep making along the way: we've touched on working with point of view, but there are also showing and telling, and psychic distance.

SHOWING AND TELLING

You've probably heard someone quoting 'Show, don't tell' but that's nonsense. Both have their value; the key is to understand their respective strengths, and use each to your story's best advantage.

- **The more I talk about Showing, the more I call it Evoking.** Showing is for making the reader feel they're in there: feel as in smell, touch, see, hear, believe the immediate physical and emotional moment of the characters: your rage beating in your ears, the wind whipping your cheeks, a beggar clutching at your coat.

- **The more I talk about Telling, the more I call it Informing.** It's for covering the ground when the narrative needs to do that: the storyteller saying 'Once upon a time', or 'A volunteer army was gathered together', or 'The mountains were covered in fine, volcanic ash'. So it's a little more removed from the immediate experience of the moment.

Certainly, there is a kind of 'telling' which is really just rather dull writing:

> *The temperature had fallen overnight and the heavy frost reflected the sun's rays brightly.*

would be much more effective if you 'show' it with something like this:

> *The morning air was bitter ice, and dazzling frost lay on every bud and branch.*

In the second version, the reader's senses are engaged with 'bitter ice', 'dazzling', and 'bud and branch' – physical, individual concrete things and strong sounds – rather than just being given the information about the temperature falling and the reflections being bright.

Anton Chekhov

The playwright Treplyov, in *The Seagull*:

'I feel myself gradually slipping into the beaten track. This description of a moonlight night is long and stilted. Trigorin has worked out a process of his own, and descriptions are easy for him. He writes that the neck of a broken bottle lying on the bank glittered in the moonlight, and that the shadows lay black under the mill-wheel. There you have a moonlight night before your eyes, but I speak of the shimmering light, the twinkling stars, the distant sounds of a piano melting into the still and scented air, and the result is abominable.'

And there will be times in your story when the narrator stating a simple fact is what's wanted. *The taller man was a carpenter, complete with the tools of his trade* gets the job done much more quickly than a careful evocation of details. You could write,

> *A saw and hammer dangled from his belt and an adze was hooked into it, the thumbnail of one of his broad, craftsman's hands was black, and when he bowed she saw several long wood-shavings caught in his curly hair.*

But does the moment want to linger on the details that long? Would the viewpoint character notice all this? Is this a moment for the reader to do maths to work out who this man might be? Maybe, but maybe not.

So, generally speaking, when you want the reader to feel closely involved in the characters' experience, you'll be working with **Showing/Evoking**: presenting the immediate, physical stuff of the moment and letting it evoke the experience in the reader.

> *They stood close and wrapped their arms round each other in a passionate embrace, so that she became aware that he had been riding, and then that he was as nervous as she was.*

This is less evocative, because it doesn't tap into the reader's own physical experience, than:

> *They gripped each other and the tweed of his jacket was rough under her cheek. His hand came up to stroke her hair; she smelled leather and horses on the skin of his wrist. He was trembling.*

Notice how, although 'showing' the carpenter takes longer than 'telling' him, if you pick the right physical details, and the right verbs, the sentence often turns out no longer: *gripped each other* is much stronger as well as shorter than *stood close and wrapped their arms round each other*. This is most important, of course, at the important moments of change in a story, the crucial events in the characters' journey through the plot; those moments, above all, must live for us as vividly as possible, by being fully embodied and evoked:

- Telling/Informing: *Giacomo was tall and attractive to women; he'd so much charm that each felt she was the one woman in the world for him, and never guessed how little he cared for her.*
- Showing/Evoking: Show us how Giacomo stands, relaxed and smiling, by the fountain as the day starts, give us what he says of greeting as he offers to fill Anna's bucket, show us Anna looking up into his face and, seeing love in his smile, agreeing to meet him after Mass … and then show us what Giacomo says in the tavern that night, about making sure that this lass – 'What's her name? Anna?' – has no means of discovering his real name.

Of course, there are times when leaving things more open and un-particularized allows the reader's imagination space to work. *They fought by the rotting willow* is vivid and particular, and so is *They kissed under the sapling oak*. But sometimes *They met at the great tree* would be better. Perhaps the voice of your story has the plainness of a chronicler. Or maybe the voice is that of someone deliberately trying not to give way to imagination and emotion, but choosing or even struggling to keep their distance from what happened. Maybe, maybe not.

Snapshot: reading for Showing and Telling

Take a favourite historical novel off the shelf and start reading it in terms of Showing/Evoking and Telling/Informing. Notice which the writer tends to do when. How does the narrative cover the ground or inform the reader, while staying vivid and satisfying – or does it go dull and flat? When the narrative is very particular and immediate, what words create that effect? Does it nonetheless keep the story moving, or do things slow down too much? Or are the pleasures of the prose such that it doesn't matter?

Key idea: the rhythm of storytelling

Good storytelling has a rhythm which is created by variations in showing and telling, and in psychic distance, which is quite separate from whether a particular moment in the story is fast-moving and full of action or slower and more contemplative. The movement between being close up, with an individual character's subjective experience, and further out, with a more objective sense of the wider world of the story, gives a story dynamism, as changes in camera shots and angles give a film dynamism, which is quite separate from the events portrayed.

PSYCHIC DISTANCE

For many beginner writers, these questions of voice, narrators and point of view, and showing and telling, pile up the choices to make and risks to worry about. It helps enormously to understand the concept of psychic distance or, as some call it, narrative distance. John Gardner first described it in his classic how-to-write book *The Art of Fiction*: the basic idea is that a narrative isn't just locked into either one viewpoint or a different one, but has a spectrum – a *range* – from deep inside of a character's consciousness to far out in a place that no individual character inhabits. Film has an equivalent range, from a super-long shot, with a wide landscape and the character in the far distance, to a tight close-up of a face where we can see every flicker of emotion. But fiction can go deeper still: right inside, into the mind and feelings. To think about how this works, Gardner sets some points on the spectrum:

1 *It was winter of the year 1853. A large man stepped out of a doorway.*

2 *Henry J. Warburton had never much cared for snowstorms.*

3 *Henry hated snowstorms.*

4 *God how he hated these damn snowstorms.*

5 *Snow. Under your collar, down inside your shoes, freezing and plugging up your miserable soul.*

Psychic distance works in just the same way in first person. Even if you have an internal narrator, as a *character* they're in the moment, but as a *narrator* they can still step back into storyteller mode, and explain things:

1 *In the far-off days of Uther Pendragon, witches stalked the earth.*

2 *When I was a child Mistress Sarebane frightened me.*

3 *I was frightened of Mistress Margit. 'Mother Mary, save me!' I prayed, hiding in the ditch.*

4 *And here came old Margit with her ragged clothes, and Mother Mary would save me, wouldn't she?*

5 *Margit was coming and her cloak like little demons dancing – Mother Mary save me – cold water and dirty...*

Each of Gardner's points on the spectrum is about the same kind of event, but the effect on the reader is very different, depending on how close we are to an individual character's consciousness.

- **The further out the narrative is (say 1 and 2),** the more the narrator is in charge, telling, describing, explaining, summarizing, setting the scene: *It was winter of the year 1853; In the far-off days of Uther Pendragon.* There's lots of information which we can take as true at least as far as the narrator's concerned: where we are, what's happening. I think of the further-out distances as 'storyteller mode': making things clear, covering the ground, setting up the next scene, explaining what needs explaining. What we have no sense of is who the man in the doorway is, let alone what he's thinking or feeling.

- **In the middle (3 to 4, say)** we get more of a sense of an individual in a particular situation: *Henry hated snowstorms; I was frightened.* But it is still the narrator's voice, and thoughts or speech are quoted directly: the character-narrator cries *'Mother Mary, save me!'* and Gardner could have added, *Why must it snow on my birthday, Henry thought.* The character's point of view and subjective experience are coming to centre stage; the narrative is showing, evoking, presenting (rather than explaining), and getting closer to real time in the particular moment.

- **As we get closer still (say 4),** instead of the thought being quoted directly and separately, the character's voice is beginning to colour the actual narrative: *God how he hated these damn snowstorms. And here came old Margit.* It's this use of free indirect style, more than anything, which draws us right into the character's experience: the character is filling the frame, excluding other characters' experience, and without the sense of context that the narrator supplied.

- **And when we're right in close (Gardner's 5)**, the character's consciousness takes over the narrative: *freezing and plugging up your miserable soul; like little demons dancing.* Our sense of it as narration begins to melt away altogether as the thoughts download along with sensory stuff: *Snow. Under your collar,* or *Cold water and dirty.* Because the whole scene is filtered through the character's consciousness, we're aware that it's subjective perhaps to the point of unreliability: that another character might experience things very differently and perhaps more accurately. At its most extreme, this kind of writing becomes a brain-download: a stream of the conscious perceptions of the moment. Indeed, the right-close-in territory is very useful for sex, battles, violence, madness and anything else which involves an altered state. But if we only had this super-close-in stuff and nothing else, we wouldn't have a clue where we were, whose head we were inside, and so on.

So of course you need a mixture. When you look at good writing, you'll see that although most novels will spend much of their time in the middle of the range, the narrative moves around and mixes things up. Almost no narratives will stay right out in 'long shot', because fiction is always about individual experience: if we're never let inside heads and hearts, the story becomes monotonous and unengaging. But few narratives stay permanently right close in either, not just because it's laborious to convey plot and information, but also because it, too, can become monotonous in tone and rhythm. Even so, it's worth learning to stretch your range, because without those two extremes in your toolkit, your storytelling will be restricted and the narrative will be even-toned and undynamic.

Snapshot: working with psychic distance

Take three or four sentences from something you've written: choose a section which is centred on a viewpoint character but doesn't have any dialogue. Rewrite those sentences three times: once at the furthest out (like Gardner's Level 1), once at the middle (say Level 3), and finally at the closest in of Gardner's Level 5. Some tips:

- It's easiest to start with the 3-ish one, and then work on the others.
- You may need to bring in more information for the Level 1 version.
- You'll probably lose some context in the Level 5.

When you've done these, look back at the examples above, and see if you could push your versions a bit further to the extreme. Ninety per cent of the students I do this with think they've done 1 and 5 when actually they've only got as far as 2 and 4.

Focus point: psychic distance solves many questions with a single answer

Psychic distance is a powerful tool because it brings together and makes sense of a whole lot of techniques which are usually thought of separately. To decide about:

- Telling/Informing versus Showing/Evoking
- handling point of view
- objective and detached versus close in and subjective
- context and understanding versus immediacy and perception
- narrator's voice versus character's voice

just ask yourself: how close in should we be to the character's consciousness at this moment?

Edit: reworking for psychic distance

Look at the scene you wrote earlier in terms of psychic distance, and see if you can make it more effective by going deeper in or further out, or both. If you were allowed to change point of view once during the scene, who would you switch to, and where in the scene would you put the switch? Rework the scene to make the most of that.

Psychic distance is never the same for long

In real writing, the psychic distance is never precisely the same for long, so it's important to learn to move to and fro along the range. Look at this extract from Hilary Mantel's *Wolf Hall*. Technically, the whole novel is in Thomas Cromwell's point of view, but that doesn't mean that wider news can't be conveyed, only that it's restricted to what, one way or another, Cromwell can find out:

> *New Year 1529: Stephen Gardiner is in Rome, issuing certain threats to Pope Clement, on the king's behalf; the content of the threats has not been divulged to the cardinal. Clement is easily panicked at the best of times, and it is not surprising that, with Master Stephen breathing sulphur in his ear, he falls ill. They are saying that he is likely to die, and the cardinal's agents are around and about in Europe, taking soundings and counting heads, chinking their purses cheerfully. There would be a swift solution to the king's problem, if Wolsey were Pope. He grumbles a little about his possible eminence; the cardinal loves his country, its May garlands, its tender birdsong. In his nightmares he sees squat spitting Italians, a forest of nooses, a corpse-strewn plain.*

Look at how Mantel directs our attention, first towards what Cromwell/Wolsey know of Gardiner's activities (not much), and then closer in to Cromwell's take on 'Master Stephen', and his confidence but also frustration. Then we are right inside Cromwell's idea of Wolsey's nightmares.

Snapshot: moving psychic distance

Take the extract that you wrote at the different psychic distances and rewrite it, either starting far out and sliding inwards, or the other way round. To give you the idea, this is my version of the example further up.

In the far-off days of Uther Pendragon, witches stalked the earth. Indeed, every village had its witch, and its people feared or consulted her according to how desperate they were. About three hours' walk from Chester was our village of Avonford, and there we all knew that Mistress Sarebane could save the crops or kill the cattle. But I was so frightened of her power that I would hide when Mistress Margit came along the street, with her ragged clothes and her big black cat, until I was shivering and praying to Our Lady because she'd save me, wouldn't she? But Old Margit's cloak was like little demons dancing so hide in the ditch, cold and wet and Mama'd be angry – and Black Peter would see me – Mother Mary, save me – save me and I'll be good for ever...

You may need to add a sentence or two, but don't worry if it doesn't read like very good writing; real prose doesn't do things so mechanically, and this is just an exercise.

Write: putting all these decisions together

Choose an historical place as a starting point (you can change things about it later if they cause you problems). Make a few notes to make the place and some people who live there present to you: concentrate on the practicalities and the 'scratch and sniff' of being a human in that place. Now imagine that a stranger has arrived. They badly need or want to live or work in this place. Jot some notes down about who they are and why they need to be accepted here, and then draft a story. Make your own decisions about:

- how many characters will best suit your story

- what each character wants and needs
- whether to use an internal or an external narrator
- how much the narrator has a point of view which goes beyond what any one character knows during the events
- point of view: is the narrative locked into a single character's point of view, or does it move between more than one?
- whether to use past or present tense
- how 'historical' the voices are – both the narrator's and the characters'
- where to begin and where to end the narrative
- where the focus is going to be: where the big turning point is, for maximum effect.

William Shakespeare

From Hamlet's advice to the players:

'Be not too tame neither, but let your own discretion be your tutor: suit the action to the word, the word to the action, with this special observance: that you o'erstep not the modesty of nature; for anything so overdone is from the purpose of playing, whose end, both at the first and now, was and is to hold as 'twere the mirror up to nature, to show virtue her own feature, scorn her own image, and the very age and body of the time his form and pressure.'

Workshop: reassessing how you put everything together

As ever, print out the story you've just written and then mark it up. First, think about how each of those basic, necessary decisions about narrator, tense and point of view actually worked out in practice. Which turned out to be the right ones? Which would you change in revision? Is there another story latent in this one, which is more promising?

Now look at the story in terms of the decisions you made as you went along:

- **structure:** did you start and finish the story in the right places? Have you made the right choices about what to emphasize and what to put in the background?
- **psychic distance:** did you make the right decisions about when to go in close and when to pull out? Was 'close' close enough? Was 'far out' far out enough?
- **Showing:** could you evoke things more vividly? Are there places where you explain or inform, where it would be stronger just to present the reality?
- **Telling:** are there places where you could have covered the ground or compressed something to get rid of trivial details? Would it be simpler or stronger just to inform us or explain something? Could you make your telling more vivid?
- **characters' voices:** are the voices convincing as people speaking? Are they consistent in how 'historical' they sound?
- **narrative voice:** does it draw the reader in? Is it consistent in how 'historical' it sounds?

 ## Edit

Edit the story, taking into account all the things you've been thinking about.

Next step

We've now thought about all the basic building blocks of the business of telling stories, and in the next chapter we'll look at how to build the structure that will become your story.

8

Different shapes of story: form

Form in fiction isn't just about how long or short a story is: your decision has implications for everything about how you handle structure, how you choose and work with characters, and who might publish your work. As well as thinking about length and act-structure, you might decide to tell the story not in the order that the events happened – or you might be imagining a story that has a sequel, is part of a trilogy, or involves diaries, letters and other documents as part of the storytelling.

Anton Chekhov

From a letter to A. S. Suvorin, 27 October 1888:

'An artist observes, selects, guesses, combines – and this in itself presupposes a problem: unless he had set himself a problem from the very first there would be nothing to conjecture and nothing to select.

You are right in demanding that an artist should take an intelligent attitude to his work, but you confuse two things: solving a problem and stating a problem correctly. It is only the second that is obligatory for the artist. In "Anna Karenin" and "Evgeny Onyegin" not a single problem is solved, but they satisfy you completely because all the problems are correctly stated in them. It is the business of the judge to put the right questions, but the answers must be given by the jury according to their own lights.'

Form and length

The difference between a novel and a short story isn't just that the former has more words (though it does), or that you need more story material in order to have enough for those extra words (though you do). That extra length has consequences for how the story is built, so what starts as a matter of word count is really a matter of *form*. Although in prose fiction the boundaries of different forms are very loose, they are there: each has its advantages and presents particular challenges. With experience it does become more obvious what form is likely to suit the new idea that's becoming a new project: a satisfying story is one which is the right length and shape for the idea.

But these different forms have also emerged in response to the economics of selling fiction, of which more in Chapter 11. So, if you do want to write for a specific market, it is worth trying to develop your sense of what sort and scale of story idea is likely to suit different forms, to help you sift possible ideas with that in mind.

However, I can't stress enough that the most important thing is to work in terms of what the *story* needs. Particularly at the literary end of the spectrum, it's impossible to be categorical about what a given form 'ought' to be, and there will always be examples which do something completely different, brilliantly.

And 'what the story needs' extends to asking yourself if the story would work better as a non-linear narrative (a story told not in the order the events would actually have happened), or by combining separate story threads in a dual or parallel narrative.

Key idea: word count isn't all that defines the form

The word count of a piece isn't the only thing which defines a piece of writing as a short story, or a novel, or some other form. The consequences of a certain length, for how a story is told, means that different lengths also create different expectations in the reader.

FLASH FICTION

These are very short stories: some magazines and competitions define them as up to 300 words, some as up to 1,000. The best flash fiction is like Doctor Who's Tardis: far bigger inside than you'd believe possible from the outside: Rose Tremain's 'Death of an Advocate', in her collection *The Darkness of Wallis Simpson*, is a nice example of a very short story.

The cast will probably be very small and the situations and problem will need to be conveyable very succinctly. The difficulty with historical fiction is that you don't have space to sneak in much help with things the reader doesn't understand already, and you may have to rely on things which aren't strange to the reader: these handy, familiar things can easily become clichés.

It is amazing how much story and atmosphere you can fit in, but to do so every word needs to be building the atmosphere as well as conveying the events, and creating a sense that these people exist in a larger world beyond the story. It can work best to think of the very short ones as being almost like poems: even a poem, if it's good, embodies a journey. 'Beginning, middle and end' still applies, and the reader needs to look up from the end and feel that something has changed in the characters or in themselves.

A first draft of such a short story may not take long to write – although revising and redrafting are a different matter – so it can be a good way to try out a voice or a situation, to keep your hand in when you don't have much writing time, or to explore some material for a longer-form story. Flash fiction is ideal, too, if you want to submit work to the competitions, online sites and print magazines, which are stalwarts of the creative writing world.

Snapshot: write flash fiction

Pick one of these prompts or choose your own, and write a very short story which has a beginning, a middle and an end:

- Pig
- I shall forgive her
- When they came home
- This night
- An embroidered kirtle
- Beyond the rood.

Edit it to exactly 200 words. (Two words together can count as one.)

SHORT STORIES

Short stories are usually thought of as about 1,000 to 15,000 words: more space than a flash or a poem, less than a novella. The short story is a form which has fascinated many of the greatest writers since Edgar Allen Poe first set out the principles which became the modern short story. However, at the literary end of historical fiction the specific challenges haven't been taken on by as many writers as you might expect. Rose Tremain has consistently written them: her story 'The Crossing of Herald Montjoy', in *Evangelista's Fan*, is a lovely example. David Mitchell's *Cloud Atlas* is, arguably, a set of intricately linked short stories, and Michel Faber's collection *The Apple* is a series grown from the characters in his novel *The Crimson Petal and the White*.

Short stories certainly do need a strong structure of 'beginning, middle-muddle and end', if the reader is to feel the sense of journeying: a good many writers would agree that a short story is the fleshing out of a single unit of change. My experience – which is absolutely *not* a rule – is that up to 2,000 words seems to have room for one main character and one or two major scenes, while a longer story could be more of a duet, as it were, and there is scope for a series of scenes or at least stages. But at the longer lengths stories can sag and loose focus, and it helps to start thinking in terms of five acts rather than three, to help you structure the middle more strongly.

As you have more space to work with, it also gets easier, although still very challenging, to cope with the specific demands of historical fiction: any necessarily explicit explanations dominate less, and it's easier to slip in covert explanations and background stuff. You can therefore work with slightly more unfamiliar places and periods, or find odder angles on known ones. But there still is the problem of being restricted in how far you can range from known historical territory; you need to be shrewd about finding fresh angles on known territory ('making the familiar strange'), or building enough discreet handholds into strange territory ('making the strange familiar') that readers are not baffled.

Snapshot: short historical fiction

Track down some historical short stories of as many different kinds as you can. Read each one, and ask yourself the following questions:

1 What size of idea is it based on? How many characters does it have? How (and how well) does it give the sense of a world beyond the edges of the story?

2 What's the basic story? How purely is it focused on that, or are there more strands to it?

3 What is its relationship to history? Is it just setting and period, or does it explore a real historical event? Is that at the centre of the story, or on the periphery?

4 How much does it rely on what the reader already knows for its full meaning and effect? Are you frustrated because you're not getting some references and details? Does it over-explain things which you didn't need to have explained? Or does the writer get it pretty much right for you?

Michel Faber

From the Introduction to *All the King's Horses and Other Stories*:

'What, then, is the secret of a good historical story – a story that keeps us securely inside a bygone world, while not annoying us with constant reminders of where we're supposed to be? How can an author recreate a past era in such a way that it isn't a theme park? ... Too often in historical fiction, characters seem aware of the momentousness of the events they're embroiled in. Real life is seldom like that. People cope as best they can, living from minute to minute, performing the small tasks they're given, trying to get along with whoever is closest.'

NOVELLAS

A length between, say, 20,000 and 45,000 words is the basic definition of a novella, but there's more to it than that. Some novels are not much longer than that (for example, Michael Cunningham's *The Hours* and Harlequin Mills & Boon's romances), but a novella is short-story-like in the intensity of its focus, the limited cast and the single narrative thread. A. S. Byatt's *Morpho Eugenia* and *The Conjugial Angel* are good examples, while Peter Ackroyd's *The Plato Papers* is a wildly imaginative alternative take on the form.

Many aspiring writers assume that their project must be bulked up to novel length to count as 'proper' writing, but the real 'proper' writing is shaping a piece to the scale and structure that does it most justice. If it's a novella, it's a novella, and if you want to write a novel, look for a different idea with the complexity to support the greater length.

For the last 50 years or so it has been next to impossible to find readers for novellas, since the cost of publishing them is almost the same as that of a full-length novel, but it's harder to persuade a reader to buy into something apparently less substantial. If anything, the market for historical fiction tends to like fat books, because readers want to feel they're buying into a whole world. However, the e-book is showing signs of changing that, because the length of an e-book is less obvious; it will be interesting to see what happens.

NOVELS

In principle, a novel is simply defined as fiction longer than around 50,000 words, but it also implies a certain substantialness: a wider canvas than a novella, more in the way of subplots and complexities, perhaps a sense that this is more than one person's story. There's also more scope to let things develop a little more gradually, which doesn't mean you can let the narrative tension slacken, only that you can tighten it more incrementally.

Novels suit the panoramic scale which comes very naturally when you're conjuring a whole, different world and transporting the reader there. This is one of the things historical novelists have in common with the writers of speculative fiction: the appeal for both writer and reader is partly in the Otherness of that different world. In terms of the book industry, most modern novels fall into the range 80,000–120,000 words for commercial fiction (literary fiction perhaps 70,000–140,000), with a very big peak in the middle of that range. There will be plenty of historical fiction at the longer end, although Susannah Clarke's 800-page *Jonathan Strange & Mr Norrell* is exceptional. Editors, agents and teachers know that most 200,000-word manuscripts have a nice 110,000-word novel inside them, which is longing for a more focused plot and tighter writing.

SEQUELS AND TRILOGIES

Historical fiction lends itself very naturally to sequels and longer series and, as with speculative fiction, many readers love the sense that they're entering a whole, rich world. But if you're finding the wealth of your material is pushing you towards thinking about several connected books, then you do need to be careful. Editors, agents and teachers know the novel which is all setting-up and no action, because all the crises and resolutions happen in the sequel; they also know the 'trilogy' which is just a 300,000-word novel chopped in three. A book which is essentially only a section of a larger narrative arc will always be unsatisfactory, because it doesn't have a structure and story which are sufficient to itself. A long, real life or big chunk of history may be intensely novel-worthy, but it's very difficult to evoke the full drama and depth of individual events while also covering so much ground, and a series which is too carefully faithful to the biographies is likely to get very ploddy during the duller phases.

In other words, a series must work so that a new reader can pick up any of the books and enjoy it by itself, while each new book mustn't bore a reader who *has* followed the series from the beginning and doesn't need the earlier events and characters explained. Stella Duffy manages it very well in her pair of novels about Byzantium, *Theodora, Actress, Empress, Whore* and *The Purple Shroud*. Mantel's *Wolf Hall* and *Bring Up the Bodies* also work as standalone novels, and I'm sure the third book will too, although it helps Mantel that many readers will have some idea of the real history underpinning them.

Focus point: a story must be self-sufficient

A story, however short or long, *must* work on its own terms and within its own structure: it must have its own beginning, middle and end. Even if you are putting in elements which might develop further in a sequel or a different story, they must work properly and fully within *this* story. In other words, a story mustn't feel irrelevant, unsatisfying or too inconclusive to the reader who has no idea that a sequel or prequel is possible. If the only answer to the question 'Why is this character/scene/place here?' is 'Because I need it for the next book,' then it's not earning its keep in *this* book, which is what matters.

Non-linear narratives

This is a catch-all term for stories which are told out of the order in time in which the events would have taken place, and they seem to suit historical fiction particularly well, perhaps because we are already extra-conscious of how different times relate to each other. Indeed, many contemporary novels, such as William Boyd's *Restless*, have a strand which could be called historical fiction by our criteria.

Joseph O'Connor's *Ghost Light*, for example, is the story of Molly Allgood, the Dublin slum child who as Maire O'Neill starred in *The Playboy of the Western World* and other plays by J. M. Synge, became his great love, after his death had success in Hollywood, but ended her life in extreme poverty in London. But the novel starts at the end: within the frame of her last days we slip to and fro between the important parts of her life, sometimes in her thoughts, sometimes in full transitions to one time or another; at one point there is even a section of 'an imagined play' of Synge meeting her mother.

William Faulkner's *Absalom, Absalom!* is a different example: the story of Thomas Sutpen in the early 1830s is told and retold by different narrators, who tell things in different orders and don't always agree, so the reader not only has to assemble the story, but decide what the truths inside it might actually have been. Ian Pears's *An Instance of the Fingerpost* is made from four standalone accounts, one after the other, which all deal partly with different facets and versions of the same events, while David Mitchell's *Cloud Atlas* nests stories from past, present and future inside each other.

At the more commercial end of things, what used to be a fairly challenging, literary technique has spread to the mainstream, as readers get used to assembling the overall arc of the story from sections which have, as it were, been rearranged.

With non-linear narratives there's scope to build tension, by cutting away from the forward movement of the story, but the real interest is that you can 'layer up' story elements which were well separated in time or place, but which resonate together when juxtaposed. As we explored in earlier chapters, during their present humans re-experience their past *and* the past of others, and this kind of narrative can evoke and work with this. Such structures enrich the reader's experience because assembling the story engages more of our own readerly mind, and makes the story seem richer and more involving. But because the chain we would normally be following is broken up, readers need help: at the beginning they need to learn (intuitively) how the novel works; they need hand-holds all along to keep them oriented in practical terms; and above all they need help to intuit *why* the story is being told in this order – to get the 'more' that is their return for putting in the extra work.

Key idea: non-linear narratives ask more of the reader

Non-linear and other narratives which don't follow a straightforward arc of a single story moving forwards in time, are more challenging for the reader because they break up the 'causally related chain of events' and rearrange the sections, or even mix sections of more than one chain together. It's your job to make sure the rewards really are correspondingly greater, in return for the extra work. And there will always be certain readers – and any reader in a certain mood – for whom the extra work isn't worth it.

PROLOGUES

A prologue is a chunk of story which comes before Chapter 1 and is very separate in time, place, voice or character from the main text. They are very common these days, not least because the online 'Look Inside' drives readers to that first page willy-nilly, so it's more important than ever to have a compelling first page. And a prologue can work well to set up an appetite-whetting 'promise' that the main story will be worth the reader's time. However, calling something a 'prologue' does announce to the reader that this isn't the main story: some readers even skip them completely. So it's important that a prologue is delicious and exciting in itself, and its structural function in the story justifies it being there. A great prologue won't cure a dull first chapter, nor will it set up mystery or suspense if it's merely obscure or confusing. If you're using a prologue to solve a problem with how the story works for the reader, the chances are it could be solved better by some other means.

DUAL NARRATIVES

This is a loose term for narratives which have two separate narrative threads, which don't overlap in time and place, or at least not till the end. Chunks of each narrative alternate, but if you took all the separate chunks of one narrative and assembled them, it could pretty much stand as a story on its own: there are no intricate links of plot as there would be with a main narrative and an important sub-plot. Arguably, Charles Frazier's *Cold Mountain* is one such, since Inman's and Ada's narratives have similar weight in the book, but they and their narratives aren't united until nine-tenths of the way through the story. Another typical form this takes is what I think of as the grandparent–grandchild narrative, such as Marilynne Robinson's *Gilead*, where the connections between the two are formed by the intermediate generation, and memories, documents and so on.

As with any non-linear narrative, the challenge for you is to not just to keep the reader oriented, but also to help them understand, perhaps only intuitively, *why* you are telling the story this way: making those extra connections and insights into theme and ideas clear and worth their doing the readerly work.

Deborah Swift

'Parallel narratives can allow the writer to draw parallels and make links between two periods for the enrichment of the themes of the story. But the switch of points of view between characters needs to be carefully handled when they are changing in time. The whole mood and way of talking are different in changing centuries. Dialogue in 1970 is not the same as dialogue in 1870.'

Parallel narratives

This is a particular kind of dual narrative, where the two stories are separated by so much time or space that they have no characters or events in common. Sebastian Faulks's *Birdsong* is on this territory, as are books like *The Love of Stones* by Tobias Hill, and my own *The Mathematics of Love* and *A Secret Alchemy*. Here the challenge of connecting the two stories and keeping the reader reading as you switch between the two is even greater, since it's harder to construct the connections of plot and story that mean it will make sense for the reader. The plot connections between the two main strands of the Hill are tenuous, but it is a wonderful book, as is Barry Unsworth's *Stone Virgin*, which straddles even more centuries. As Deborah Swift points out, the big challenge is to find the way to write each narrative which is right for itself, and distinct from the other one.

A. S. Byatt's *Possession* is a different kind of parallel narrative, since the Victorian love affair between the two poets, Ash and LaMotte, scarcely exists as a narrative at all. The reader constructs it through an out-of-sequence mixture of private writing – diaries, letters – and public writing: poems, stories and literary criticism. The story of Maud, the modern LaMotte expert, and Roland, who studies Ash, is told by a knowledgeable, external narrator, and it forms the bulk of the narrative, which is formed by the investigation of this mystery: Maud and Roland are, if you like, our representatives in assembling the 'story', which is never actually told *as* a story in the sense of a unified narrative. Only at three points in the novel does Byatt give us the Victorian story directly, using a knowledgeable, external narrator specifically to relate events which would have left no written traces.

Focus point: readers expect separate narratives to make sense together

In dual and parallel narratives, nine readers out of ten *expect* the two threads to make sense as a single book, and will spend a lot of mental energy and attention – even if only subconsciously – wondering *when* they're going to make sense in that way. So, even if (as with *Cold Mountain*) it's a long time before the two strands converge, it's important that it's not long in the novel before it starts to become clear, even if partially and slowly, how they're related. Obviously, if the narrative is split across time then, unless you're working with ghosts, there's more scope for the later story to be affected by the earlier one, than vice versa. But themes, ideas and the roles of characters and settings can and should be reflected backwards and forwards, to illuminate the earlier one just as much.

HANDLING NON-LINEAR NARRATIVES

There are many ways you can help to keep the reader straight when you're telling a story out of sequence, or plaiting two stories together. Remember that the first 20 per cent or so of the novel is absolutely crucial to the reader learning how this text works, and so how to read it. If the reader at any point suddenly can't remember who 'he' is, or what 'school' you mean, or has to turn back a page or three to find out where they now are, then you've failed.

The points where you switch the reader from one place or time to another are particularly important: you need to ground the reader very quickly and firmly in the new place, so try to make the text particularly characteristic at this point. Not that you can relax for the rest of the section, obviously, but these are all things which can provide 'handholds' for the reader as you move them:

- **Practical details** – names, places, things – which are specific to the time and place we've landed in and not the other thread.

- **Voice** is the most intuitive way of clueing the reader in immediately. If the different elements have different narrative voices, then make them as contrasting as possible, especially at the switch. Even if it's all in one voice and point of view, the more you can exploit the difference in mood or action on opposite sides of the switch, the better.

- Let the narrator 'tell' the reader: there are times when 'Ten years earlier, in Vladivostock' is the best way to move the reader.

- **Heading new sections with times and places helps,** but many readers skip them, so such headings are only a fallback; integrating handholds into the narrative should be your primary way of keeping the reader straight.

Think hard before you have several separate narrative strands, *and* mix up the order in which each strand is told. It can be done, but the more fragmented things are, the harder it is for the reader to stay on track and engaged. I would suggest (though it's not of course a rule, since there are no rules) that if you are alternating chunks of separate story strands, then it's safest if each strand in itself is told in chronological order. There *may* be scope, within a strand, for a very thin 'frame story', which frames the main narrative of this strand, but all the rules of how to help the reader apply all over again within that narrative: when you slide backwards in time, be careful to take us with you.

Snapshot: different shapes of story

Browse for historical fiction which has more than one strand to it. For each novel ask yourself:

- How many separate narrative strands does it have?
- Do they alternate, or do we get the whole of one, before we get the next?

- Is each strand told in chronological order within itself?
- How distinct are the voices?
- How are the strands related in storytelling terms?
- How are the strands related in thematic terms?
- Did you (or would you) find it easy to stay on track and not get confused? How does the author help with that?

Are you drawn to particular shapes of narrative? What is it that you like about them?

Using documents

Possession and many other novels work with what I call 'documents', as a catch-all term for the different written texts that a novel might include inside itself: letters, newspaper cuttings, bits of memoir, shopping lists, poems, etc. Using real or purported documents does seem particularly common in historical fiction, concerned as it so often is with the relationship of the individual life to the continuum of time: one of the great twentieth-century historical novels, William Golding's *Rites of Passage*, is built of one long diary-letter, which encloses, literally as well as figuratively, another diary-letter.

 ## Sara Sheridan

'Research material can turn up anywhere – in a dusty old letter in an archive, a journal or some old photographs you find in a charity shop... Occasionally a particular word or phrase in a letter or diary has sparked an entire plot – like an echo from history, still very alive.'

USING REAL HISTORICAL DOCUMENTS

This can be an effective way of enhancing the air of authenticity, and obviously if your story is centred on real historical characters then what they actually wrote may have been your inspiration, and will certainly need taking into account.

But do be careful to make sure that the document is earning its keep as part of moving the story on. And the other question is voice. Readers will read authentic documents in a different spirit from the fictional narrative they're bedded in, as in a biopic which mixes jerky black-and-white documentary footage of the real character with smooth full colour of an actor playing the fictional version. But the voice you give to an historical character does need to align, as it were, with the voice that we hear in their genuine writing: we need to sense a continuity between the two, even if they're not the same. And if you mix, for example, real letters with fictional letters, you're going to have to be careful that the latter really do sound like the former, just as in a biopic it works *less* well, paradoxically, when the vintage footage is closer in style to the fictional footage.

Focus point: copyright in real documents

If you plan to use the text of any genuine document in your novel, you must check the copyright position, however little you plan to quote. In the UK, published texts are in copyright for 70 years after the death of the writer, and if you plan to use the words of so much as a sentence, whether or not you specifically show it as a quotation, you will need to ask the copyright holder (usually the author or their estate) for permission, and pay whatever fee they ask. Ignore anything that anyone says about 'fair dealing' (UK) and 'fair use' (US); these rules do not apply to fiction but only to non-fiction.

There are other complications. Whether and when a text was published makes a big difference, and the person who owns the physical letters and shows them to you may not be the person who owns copyright in the words. Copyright may still exist in translations and editions even when the original text is no longer in copyright. The Society of Authors website has more advice and fact sheets.

Write: a story from a real document

Browse books and websites, looking for real historical documents such as letters, diaries, court reports or newspaper items. Pick one which feels as if it has a story inside or behind it that you'd like to explore; feel free to fictionalize names and so on, if you don't want to be tied to the specifics.

Copy out the item – longhand or copy-typing – to get the words and rhythms into your ears, then work out a story in which this document isn't just a record of something that happened, but has a function in the plot. When you write the story, quote as much or as little of the actual text as you like, and try to find a narrative voice which complements it without necessarily imitating it or pastiching it.

USING IMAGINARY HISTORICAL DOCUMENTS

In *On Histories and Stories*, A. S. Byatt describes invented documents as 'ventriloquized' rather than 'parodied' or 'pastiched', and because written forms are the main way we can hear real, historical voices, they are the way in to historical voices for many writers. It's possible to make the voice of a letter, say, more strongly historical, than you could the voice of a whole novel, and there's real pleasure for readers and writers in what documents can add to a narrative: they might cast a different, selective and perhaps subjective light on the story, amplify our sense of period, character, setting or event, or indeed offer us the readerly pleasures of ventriloquism or parody.

Documents offer all sorts of plotting opportunities: letters go astray or have their secrets betrayed and acted on; newspaper reports can cause someone to abandon their home or their job; a diary entry can bear witness to a character arguing their way from wanting to save their marriage to deciding to get a divorce. In *Possession* the documents are the clues to the mysterious Victorian love story, and the letters are crucial to it, but the modern hunt for more documents is also the story-engine of the novel. Choderlos de Laclos's novel

Les Liaisons dangereuses is not historical fiction, but it is a peerless example: it is entirely made of letters, and every letter is written by a character as part of the main story, *in order to make something happen.* The writing, sending and reading of each letter moves the plot and the story on, and not always in the way the sender intended.

However, it's easy to use documents badly: a character isn't the type to write letters like this or they don't have time in your plot; diaries over-explain states of mind which are more powerful when simply evoked in character-in-action; newspaper extracts try to get you out of the hole of having an internal narrator who wouldn't know these things; letters to a friend, of the 'I must just tell you what happened on Tuesday' kind, are a last resort to convey something vital. If these don't enrich the story but only explain it, readers will sense that you're taking the easy way out.

With what one might call 'public' documents – newspapers, histories, poetry – the difficulty is chiefly making them sound authentic. Whereas the reader accepts the narrative voice as being in the business of evoking an impression of the time, something which purports to be an Elizabethan play script, or a newspaper report of the Gordon Riots in 1780, is up against the reader's sense of the real thing, and inauthenticity will really jar.

The gap between what a narrative says and the individual, subjective take in letters and diaries is rich territory: the reader is aware that the written account is filtered through the character's personality and their reasons for writing. (Indeed, my novel *The Mathematics of Love* originated in my exploring the gap between what a Peninsular War veteran would write of his experiences, and what those experiences actually were.) But letters and diaries are written after the event, and it's easy to be lured into summarizing, explaining and reporting: staying too far out in psychic distance and making this kind of narrative very even-toned and undynamic. You will have to decide how much to switch into showing/evoking mode, quoting speech directly, for example, in a way which may not be true to the reality of diary- and letter-voice. Certainly, whole novels written as a diary generally have to do a lot of 'cheating' of this kind, although it helps if the writing of the diary interacts with the action. An excellent example of this, though not historical fiction, is Dodie Smith's *I Capture the Castle*. A novel which simply interweaves documents with narrative can afford to be more faithful to the after-the-event nature of documents, and exploit the contrast of voices.

Snapshot: documents in different voices

Documents are the product of a writer, a form for the writing, and a recipient. Think of three very different characters, perhaps these or some of your own:

- a rich and religious businesswoman or -man
- a reluctant debutant(e) about to be launched into the high society of the time
- a tramp or hobo.

Think of three different kinds of writing, for example:

- a secret diary
- a letter to a beloved uncle, aunt or godparent
- a written speech for some kind of celebration.

Try out different pairings of character and writing till you find a promising combination: the document is going to reveal an important secret about themselves, for example, 'I've just discovered that I'm not my parents' child, but was found as a baby on the battlefield and adopted'. Write a crazy first draft of that part of the document.

You could also explore, for example, how different the same person sounds in three different forms, or how different people write the same secret.

Key idea: diaries and letters need a story-reason for existing

It's tempting to use diaries or letters when you need to convey some background or information: just park it in a diary. But, as with any info-dump, the reader will quickly realize what you're doing.

The fact that this character writes this stuff must be psychologically likely and, ideally, the existence of this writing should be part of the plot, not just a convenient way of conveying information.

Write: how differently a story can be told

Pick a place and a period, and think of an incident involving a small child, teenager or young adult, when their parent (or grandparent) was also in some way involved. Make a few notes about who these people are and the basic series of events. Then choose two *different* narrative perspectives to write it from, one of the child's, one of the parent's, which will be interesting both in terms of how long it is after the event, and what form their version takes. Don't worry if your first try is a bit of a mess – this is a complex project for such a small compass – but it should help you to get a feel for the thinking that this sort of story needs.

Some possible combinations might be:

- Small child in first person at the time; parent in first person remembering the moment years later.
- Teenager's diary later in the day; parent explaining what happened to the police, magistrate or secret police.
- Parent's letter to the child's other parent, explaining what happened; child describing it to a friend at school.
- Parent telling a friend over a drink or some such, a day or two later; young adult describing it to their priest or psychotherapist.
- Later biographer of the child/teen/young adult; parent with slight dementia or a high fever years later.

You are going to form the story by alternating sections of the two accounts; it's up to you whether you write the whole of one and then the other, or write chunks in the order that the reader will read them. Remember 'get in late and get out early', and make your own decisions about whether each of the two strands, within itself, should be told in strict chronological order. In real life the oral, informal accounts in particular would quite likely hop to and fro in time, so balance this verisimilitude with the need to keep the reader clear.

Workshop: looking at how far you've come

Collect together *all* the Write exercises you've done so far, and print them out (or switch on Track Changes and remind yourself how to do comment balloons). Read them through in the way you've got used to: noting what doesn't work and what does work, and finding problems but not solving them.

- Which exercises sparked the best writing? Why do you think that might have been? What have you learned, and got better at, so far? Have the exercises, between them, shown you which aspects of your writing most need work?

- Which voices are most effective? Is there any common factor in the ones which came alive relatively easily? What do you need to do to learn to make other kinds of voices more vivid?

- What made your imagination run more freely: telling yourself accuracy didn't matter for now; having material already in your mind; or researching new things?

- Are there places where the historical information and researched material is a bit lumpy and undigested? Are there places where the lack of vivid, accurate detail has made things bland and unconvincing?

- Do particular themes, ideas, or characters keep recurring? How might they work in different periods? Did particular periods keep recurring? How might you find different stories in those periods?

- Do non-linear structures excite you? What did experimenting with them show you about the opportunities and pitfalls?

Edit: making your own decisions

Pick one of the 16 Write exercises you've done so far, and develop it in whatever way you feel will make it most powerful, convincing and coherent, thinking about everything we've explored. Don't be afraid to depart radically from the origin of the piece, if that's where your thinking seems to be leading you. Some of the things to think about are:

- Might the ideas and characters work better in a different period or setting?
- How might 'the journey you make' be stronger and more dramatic?
- How might 'the route you take' work better and more convincingly?
- How could you use structure to help that?
- What voice or voices would serve your story best? Does that affect how you handle point of view and showing and telling?
- How best can you avoid getting stuck in the mud of information, while being vivid and particular?
- Might you use real or invented documents? What would they add? What might the pitfalls be?
- Would a wider range of psychic distance work better? Where might you close right in? Where might you pull right out?

Next step

We've been looking at the different forms that your story might take, both in length and in structure. Now we're moving from form to genre: thinking about what sort of 'journey' and 'route' your reader might be making along the roads of your historical world.

9

Different kinds of story: genre

'Genre' is a term which gets used in confusing and contradictory ways, because it may mean the kind of story this is, or the setting, or where a bookshop might shelve it. All the major bookshop genres have historical fiction forms, and there are other genres which have important historical aspects. Or are you 'crossing genres'? If so, there are creative and commercial opportunities but also large pitfalls, as there are with trying to straddle the literary/commercial divide.

'Genre' is a term which has been used in many different ways over the centuries, and can still cause much confusion. For our purposes, however, there are two basic, though overlapping, ways in which the term is used:

- First, *genre* **as the nature of the story**: romance, thriller, comedy, action-adventure, drama, detective story/mystery. This is about what's at stake in the novel, and what satisfactions it provides for the reader, and of course those can take an historical form: what are we hoping for, and what are we dreading? For example, adventure and thriller stories are about physical and psychological survival in tackling threats and dangers (although a thriller, in particular, may have a mystery inside it). In romance and romantic comedy the survival is just as desperately important, but the threats and dangers are social and interpersonal, and the goal is psychological and emotional survival. Of course there will be elements of others – the thriller's protagonists falling in love, the comedy heist story – but a story which doesn't have one dominant drive built on what's at stake will have much more trouble holding on to readers.

- Second, *genre* **as one of the book industry's fundamental classification systems.** Selling books is the business of finding the readers who are looking for a certain set of satisfactions – a certain genre – and showing how this book (your book) will deliver them. So genre affects everything about how the book industry works: how authors focus on those satisfactions and deliver them; which magazines might publish your stories; the typography, blurb and cover design of a book; whether your publisher will pitch it to the supermarkets or the literary prizes; where in the bookshop it will be shelved and displayed; and, increasingly, what sub-sub-subsets of genre might get it high up in the rankings of the online booksellers. Because of this, 'historical', 'literary' and 'fantasy' are also bought, sold and talked about as genres, even though those labels tell you nothing about what kind of story it is: love story? action-adventure? mystery? You will therefore often hear subsets talked about: 'literary romance', 'fantasy thriller', 'historical crime', and the fact that a book can be sold as 'historical fiction' sometimes grants you a bit more leeway in fitting the other half of the description.

Just to confuse things, since highly commercial fiction focuses on delivering with super-efficiency the satisfactions proper to that genre, it's often called 'genre fiction': i.e. plot-driven, easy reading such as beach reads, popular women's magazine stories, 'airport fiction', and 'category' or 'formula' fiction such as Harlequin Mills & Boon.

Key idea: 'genre' can mean different things

When writers and readers talk about genre, it can mean one of two things, or both interacting: what the main drivers of the story are, or the setting and society in which it takes place.

It's the genre subsets of historical fiction, and the opportunities and challenges of an historical setting, that this chapter explores. Which might offer you the best opportunity to learn and develop as a writer. Which would mean you were playing to your strengths if you're trying for publication or competitions.

Of course, there's no reason an adventure story shouldn't be full of gorgeous clothes, or a romance involve a crime; it's good for thriller writers to think in terms of the emotional depth that is the native territory of character-led stories; crime writers have a lot to teach literary writers about plotting and narrative drive. To explore how to do small amounts of these well in your genre, look towards a genre where they're central.

Focus point: genre is different from form

Some aspiring writers use 'genre' in completely the wrong sense: novel, poetry, short story, play, novella, non-fiction are not genres but *forms* of prose narrative, just as sonnets and ballads are two forms that poems can take. As well as causing confusion, it also suggests that the writer doesn't understand what it is about genre that is important.

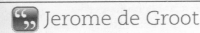

Jerome de Groot

Jerome de Groot is Senior Lecturer in English Literature at the University of Manchester, and author of *The Historical Novel*

'Historical writing can take place within numerous fictional locales: romance, detective, thriller, counterfactual, horror, literary, gothic, postmodern, epic, fantasy, mystery, western, children's books. Indeed, the intergeneric hybridity and flexibility of historical fiction have long been one of its defining characteristics. A historical novel might consider the articulation of nationhood via the past, highlight the subjectivism of narratives of History, underline the importance of the realist mode of writing to notions of authenticity, question writing itself, and attack historiographical convention. The form manages to hold within itself conservatism, dissidence, complication and simplicity; it attracts multiple, complex, dynamic audiences, it is a particular and complex genre hiding in plain sight on the shelves of a bookshop.'

HISTORICAL ADVENTURE AND THRILLER

If the basic drive of adventure plots is 'Will they achieve their goal and survive physically?', then history offers us enormous scope for scale, drama and grandeur in storytelling: survival is much more up to the individual and medicine is not much help; magic, hell and heaven are all real and only round the corner; monarchies are personal; weapons are a historical nerd's delight; combat is hand-to-hand; and surviving and pursuing your goal are inherently physical and dramatic, from the horses that might (or might not) let your character ride to the enemy's gates, to the underwear your character might (or might not) have to take off in the sex scenes. Even quite recent periods offer settings where the stakes are very high indeed, and which we know enough about to want to visit: 1930s Berlin, Cold War Shanghai.

The main pitfalls of an adventure plot are that the engineering of the plot asks your characters to act in ways which aren't psychologically credible, or that all the details of weapons or politics don't leave enough space for their inner life. It's not that we need pages of analysis and introspection, but that what we *do* sense of their past, and the hopes, dreams and insecurities that form their personality, are vivid, consistent and engaging in the strict sense: the reader must want to stay engaged with them, want to find out what happens, and believe in how their personality changes and develops through these events.

Bernard Cornwell's *Sharpe* series is a classic example of historical adventure, and a clear descendant of C. S. Forester's Hornblower, by way of Patrick O'Brian. However, as with series detectives, the key to a long-running lead character like Sharpe is for his personality to remain fairly static through the books: the emotional change and growth in each book is minimal, so that each new book can supply the mixture as before. Inman's strand of Charles Frazier's *Cold Mountain* is also essentially an adventure, as he struggles to get home. M. C. Scott's Boudica series is grand-scale adventure built inside the known boundaries of early Roman Britain, and 'swords and sandals' is a whole commercial subgenre of its own, while for something more literary you could look at Patrick deWitt's *The Sisters Brothers* or Paul Kingsnorth's *The Wake*.

As I mentioned earlier, thrillers are essentially adventure stories with a mystery built in. Staying close to well-documented history, in *Pompeii* Robert Harris builds in mystery at the beginning, as the protagonist tries to get his fears heard that a series of odd but apparently unrelated events have a common cause; mystery gives way to thriller as he has to act to find the cause and solve it ... and then the eruption begins. Antonia Hodgson's *The Devil in the Marshalsea* is very different: a mystery within the walls of the prison must be solved by the protagonist, who is himself imprisoned for debt and in danger from the unknown criminal; if he fails to solve the mystery he will be transferred to the Common Side and certain death.

HISTORICAL CRIME AND MYSTERY

The basic plot of crime stories is 'Will they get justice and set the world to rights?' In crime and mystery traditionally there's a murder, since murder demands justice more loudly than any other crime, but it might also be that there's something rotten in the state, or even that for a long time no one's quite sure *what* the mystery is, as with Iain Pears's *An Instance of the Fingerpost*. In historical settings official forces of justice are less comprehensive and well organized, so it's easier to put the burden of setting the world to rights on to a non-professional protagonist. It's also fascinating to explore the beginnings of professional investigation, as with R. N. Morris's novels, beginning with *A Gentle Axe*, which are set in 1860s St Petersburg and star Porfiry Petrovich, the examining magistrate from Dostoevsky's *Crime and Punishment*. Plots are easier to construct (except when they're harder) when it takes a fortnight to ride from New York to Boston; forensic science and the rules of evidence are both primitive; saving the wrongly accused is even more urgent when their fate will otherwise be hanging, drawing and quartering.

So the mystery might be political or personal, but the consequences of it not being solved and justice not being achieved must really matter to the protagonists: to keep the tension rising, you're going to have to think of more and stronger reasons why the protagonists keep on trying to solve the mystery, even as you put ever bigger obstacles in their way ... and all the while keeping our emotional engagement with them as characters-in-action. And while your modern readers will want to be satisfied by the outcome, there is a danger of the resolution losing touch with the historical likelihood.

Umberto Eco's *The Name of the Rose* is a classical detective story in every way (and his little book *Reflections on The Name of the Rose* is a fascinating rumination on the business of writing historical fiction). In C. J. Samson's detective series, the fictional lawyer Shardlake tackles crimes centred on the real politics and personalities of the Tudor court. Andrew Taylor's beautifully written standalone detective stories, such as *The Anatomy of Ghosts*, show how the classical mystery ingredients – a closed society, crucial evidence of who-was-where-when – can be combined with sophisticated and thoughtful themes. One of my personal favourites is the exquisitely written *Morality Play* by Barry Unsworth, while Margaret Atwood's *Alias Grace* is arguably a crime novel, although of the 'Whydunnit?' rather than 'Whodunnit?' kind; *When We Were Orphans* is Kazuo Ishiguro's literary reimagining of the Sherlock Holmes tradition, set in 1930s Shanghai.

ROMANCE AND ROMANTIC COMEDY

The basic plot of romance is 'Will they achieve love and survive emotionally?': love, sex and marriage are all more high-stakes in a world without divorce, contraception, antibiotics or missing persons bureaux, and you can have fun – or drama, luxury or downright weirdness – with the clothes. Since the survival is emotional and psychological as much as physical, there's scope for the 'journey you make' to be as much about how the character changes emotionally as practically.

The risk – especially with literary fiction and light romantic comedy – is of losing sight of the need, yet again, for the stakes to rise. If the plot centres on finding love, then however light the touch with which you're writing it, the love needs to deepen even as the risk of it going wrong increases. The love also needs to be psychologically credible: it's very easy, in constructing a romance, to treat the love as a given, rather than as a living, changing mainspring of character-in-action, in which two people earn the realistic hope of staying together, or fail to do so and fall apart.

One modern mega-seller of this kind of story would be Louis de Bernières's *Captain Corelli's Mandolin*, and Andrew Miller's *Pure* has a romance at its heart, as does his *Casanova*, while Elizabeth Fremantle and Suzannah Dunn both write beautifully, and very differently, within the tight margins of well-known and well-documented Tudor lives. Susan Sontag explores the triangle of Lord Nelson and William and Emma Hamilton, in the subtle and literary *The Volcano Lover;* in the realm of almost-pure fiction, Rose Tremain's *Restoration* is profoundly thought-provoking as well as comic; and the three wholly fictional lovers of Barry Unsworth's *Stone Virgin* experience three different ways in which love can be a catastrophe.

At the commercial end, what the book trade calls 'clogs and shawls' books – as exemplified by Catherine Cookson and Nora Roberts – are usually built round a romance *as one aspect of the heroine's self-realization*. Gone are the days when finding the right man and settling down are all that's needed. Moving towards romantic comedy, Georgette Heyer's Regency-set novels are always worth returning to for lessons in stylish prose, handling researched material and setting up real emotional engagement between hero and heroine: indeed, a whole sub-genre, the Regency novel, has grown up from the roots she planted.

COMEDY

There's plenty of comedy in novels that aren't sold as comedy, such as Tremain's *Restoration* and the sequel, *Merivel*; Hallie Rubenhold's *Mistress of My Fate* series follows Henrietta Lightfoot through the lowest and highest life of Regency London, while Patrick deWitt's *The Sisters Brothers* is also very funny in places. Angela Carter's *Wise Children* and *Nights at the Circus* are rare in pulling off the trick of being comic to their bones in how we laugh at the characters and their predicaments, while we still mind painfully about their fate. But novels whose chief project is to make you laugh at the ridiculous form a rather small and particular corner of the book world.

Making things funny enough is not easy: there's a risk that you just resort to overstating every character's reactions to everything, whereas how people react still needs to be proportional to the events. Voice has a lot to do with it, too: the narrator's take on what's happening is crucial in getting the reader to laugh as well as cry – or, best of all, cry with laughter. George MacDonald Fraser's Flashman books, built on a cad and a bully getting away with it, form a comic twin of, say, Patrick O'Brian's Aubrey and Maturin books.

Setting your comic novel in history offers lots of scope for jokes which fit modern tropes to a past which we don't usually think of in those terms: think of Marc Norman and Tom Stoppard's script for *Shakespeare in Love*, and the ferryman's, 'I had that Christopher Marlowe in the back of my boat once'. Comedy can also play with the received idea of a certain place and setting: Tom Holt's *The Walled Orchard*, set in ancient Athens, has a scope and sweep which are relatively rare as well as being extremely funny, without cheating his brilliant research, while his *Alexander at the World's End* forms a comic twin for Mary Renault's fiction. Some strands of David Mitchell's extraordinary *Cloud Atlas* are comic in a more fantastical way, and there's an overlap, too, with speculative fiction and steampunk.

DRAMA AND PSYCHOLOGICAL THRILLER

I've lumped these together, to cover books which have plenty of action, feeling and thought, but don't really fit under one of the traditional headings. Indeed, some editors would say that books labelled 'psychological thrillers' are neither thrillers nor much more psychological than many other novels; it's a catch-all term to label stories in which character and personality drive much of the story, but there's plenty of action and narrative excitement, and some of the most rewarding books fit best under this umbrella.

If there is a common pitfall in writing such a book, it's probably a lack of focus on what you're trying to do. Just because no one traditional type of story dominates doesn't let the writer off the hook: it still needs a compelling voice, a strong, central narrative drive, and characters whose fate we really, really care about. Sebastian Faulks's *Birdsong*, Angela Carter's *Nights at the Circus*, Helen Dunmore's *The Siege* and M. L. Stedman's *The Light between Oceans* are all good examples. The novels of Catherine Cookson and their descendants, and Dorothy Dunnett's Lymond Chronicles, are family-based dramas as much as romances, while Elizabeth Jane Howard's Cazalet Chronicles, while not qualifying under our definition of historical fiction, do have the quality of pinning down a historical moment which has now long gone.

Moving towards psychological thriller, Maria McCann's *As Meat Loves Salt* is on the border with crime, while Jane Thynne's novel *Black Roses* and its sequels, set in Nazi Germany, are driven as much by psychology as the mechanics of spying. There's also a flavour of Gothic to many such novels: Daphne du Maurier's *My Cousin Rachel* is much scarier and more powerful than *Rebecca*, while more recent examples might include Sarah Waters's *Fingersmith* or Essie Fox's *The Somnambulist*. Peter Ackroyd's parallel narratives in books such as *Hawksmoor* and *The House of Doctor Dee* are psychologically dark as well as comic, and powerfully evocative not just of a particular place and time, but of how different times overlap and seep into each other.

Sara Sheridan

'You spill a lot of beans in historical fiction. Crime fiction is about spilling no beans at all: you spill the least beans you possibly can. So, because I had already written historical fiction before, I was really good at the spilling-beans section, but the new skill I had to learn when I was writing [crime novel] Brighton Belle *was difficult. I had to avoid the equivalent of shouting, "This character's a murderer! Look who did it!".'*

Snapshot: genre satisfactions

Pick an historical genre which you have little knowledge of: you don't read much, and you certainly don't write. Nose around on the library shelves and the Internet – reading actual texts, not just the forums that discuss them – and try to get a feel for what it is that fans of the genre like about it. Make a list, and think up the outlines of a story which would provide some of those satisfactions.

Literary historical fiction

The division of books into 'literary or commercial' is a commonplace – although contested – distinction among both writers and the industry. At one end of the spectrum is the super-literary (John Fowles's *A Maggot*, say, or Paul Kingsnorth's *The Wake*) and the other is super-commercial (perhaps Conn Iggulden or Diana Gabaldon and beyond that 'category fiction'). But there really isn't a binary, either/or test: all sorts of things can tend to site a book at a particular point on the literary–commercial spectrum. More literary historical fiction is likely to:

- pay greater attention to the originality and quality of the prose, even if that asks the reader to read more slowly and attentively
- drive the reader's interest not only with story and plot but with themes, ideas and psychology; stories may be more 'character-driven' or may have dislikeable protagonists who are not the seductively 'glamorous baddy' type
- play with genre satisfactions rather than simply delivering them; explicitly parody or pastiche genre conventions; be harder to characterize and identify in genre terms
- explore history as an idea: the human consciousness of existing in historical time; perhaps 'break the frame' by making explicit that this narrative is a constructed thing
- ask harder work of the reader: assembling the story, drawing on their own historical and other knowledge; getting literary references, as with Jo Baker's *Longbourn*
- allow the story to be equivocal, unresolved, morally ambiguous, less easy to 'get'

- do well in terms of visibility at literary festivals and in the press, have a hope of prizes, sell in smaller numbers.

All these are only possibilities: readers get more sophisticated, films introduce more readers to classics which can then be drawn on by modern writers, and devices that were pretty literary 40 years ago (non-chronological structures, say, or present-tense narratives) are now commonplace in commercial fiction.

Still, more commercial historical fiction will tend to:

- be written in a way which is chiefly concerned to convey the story well and clearly
- let story be king; novels are 'plot-driven', with ideas and themes subordinated to the brisk forward movement of the story
- fit the conventions of the genre so the reader who buys it knows what satisfactions are on offer
- keep the traditional contract between writer and reader so that inside the story everything is told as if these events really happened
- make any work the reader needs to contribute in assembling the story clear and easy; not assume historical and other knowledge
- be morally complex but not usually ambiguous, and outcomes will be resolved into more-or-less good, or more-or-less bad
- sell in large numbers, but not get much get much coverage in reviews or prizes, or space at literary festivals.

Key idea: 'Literary fiction' may not be literature

Literary fiction, in book industry terms, is a genre: a particular kind of book that a particular kind of reader likes reading. Whether or not it's a good book, and will stand the test of time and critical opinion to become 'literature' in the sense of writing that's admired as art and ends up on syllabuses, is a completely different question.

Focus point: learn from the best in genres you don't like

It's easy to be scornful about genres you don't like, especially at the opposite end of the literary–commercial spectrum from your own taste. The worst commercial fiction *is* like junk food: satisfying the human desire for story in the cheapest way possible, leaving you faintly nauseated. The worst literary fiction *is* like ridiculous super-starred restaurant food: satisfying the human desire to think in the most superficial way possible, leaving you hungry.

But when you see a book that you're tempted to despise but which is selling very well, or winning prizes, dip into it and think instead about why a publisher might have chosen to take the expensive gamble of publishing it. What satisfactions does it offer to a reader? How might your project supply those satisfactions, while staying true to the kind of story that you want it to be?

Snapshot: genre in practice

Grab three or four books from the full spectrum of the historical fiction you enjoy. Study each one in terms of genre – including what the blurb says and how it works out in the text. What basic plot dominates? What do you as the reader hope for, and what do you dread?

Can you see elements of other genres? Do they work successfully in with the main plot? What opportunities do they give to make the main plot work better? Are there times when this doesn't work?

Snapshot: literary fiction

Look online for the short- and longlists of the big literary prizes over the years. Look for their historical winners and nominees, particularly those such as the Goldsmiths and Folio prizes, which specifically reward challenging literary fiction. Dip into several: it's easiest to get a sense of structure and story with a physical book, but even the 'Look Inside' facility online is better than nothing.

Some suggestions of books to try are: Ali Smith, *How to Be Both*; Neel Mukherjee, *The Lives of Others*; Colm Tóibín, *The Master*; Andrea Levy, *The Long Song*; Patrick deWitt, *The Sisters Brothers*; Esi Edugyan *Half Blood Blues*; Peter Carey, *Parrot and Olivier in America.*

If this isn't your usual kind of reading, try to understand what readers who love it are looking for, and look yourself for things to like: the prose and ideas, the characters and their times. Very often, too, such novels will explore how storytelling itself works.

If you already read this kind of fiction, try to put yourself in the place of a reader who finds this kind of writing difficult or uncomfortable. What makes the story harder to follow? What makes it more slow-moving, more quick-moving, or less emotionally engaging?

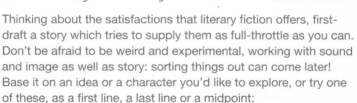

Write: try literary fiction

Thinking about the satisfactions that literary fiction offers, first-draft a story which tries to supply them as full-throttle as you can. Don't be afraid to be weird and experimental, working with sound and image as well as story: sorting things out can come later! Base it on an idea or a character you'd like to explore, or try one of these, as a first line, a last line or a midpoint:

He seized my ankle and I begged him softly to let me go.

She swore she did no wrong and I laughed, for in those days I knew no better.

They came in the night and took my father away.

As the wind rose the roof began to creak.

Quasi-historical fiction

There are various other genres that share a border with historical fiction. They are basically outside the scope of this book, but here's a quick run-down of the ways in which they present the same opportunities and challenges as more mainstream projects:

COUNTERFACTUAL HISTORICAL FICTION

Counterfactual historical fiction is set in an alternative world (hence its usually being categorized as 'alternate' fiction) in which one crucial aspect of a historical period is different. 'What if Germany had won the Second World War?' seems to dominate: Robert Harris's *Fatherland* is a thriller set in 1950s Britain as conquered the Nazi state. Joan Aiken's classic children's series *The Wolves of Willoughby Chase* is set in a recognizably Victorian England, except that the Glorious Revolution never happened, the good Stuart King James III sits on the throne, and the Hanoverians are dastardly terrorist rebels.

Historians play 'counterfactuals' like a scientific control experiment: exploring how one change would play out illuminates both real and counterfactual worlds. Similarly, counterfactual historical fiction needs to be very accurate and convincing in historical texture and detail, but for that single, crucial difference.

Snapshot: counterfactual history

You could say that any historical fiction is counterfactual: it takes a real world and puts invented things into it. So it can be useful for any writer to think about how the experience of an historical period is a mixture of perennial human nature and contingent circumstances that produce a particular society. It's also good practice for spotting those 'white spaces' between the facts where you might write your story. So pick a big historical event and change one thing about it. For example:

- Brutus and Cassius didn't manage to murder Julius Caesar.
- Henry V lived to succeed to the French throne.
- Lady Jane Grey was successfully crowned Queen Regnant.
- Doctor Dee discovered how to turn base metal into gold ... but with a substance that can only be found in the North West Passage through the Arctic.

Brainstorm a few ideas of how you might develop a story from this basic change.

STEAMPUNK

Steampunk has a common border with counterfactual: the Doctor Dee example in the Snapshot just above is on this border. Gibson and Sterling's *The Difference Engine* assumes that Lord Byron survives to lead an early Victorian radical party just as Charles Babbage's Difference Engine – the first computer – results in a steam-driven age of ubiquitous computers. Steampunk is usually promoted and sold as speculative fiction more than historical fiction, but the same issues apply: it needs solid anchorage in a convincingly structured and textured version of 'real' history.

FANTASY FICTION

Fantasy fiction shares with historical fiction the need for 'world-building': creating the sense of a world which is 'Other', but believable. It goes beyond the borders of actual historical events and characters, but doesn't entirely lose touch with them or their voices. You will need to orient the reader and make clear the urgency and importance of the characters' problems, without info-dump or screeds of plodding explanation. Its roots are in the medievalist Tolkien's channelling of the great northern sagas into the *Lord of the Rings* books, and the genre has grown up to be largely Dark Ages and medieval in spirit. And Marie Phillips's *The Table of the Less Valued Knights* continues a tradition which began with Mark Twain and *A Connecticut Yankee in King Arthur's Court*: playing for comic effect with myths and traditions that we were all brought up on.

Snapshot: genres with a historical element

If you're interested in some of these genres, pick up a favourite book or three. Read a few pages of each. What is/are the main imagined or counterfactual elements? Which elements are taken straight from 'real', factual history? What changes have followed on from the main non-historical, imaginary element?

CHILDREN'S AND YOUNG ADULT FICTION

Children's and Young Adult fiction is beyond the scope of this book, although the basics of good writing and good storytelling are no different. Writing for children and teenagers brings its own particular constraints and freedoms, which you can explore more in *Complete Writing for Children* by Clémentine Beauvais. You can't assume a wide historical knowledge in children and you may need to explain a bit more; on the other hand, children respond to historical voices with glee if not erudition. Genre boundaries are much more blurred, while time-slip stories, which embody our sense of the nearness of the past, are only a small corner of adult but a staple of children's historical fiction, including some of the very best: Linda Buckley-Archer's Gideon Trilogy is a recent prizewinning example.

 ## Blaise Pascal

Pascal's *Pensées* were collected after his death in 1662.

'Eloquence is an art of saying things in such a manner, 1, that those to whom we speak can hear them without pain, and with pleasure; 2, that they feel themselves interested, so that self-love leads them more willingly to reflect upon what is said. ... We should put ourselves in the place of those who are to listen to us, and make experiment on our own heart of the turn we give to our discourse, to see whether one is made for the other, and whether we can be sure that our auditor will be as it were forced to yield. ... It is not enough that a phrase be beautiful, it must be fitted to the subject, and not have in it excess or defect.'

 ## Edit: increasing satisfactions

Pick whichever of this chapter's Write exercises you found most challenging, and revise it to make it work better in terms of the exercise: whether it's the new-to-you genre story or the literary story, try to make it more satisfying for fans of that kind of story. If you know someone who likes that genre, explain that this is an exercise to explore something new, and persuade them to read it and give you feedback in that spirit.

Workshop: working out of your comfort zone

Look at that story again. What did it feel like, at first, to go so far out of your writerly comfort zone? Did that feeling change as you drafted it? What about when you were editing it? Which aspects of the genre (counting 'literary' as a genre for now) did you find it easiest or most enjoyable to work with? Why do you think that was? Which aspects did you find hardest or least enjoyable? Why was that?

What can you take away from this exercise? What might you learn from thinking about how this genre works? Do you want to explore it further as a reader? As a writer? What have you discovered or understood that you can take back with you to your own writerly territory? Has this exercise changed your sense of what that territory is, and what it might become?

What if your story mixes genres?

We've seen how all genres may quite naturally have elements of other genres. Some aspiring writers also worry about every last detail being 'correct for the genre', when in fact none of the definitions and details are stable or uncontested, and that kind of self-consciousness and anxiety can really confuse your sense of storytelling.

But if you're really not sure what kind of story you're trying to write, it is an alarm bell you should listen to. Editors can only buy a story if it will appeal to a particular market which they know how to find and sell to, so everything about publishing a book is conditioned by the business of sending out the right message to the right market. If you're thinking of self-publishing, the problem of presenting your work in a way which appeals to two markets is exactly the same. Whatever market you're aiming for, it's not impossible, but it is harder, to find and satisfy two kinds of reader at once: each set knows what satisfactions they're looking for in such a story, and you need to deliver those in full.

Readers looking for thriller pleasures get bored if those are sacrificed to the romance; the complexities of the family backstory and emotional dynamics may get distorted or skimped when you're constructing the detecting of crime and sprinkling the red herrings. So mixing genres demands that you combine the two sets of satisfactions without sacrificing either, and for that you need to understand both genres deeply. Only then will you be able to integrate and bend their different conventions to your will without compromising them.

Then there's the different crossing-genre problem which is really the writer trying to have it both ways: tacking half-baked intellectual or literary tricks on to a traditional body-on-page-one detective story in the desire to make it more literary; sugaring a satirical pill with a half-hearted love story to make it more saleable; putting in a 'clever' twist or epiphany in a story which has been ditchwater-dull up till then. Readers quickly know when their tastes aren't being taken seriously, and resent it, so don't do something unless you're willing to do it wholeheartedly, even if it's a secondary aspect of the book.

Focus point: cross-genre stories are harder to sell

If the appeal of your story is divided between different kinds of reader, then everything about it has to be extra good – twice as good, if you like – so that it becomes irresistible to an editor. Only then will it transcend the 'handicap' – from the marketing, sales and publicity point of view – of being difficult to pitch and therefore difficult to sell.

LITERARY–COMMERCIAL CROSSOVER

Somewhere near the literary end of the literary–commercial spectrum is a ditch which separates 'high-end commercial' from the 'literary' and, as with any kind of genre-crossing, if your story is trying to deliver a mixture of pleasures from both sides of the ditch, you have my sympathy and fellow feeling, because the same problem arises: satisfying one set of readers without short-changing the other.

It has become easier since books of this kind were relabelled as 'book-group books': substantial, well-written stories, in other words, which are absorbing and intelligent without being too tough a read, which raise interesting questions and provide plenty to discuss, and appeal well to women since women make the majority of book groups. However, whether your hope is to sell your literary–commercial crossover writing through a publisher or through your own self-publishing efforts, it's worth trying to push your work to sit more clearly on one or the other side of the ditch. And since 'literary', to the industry, is almost synonymous with 'doesn't sell', if you hope for any kind of future in continuing to write books that you can publish or self-publish, then arguably 'commercial' is the wiser side.

> ## Key idea: finding a readership
>
>
>
> If you want to find any kind of readership for your stories, you need to know what kind of reader might like them. How far you can, and want to, push your writing away from your natural territory and towards the centre of a certain genre is your decision.

Next step

We've finished anatomizing how storytelling works by exploring the opportunities and problems built into historical fiction which works with different genres, and then other genres which have things in common with historical fiction. Now we move on to think about how *you might actually write a story: the processes of getting going, keeping going, and finishing.*

10

Bringing it all together: process

Even when you understand and have worked on the techniques of imagining, researching and storytelling, it can still be baffling to know how to go about writing a story, let alone a novel. The order in which you might do things is partly to do with whether you are by nature a 'planner' or a 'pantser', or something in between. But it's also about learning techniques to help you keep the beast under control through all the stages of writing and revising, and discovering how to persevere with that for long enough to perfect the story, without putting off sending it out for ever.

Process and product

Writers such as Dorothea Brande and Julia Cameron make a distinction between 'process' – how you set about creating something – and 'product': the something you are trying to end up with. This chapter is about process. In historical fiction it seems obvious that you need to know the history, and the genre, before you can write a biographical novel based on the life of a Boston tea merchant, or a romance set in Mochica Peru which is better than the romance you've just read. But it's not easy for your writerly imagination to run free when your nose is glued to a textbook about late eighteenth-century tax tariffs, or examples of good romances. So it's not a given that, for example, you should do research before you write a first draft. Nor is it always the case that you must stand back and think about big structure before you close in and think about prose, because sometimes it's the close-up process of writing which reveals the big problem. When a character 'won't do what I want', as the writerly mystique puts it, or a scene *will* not come out right, it's usually because your intuition is trying to tell you that this is not what the story needs at this point.

On the other hand, it can be very difficult for your imagination to run until it does have a place to start or a place to run towards: you may know that your Peruvian astronomer ends up as chief priest, and imagine backwards to the life that created him. Clearly, that episode in Boston harbour is central to your tea merchant's life, but perhaps what's really exciting is that it's not so much what drives her to that crisis but what happens *after* her business is destroyed by the Boston Port Act; it's that which will test who she is and how she survives to make a new life.

So the process by which you find, plan, draft, redraft, revise, edit and polish a story ideally needs to take into account where it ends up or where it starts, but also leave open the possibility of new and different things emerging as you write.

 Key idea: there are no rules about process

There are no rules and very few rights and wrongs about the writing process, and different projects may well need to be tackled in different ways. What matters is that you understand the possibilities, and the advantages and risks of each, and think about which processes will suit *you* best.

Robyn Young

Robyn Young's most recent books, the Kingdom Trilogy, centre on Robert the Bruce.

'When writing about real figures from history, research all you can about them, from as many different perspectives as possible: friends & enemies, those who followed them into battle, those they battled against. When you've built a full picture – when you think you know them – let it go. Write them, allowing who they are for you to come to life on the page.'

PLANNING VERSUS PANTSING

Writers often divide themselves into 'planners', and 'pantsers'. Planners, it's assumed, work out who the characters are and what they're like, decide in some detail what the story and plot will be, research what needs researching, and then put those plans into the actual words of the draft. Pantsers fly by the seat of their pants: they have only the vaguest idea of the story (although they may do a lot of work on the characters), and only find it out fully as it emerges, sentence by sentence, on to the paper. Then there's the hybrid writer who 'pantses' short stories but plans novels, and that's the giveaway of what this discussion is really about.

It's easy enough, in a 2,500-word story, to work word by word; it's like moving to a strange city and setting out to find a house which you know is round a couple of corners; you'll know pretty soon whether you've taken the right turnings. Writing a novel is more like setting out to find a house on the other side of the city. You leave your house, but which way do you turn then? And after that? And after that?

A plan – a route-map – helps, but there's a risk that you're so busy sticking to that clear, strong route that you miss the better, more exciting possibilities which your intuition and imagination might serve up, and end up with a draft in which dull or unconvincing characters do things purely to fit that predetermined route. And if your plan says one thing, and your intuition is telling you it's not right, what do you do? If you change it, will the whole plan collapse?

The first risk with pantsing is that you never start at all, because you get stuck on that first turn out of the door: there is the blank page, and how on earth are you supposed to fill it? And the next risk is that you guess that turn, and the next, and the next, and end up with a story with no spine, no worthwhile journey or vivid route, however vivid the writing and evocative the scenes. And although every single word in a first draft can be changed (and many writers have done just that), as writer Mary Flanagan says, changing the big structure of a novel is a bit like turning round an oil tanker.

Some writers feel a real, instinctive revulsion from the idea of 'a plan', but I'd suggest that's to misunderstand what planning might actually be. It's not a strict itinerary complete with roadmap and Big Brother watching you, but a guidebook full of suggestions and helpful information. Some successful authors say they don't plan at all. I'd suggest that those authors tend to have a very strong sense of story and usually lots of experience: with only a vague idea where they're going, when they think 'Right, what happens next?' their imagination sorts through the possibilities intuitively.

In other words, some writers use getting the first version on to paper as the way to set their imagination to work, while other writers do their imagining-on-paper in other forms, and only later start to write continuous storytelling.

PLANNING SHORT STORIES

With short stories there's less risk of going badly astray, but that doesn't mean that 'pantsing' doesn't still carry risks, or that the story won't need just as many processes of revising. Indeed, there's an argument to be made that short fiction takes more work and scrutiny *per word* than long fiction does, because there's nowhere to hide. A slack sentence or two in a novel, though annoying, won't be the thing that makes or breaks it as an experience for the reader. But it might be the death of a short story.

Certainly the basic processes of drafting, revising and polishing are the same, and short stories, too, can benefit from all sorts of imagining-on-paper which is separate from the draft itself. Even if you only write short fiction, don't assume that plotting grids or timelines aren't for you.

Attributed to Blaise Pascal

'Pass me a pen; I need to think.'

IMAGINING-ON-PAPER

We've talked about drafting as one kind of imagining-on-paper, but there are many others. Here are some, and quite likely you will have your own:

- **clusters**
- **freewriting**
- **sketch maps**: distances affect travel times, and is it significant that she always has to ride past her estranged husband's house to reach her best friend's?
- **sketch plans of real and imagined buildings**: it isn't just the crime writers who need to know whether you can see the water closet door from the top of the cellar steps
- **family trees** and 'family' trees of friendships and colleagues, including how people feel about each other: love, scorn, (un) friendly rivalry?
- **mind maps** of themes, relationships, how an event or place affects different people, a sequence of 'fortunately–unfortunatelies'
- **sketch narratives** which aren't part of the novel: mini-stories, pen-portraits, scenes written from another point of view, scenes which in the novel take place 'off-stage'
- **drawings**: if you can draw, this is a way of really inhabiting characters and settings; others collect photographs or pictures which evoke them
- **timelines**: your character's backstory of childhood, school or war service; real historical events that are running in the background

- **charts** of things like characters' ages in past and future: was elderly Annie 6 or 60 when her grandfather died aged 100?
- **index cards** or sticky notes listing, say, scenes which you stick to the wall or string across the room; or do the equivalent in Scrivener
- **synopses** aren't just for when you're submitting work. A one-sentence 'hook' line focuses you ruthlessly on what the overall drive of your story is; a six-page breakdown of the plot engineering in whole sentences may make it clear how the 'causally related chain of events' is constructed and if you haven't connected it up properly
- **plotting grids** which lay out the chain of events schematically, but also have space for other things you want to track; there's an example in Appendix III
- **drafts** which are more or less a series of tries at the actual text of the novel, and will resemble it, roughly, in size and structure.

Snapshot: imagining-on-paper

Of that list, or any other methods you can think of, which do you do already? Which might you do? Think about your own process of writing a story – from the first flicker of an idea to polishing the last comma for the twentieth time. When, during that process, might each of these methods be useful?

Barbara Baig

Barbara Baig has taught writing for many years. From *How to Be a Writer*:

'*At a certain point in your process of collecting material and engaging with it, you will feel that you have enough material – or you will feel that you have so much that you're getting overwhelmed. This is a good time to put together a zero draft. This kind of draft gives you a way to see what you have and what you might still need. It's also a way for you to make choices about what to include and what to leave out.*

'*A zero draft is a draft that comes before your first draft: It consists of everything you think you want to include in your piece written down on the page, somewhere, in a single document.*'

DRAFTS

What Barbara Baig describes as a 'zero draft' is definitely one kind of 'imagining on paper': if you write scenes out of order then you are already working this way, and much may change when you start to stitch things together. But at some point you have sit down and start the writing which is your first shot at the text of the actual story. Of course, in the days of the typewriter or the quill-and-parchment, what counted as a draft was much clearer than it is for us, with our ever-perfect, never-ending word-processed documents. But drafts are worth thinking about, and there's an old writerly saying: write your first draft for yourself, your second draft for your reader and your third draft for your agent. In other words, use the first draft to find out what this story actually *is*. The 'second draft' work (which may start with typing up) is about revising to make the story you now know come alive for the reader: revisiting the decisions about tense, voice, structure, psychic distance and so on. The 'third draft' work is about making it even more appealing by editing and polishing to draw in even the reader who isn't convinced they want to read it.

But none of that helps if you have a blank screen or page in front of you, and are so terrified of putting down the wrong words that you don't put any words down at all. A few writers never have this problem; some writers are almost permanently paralysed by it; most of us are somewhere in between. Here are some things which may help.

- **Decide where the characters need to be by the end of the first scene**, mentally and emotionally, or physically (or both), make a few notes to get your imagination running, and write your way there. You can work everything else out later.

- **Remember, you don't have to start with the first scene.** You can go straight to one which is already present in your imagination.

- **Think of your first draft as just a giant freewrite, or brainstorm**: one more kind of imagining-on-paper, the words just placeholders for the *real* words, which you'll discover later.

- **Try writing the first 10,000–15,000 words of your draft longhand.** The human imagination is analogue, not digital, and research into e-books and note-making increasingly suggests that reading and writing are more bound up with kinaesthesia than you'd think, so longhand comes naturally to many for the brainstorming stages. Typing up is a very good way of finding out what you've got and knocking it into overall shape.

- **Hemingway said that all first drafts were rubbish,** and the concept that Ann Lamott developed from that, of the 'shitty first draft', can be very freeing: if what comes out is rubbish, well, that's just a natural part of the process.

- **Remember the journalists' maxim 'Don't get it right, get it written'.** 'Right' can come later. Keep writing forwards, so that you stay reasonably close to the reader's experience, making a note of any problems, questions or ideas about past or future chapters. Personally, I write on the right-hand side only of the notebook, and on every other line, so I can make notes and immediate corrections without losing that forward drive.

- **Ceramic artist Grayson Perry says 'Creativity is mistakes',** and good teachers know that if a thing's worth doing, it's worth doing badly, in the sense of the outcome not being good. Nothing you write is ever wasted, even if not a single word ends up in the finished piece. Its value is in what you discovered by doing it.

Key idea: a first draft is just more imagining-on-paper

It tells the story roughly as you imagine the final draft will tell it, although of course a million things could still change. But a first draft is, essentially, just one more form for your imaginings to take.

Some writers write a whole novel, longhand perhaps, pell-mell to the end, without ever looking at a single word they've already written: some will be zero-drafting, others will have worked out a great deal of the story before they started. Others write and revise and edit each sentence until it's just how they want it, and may scarcely change a word later. Most are somewhere in between: some use basic revisions of yesterday's words to get back into the world of the story and then launch into today's; some writers write a chapter longhand, then revise it by typing it up and knocking it into shape; some hurl themselves through the first 30,000 words and then take stock; some write out-of-order, whichever scenes they can best imagine, and then stitch everything together and revise it all to iron out the wrinkles. Try new processes, but listen to yourself: don't meekly assume that what suits your writing buddy or some big-name writer will suit you.

Snapshot: setting yourself up for a crazy first draft

Flip back through your notebooks, and some of the sketches and Snapshot exercises, find a story idea that you haven't developed yet, and think of a character to build it round. Focus your imagination, bring the character to the front of your mind as a character-in-action, and think about what pressure you could put them under. What world would it happen in? If you need to, do brief, free-form research for voices, images or places, but don't make proper notes: just let whatever sticks stick.

Write: crazy first draft

Put the research aside, and write a 'crazy first draft' of a story with that character in that situation of pressure. Ideally, write longhand, and as fast and close to freewriting as you can: ignore 'correctness' in spelling, research, etc. Don't worry if it goes off the rails in terms of story, and be brave with the voice and language: no one's looking, and you can check things later. You are just trying to get words down on to the page that get you to a resolution.

When you finish the first draft

Huge congratulations: if you can get to the end of a first draft you can know the story will some day be finished. It has a beginning, a middle and an end, and you've solved at least some of the problems. If you've finished the first draft of a novel, then you've done more than 90 per cent of people who want to write a novel ever manage: there *is* a novel, however flawed or provisional, sitting on your desk or your hard-drive. And now comes the real work. Yes, you rewrote things as you went, but this is a different order of revising.

The thing is, to write the first draft you have to be inside the novel, inhabiting it and experiencing it, but that, almost by definition, precludes experiencing it as a reader does: cold and fresh. And to make sure it works on the reader in the way you want it to, you need to find ways of experiencing it as a reader, and then bringing that experience to bear on the text.

 ## Key idea: why you should 'murder your darlings'

This well-known phrase isn't a puritanical insistence that anything you like in your writing must by definition be sinful, and should be expunged. 'Darlings' are the bits which your readerly instinct tells you aren't earning their place, but your writerly mind keeps finding reasons to keep. They're usually sections which cost you hard work or emotional energy, which evoke a place which is potent for you in some way, or were genuinely important in a previous draft; or they may say something you want to say or are just a really good piece of writing. Yes, they're important to you, but *not to the telling of the story* and so not to the reader.

Get that knife out.

RETROSPECTIVE PLANNING, MICRO-PLANNING AND THE 30,000 DOLDRUMS

All the different kinds of planning and imagining-on-paper, of course, don't have to be things you do *before* you start that first draft. Many writers will 'pants' for a while, then use some planning techniques to work out where to go next. A quick family tree or sketch map will help you imagine and structure the next scene more strongly. Sometimes a novel gets out of hand and it needs a new grid to rework the structure, or a timeline because everyone's ages are in a muddle.

When the words don't seem to want to come, perhaps you don't know quite enough about what story you're trying to tell: do a micro-plan of what needs to happen in the next scene. This is a brilliant way of giving *any* new scene good narrative drive, even if you're not much of a big-scale planner. It saves writing all sorts of surplus description and bland dialogue as you 'write your way in' to the heart of the scene.

If one of your characters won't behave, you have two options: follow what it seems they *would* do, and do some replanning to sort out the consequences, or go back much earlier, and do some reimagining of that character, so that by the time you and they get to this sticking point, the behaviour you need is convincing. You may not need to go back and actually rewrite: make some notes about what you've worked out happened back there, then just write onwards *as if* you'd made those changes.

One incredibly common sticking point for many writers, whether they're arch-planners or super-pantsers, is around 30,000 words. Your mind's a blank, and every possibility seems stupid and clichéd, or will scupper your plot. Is the basic premise a terrible one, or do you not have the skills to write it? It seems that most of us have enough story-fuel in the tank to get us that far, before the tank is empty and we must fill it again. Stop, take stock, do some retrospective imagining-in-paper and some research to support it. At some point, one idea or another will start to glow and light the road ahead again.

WHEN TO RESEARCH

I've left it till now to discuss where research fits in your process, because it's so important that the research serves your creative process rather than replacing it.

- **Researching before you write the first draft** gives you lots of material and gets your imagination going. It may be essential for basic facts for the plot and structure of the story, but it has risks too: it can swamp you with material and trap you into merely reproducing your research. And if you suffer from the terror of the blank page, or nerves about 'getting the history wrong', it's very easy to use research as procrastination, and never start writing at all.

- **Researching during writing the first draft** means you can get on with writing, while pinpointing exactly what material you need. But the risk is even bigger that the pages fill with Tremain's 'inert data' and, because research-as-you-go will mean the drafting goes much more slowly, you risk losing touch with the larger pace and structure of the story, or simply losing hope that you'll ever finish. And research-as-you-go is crack cocaine for procrastinators.

- **Researching after writing the first draft** has the advantage that the story has told you what *it* needs, and you're less likely to feel swamped. On the other hand, restructuring because a guess turns out to have been seriously wrong is a nightmare, and you may stumble on wonderful material too late for it to have an organic part of your story's development. It's also so easy to look at your generic, standard-issue placeholders, and decide that they will, in fact, do, and you can spare yourself the extra work to find new, fresh words and ideas. You can't.

- **Researching when you can** is often the only possibility: when you can get to the library or the places, park the children or find the expert. Don't despair if life gets in the way: just do your best to understand and overcome the drawbacks. It's no sign of failure to go back to places and books: the first visit was to get the basics, the second to fill in the gaps that the story told you needed filling. And I am a very good customer for my local independent bookshops because if I own a book then, as soon as I have time for it, it's at hand: I can pencil in the margins and read it in the bath, and I save on the library fines too.

HOW TO RESEARCH

The function of research is to fill the larder of your imagination with food and fuel for your storytelling mind. You are not a historian, and you don't have a set of necessary professional standards to live up to or be sacked, only your own creative standards and what you choose to take on of other people's. Your novel, your rules. So it's up to you a) what you research, b) how much depth you go into and c) what you take away with you. Chapter 4 explored the different sources of information, and here are some approaches which I and various friends use in dealing with them.

- **Rolling around in the material:** sitting in the places, listening to the music, looking at the art, reading the writing of the time as a reader does, reading books about the period immersively.

- **Reading round the topics:** filling your knowledge banks in an open, receptive way, to find out what's there. This is what poet Philip Gross calls 'free-search'.

- **Listening for voices:** read writing of the period (and perhaps make notes) for vocabulary, cadence, sentence structure, world view, tone, humour (or lack of it). Try writing a bit of pastiche, just to get the feel of those voices.

- **Note-making/marking up:** *if you own* the book or printout (and obviously not if you don't). But there's no point in underlining or highlighting if you don't show what it's about: make an indexing note in the margin so that later you can easily find what you need: for example 'CLOTHES: children's'; 'RELIGION: god-fearingness vs relig. ecstasy'; 'THEME/LOST CHILDREN: illegitimate, ?Stephen'.

- **Note-making for your memory:** things stick in your head only if they pass through your brain, which is why note-making in an outlining or mind-mapping form is so much more effective than word-for-word copying, copy-and-paste or highlighting, or recording a talk without transcribing it.

- **Note-making for reference:** you almost certainly only need to do this for a minority of what you read: the central details of real, important events or major real characters' lives. If you own the book, dense marginal indexing can do a lot.

- **Taking pictures:** use these to prompt your memory of a place, but don't let snapping be a substitute for absorbing the atmosphere through all your senses. Many digital cameras and phones have a 'Text' setting for clear images of books and articles, which is quicker and kinder to the book than photocopying. Check the library's rules, but it's not usually a problem.

- **Collecting material:** leaflets, postcards, posters, booklets. They're evocative, as well carrying information, while graphic design is very culturally specific. Even a language you don't really speak can offer you names, words and phrases.

Moving on to the second draft

First, you need to find ways to read your first draft 'like a reader', trying to see it anew and recording your readerly reactions: a problem-*finding* process. Record *everything* that occurs to you as you read: not just typos or small-scale changes of mind, but that vague unease that the prison scene isn't grim enough, or that realization that you were working so hard at the grim that the chapter goes on for far too long without any plot happening. Write those whispers down: you may change your mind later, but now is your best chance to recognize the saggy middle, before a competition judge does. However, reading-like-a-reader isn't easy when you know a text as well as you know this one. Some of these techniques can help:

- Put the story away for some weeks or, better still, months, and write something else to cleanse your palate.
- Print it out and read it away from your desk: maybe even in the park or a café.
- Read it aloud. This is a superbly powerful process, because in order to speak the words your brain has to understand them, and it will alert you if the grammar doesn't make sense, sentences are awkward or repetitious, voices are clunky or unconvincing, punctuation doesn't work, or there are typos. What's more, the brain processes words for reading aloud in a different place, so it's more like coming to something unknown: you're much more likely to spot things like unconvincing reactions, over- or underwriting, mixed metaphors or places where the action doesn't join up. Go on, be brave!

- A distant second best to reading aloud yourself is to get your computer to do it while you mark up a hard copy.
- Change font and page layout.
- Upload it to your e-reader (although this means it's more fiddly to make notes).

But once you've got a marked-up script, and a new to do list alongside, where do you start? So much is interwoven: how do you deal with everything without ending up fiddling and getting in a muddle? Here are some possible processes:

- Start at the beginning and go forwards. On each page, ask yourself, 'What do I need to cut? What do I need to expand? What do I need to change?' and do it.
- Tackle it chapter by chapter: ask yourself the same questions, but about the whole chapter.
- Tackle particular big issues: a chapter that really doesn't work, a character who doesn't convince as a lover, a Californian who needs to be an Acadian. Sort out that issue wherever it crops up, and then tackle the next one. Then move on to smaller or more local problems.

DON'T FIDDLE

One rule that is worth sticking to is the one my students know as *don't fiddle*. Don't keep popping back into the file, changing a word here, a word there, rereading a little bit after supper and drinks, and tinkering. It's also tempting, when one revision makes you think of other changes, to go dashing off to sort those out before you forget. Either way, you will get in a muddle, fail to see through changes you started, forget about the larger context, lose track of what you've done and lose touch with the sense of the larger structure. Even if you just correct the odd typo and fiddle with the punctuation, your eye becomes jaded, the text shop-worn: it goes dead to you, and you cease to be alive to it.

So, whenever you start work, decide what you're going to do, and do it: 'Continue battle chapter'; 'Make Sgt Rainsby Cpl Renny'; 'sort out lost-letter plot'; 'check geography of Quebec chapter'. If the work throws up something else, don't be diverted: put it on your to-do list and keep going. When *this* job is finished, save it, then close the file or start another specific job.

This is one reason for working on hard copy (or at least using Track Changes): you can mark what you *think* needs changing but then review it, because it doesn't sink back to looking perfect. You're also much more conscious of where you are in terms of the structure and pace of the thing, and which bits you've dealt with and which you haven't.

Edit: Crazy first draft towards good second draft

If you wrote longhand, type up the crazy first draft that you wrote earlier in the chapter. Print the story out, read it through with the usual process of problem-finding, and do any research that you need to. Revise the story, using the research, *and put it away*. Resist the temptation to go back to it.

Focus point: keep an eye on your process, but don't obsess

It's worth cultivating an awareness of what processes you tried, what worked, and what didn't, and ideas about why. You'll learn how your writerly self ticks, which should also help when real life, or a new project, means that you have to abandon your tried-and-trusted ways. But don't get perfectionist about it, and then despair or procrastinate when you can't do things as you like to: nothing that you might do to a story is irreversible, once you've actually written it.

Martine Bailey

'As I got close to the end of **An Appetite for Violets** I realized who the murderer had to be. I then had to go back to the beginning and tweak scenes, seed clues and misdirect the reader. This sounds easy but there were lots of headaches, highlighter pens and post-its involved!'

Snapshot: assessing your stories

Collect together all the stories that you've written so far. Read through them quickly, and 'triage' them, letting your instincts label each of them with one of the following diagnoses:

1 The story works in terms of what it's trying to be, and feels fairly nearly finished.

2 There's potency in the characters, setting, ideas or events but the story isn't working yet.

3 One day you'll know what to do with these characters, settings or ideas, but at the moment you don't.

4 You're never going to be interested in developing this story.

Key idea: grammar, syntax and spelling really matter

Grammar, spelling and syntax are the systems that we use to transmit meaning from one person to another, so anyone who wants to get their meaning across has to work with these systems. That means you can't ignore what you learned (or didn't quite learn) at school. But what you're trying to do with that system is different: not avoid Teacher's wrath or get an A, but work on the reader so they experience the story as you want them to.

So you sometimes need to go beyond 'correct' to 'right for the story'. However, just as jazz musicians have to learn the jazz scales, melodies and harmonies before they can improvise satisfyingly, you need to know the systems of your language before you can mix and flex the elements to say says something new in a way *which will communicate to the reader*.

Focus point: 'editing out the freshness'

Writers sometimes worry that if they go back over their first draft too microscopically, they'll 'edit out the freshness'. But the freshness will only fade if you lose touch with the overall voice, energy, spirit and tone of that first draft. This was your first, natural, creative response to what your imagination and sense of story served up. When something isn't doing its job as well as it could, and you think of a change, ask yourself if the new version will still be in touch with the voice and spirit of the story. If it will, then great. If it won't, then don't just give up: persevere in looking for another way of solving the problem which *doesn't* flatten out the story's individuality.

Snapshot: developing a story

Go back to the stories you triaged. Now look harder at categories 2 and 3 and decide which one will teach you most if you work on it. That isn't necessarily the one which you feel is most likely to come out well: this Snapshot is all about heroic failures, not timid successes. Then, thinking as laterally as you can, look for what isn't working yet, and think freely and widely about how you might develop the story into something that works better. Might it have what I call a *doppelgänger* story: a better story, perhaps centred on a different character, in the events and actions before, after or alongside this one?

Key idea: heroic failures will teach you more than timid successes

As a writer, you learn far more from setting out on a project that will stretch you, even if it means you struggle or fall short, than you ever will from writing something you know you can make work. That's not to say you should always deny yourself the fun of an easy game which you know you can win, only that, as all good teachers know, if a thing's worth doing, it's worth doing badly: it's a necessary step on the road to doing it well.

Write: developing a story

Look at your triaged list of stories and your ideas about how you might develop one of them. If that doesn't appeal, do the same kind of working-out for another of those seed-stories.

Put the original story away, and use those ideas as raw material for a new story. What's crucial is that you *don't use the old text*; don't even look at it. Just set out to plan and write a new story, treating the original material as no more or less useful than all the other things you might draw on from your imagination, memory and research.

WHEN YOU GET FEEDBACK

So you've revised your draft, but because you can never wholly read your work as others would read it, you need some other readers. There's more about where you might seek feedback in Chapter 11: what we're thinking about here is what to do with that feedback. I think of this as kind of triage: *Accept, Ignore, Adapt*.

- **Accept**: otherwise known as the 'Doh!' moment. The feeder-back is right. They've told you that Mississippi has four ss; they've pointed out that all the exciting stuff happens in the last third; they've told you that your main character is boringly passive ... and you know they're right. (And, yes, that last one is pretty devastating.) Now you just need to work out what to do about it.

- **Ignore**: they're wrong about what medieval peasants ate at Christmas; your novel is a thoughtful romance, whereas they mainly read action adventure. You can safely ignore that part of what they've said, with the proviso that if other people start saying it, you might have stop ignoring it and do something.

- **Adapt**: it's not a 'Doh!' moment, but you know there's something in what they say and so you must take the problem seriously.

However, they may blame their reaction on the wrong thing, and so suggest the wrong solution. You might need to tweak how that Christmas meal is written, to make sure other readers are convinced. The cure for the 'boringly passive' main character may not be that you should make them more peculiar or outlandish, but rewrite them so that their humour and thwarted energy comes over more strongly, and then put them under more and more pressure, so the reader's on tenterhooks waiting for the explosion. To cure the dull first two-thirds, you could change the plot or cut it drastically. But maybe the plot is fine: you just need to use the viewpoint of a different character who's closer to the centre of events and more active in them. Or it could be that the voice is dull, or you're not exploiting a wide-enough range of psychic distance, so the narrative is flat and homogeneous. Non-writers, particularly, don't think about voice and viewpoint, and they don't know about psychic distance, but how you handle all three makes an enormous difference to how gripped any reader is by a story.

Digesting the feedback like this may take a while, and then you need to make a plan of campaign. Again, don't just launch into the file: at best you'll get in a muddle and at worst you'll succeed in avoiding the really difficult job that involves cutting things you love. Decide on a sensible order for the work, and see each job through as fully as possible, before you move on.

Moving on to the final draft

This cycle of drafting – problem-finding, perhaps feedback, problem-solving, printing out, reading, problem-finding – can go round several times and probably will, especially when you're not yet very experienced. But there comes a point when this is as fundamentally good as it's going to get, and no amount of tweaking will change that. You've reached the moment of calling it the final draft: the one 'for your agent'; the one which you will be sending out.

And now you have to become tediously nit-picky, because sending a story out with mistakes in the presentation is like asking your readers to watch a beautiful journey through dirty windows because you couldn't be bothered to wash the car. True, many readers won't notice very minor typos, but some will, and it doesn't take many errors before no reader will be experiencing the story as vivid and convincing. And if you're sending it to professionals – agents, editors, competition judges – it matters just as much. They can all spot a typo, a mixed metaphor or a continuity error at 50 yards; if they like a story, a few typos won't make them change their mind, but a sloppily edited manuscript suggests that you don't know that these things matter, or that you *do* know but can't be bothered to correct them, or that you don't have the good manners to respect the industry's professionalism.

Publishers spend time and money on several separate editing stages because they *know* it makes a difference to the reader's experience. Both MegaBooks Publishing and The MiniBook Press will do the following with a novel:

- the **structural edit** is about the big issues of storytelling, characterization and voice
- the **line edit** makes sure that all those things are embodied in the best individual words possible
- the **copy-edit** checks continuity, consistency, punctuation, spellings, factual details and foreign words, and marks up the script for the typesetter
- **proofread 1** does what no machine can do and **proofread 2** does it again.

The serious writer takes a similar, professional attitude, although final-draft work is like a mix of line edit and copy-edit: checking for mis- and inconsistent spellings and continuity errors, picking up inaccurate grammar and syntax, polishing punctuation, checking that things like dialogue are punctuated and formatted correctly, spotting pronoun trouble, and noticing repeated and missing words and so on. Reading aloud is hugely valuable at this stage.

Because in some ways the writer is the least likely person to spot some kinds of errors and inconsistencies, if you're thinking of self-publishing, you should seriously consider paying a professional for, say, a combined line- and copy-edit, even if you've done free beta-reading swaps up to now. Your friendly retired English teacher may be very cheap or even do it for fun, but professional copy-editing is a very specific skill and process.

If you're dyslexic or for some other reason find it very difficult to spot slips, then you may need to focus extra hard on getting help for this stage, and reciprocate in other ways. After all, *any* thoughtful readerly feedback is valuable for a writer, even if spelling isn't your great strength.

Focus point: spell- and grammar-checkers

Don't rely on the wonders of modern software to do the work for you. True, spellcheckers are very handy for the first-pass picking up of errors, but they're not enough. They don't know which you meant of homophones like *stationery* or *stationary*, *discrete* or *discreet*, or *born, borne, bourne* or *bawn*. Nor will they spot when you've written *Hell* when you meant *He'll*.

Automated grammar-checkers, on the other hand, are completely useless for creative writers, and will probably do your writing more harm than good. They're calibrated for business English, not creative writing, and work crudely even at that level. In the short term, use writer friends as beta-readers. In the long-term, you need to develop *your* sense of how language works. Read thoughtfully, and get hold of decent reference books based on UK or US English, as appropriate. Don't only look things up when someone tells you you've made a mistake, but also whenever you're puzzled, interested or realize you don't understand something: that way you will develop a wider, more accurate and less inhibited capacity to use the language.

Workshop: think like an editor

Take one of the stories that you edited in an earlier chapter: preferably one from a long time ago. Print it out and take a pen. Work through it in several passes, as a publisher's editor does:

Structure: Is this the strongest story that you can make from the material (characters, setting, themes) of this project, or might it have a *doppelgänger* story? Does the story start and finish in the right place? Are the proportions right, so nothing that matters is skimped, and nothing takes up more space than it deserves? Did you make the right decisions about narrator (who, where, etc.), overall voice, narrative tense, point of view and tone? Are each character's actions and reactions convincing and well proportioned relative to what triggers them?

Paragraph by paragraph: How do those structural decisions play out in each paragraph?

Psychic distance: Were the moves closer in and further out at the right moments in the story, and to the right distances? Would a wider range bring more dynamism to the story? Are you Telling where you should be Showing, or vice-versa?

Point of view: Is it consistent, and have you handled any moves well, so the reader stays with you? If it seems awkward, should you smooth it out, or find another way to convey what you were showing us through that viewpoint? Or is it telling you that your original decision about point of view needs rethinking?

Voice: Is the voice consistent and engaging? Anything too modern, or too clunkily olde-worlde? Do the characters' voices all sound different, and right for each personality? Where you've used free indirect style and reported speech, does the character's voice come through clearly, even though it's in the narrative?

Research: are there any places where more reality and detail would make things more vivid, individual and convincing? Are there places where your research data is still in inert lumps on the page? How could you compost it down? Have you mistakenly assumed that what you know of one historical period (including how our own twenty-first century works) is true of the period of your story, or all periods?

Sentences: Are there any facts which need checking? Is it crystal clear who says each line of dialogue and have you paragraphed and punctuated it properly? Is there any dubious grammar, syntax which doesn't make sense, or punctuation which doesn't conform to convention or doesn't express what you want it to express? Check for mixed metaphors, dangling modifiers, and places where you've used a verb or image metaphorically and it clashes with the actual physical facts of the moment. Did you change the name or word for anything, and miss an example?

> **Presentation:** Is it properly presented on the page: double-spaced in Times New Roman, with generous margins, indented first lines for each paragraph, no extra space between paragraphs unless you intend a clear break, and page numbers, headers and footers all present and correct?

STOPPING

In the end, you have to stop. If all you want to do is put the manuscript under the bed or park it on your e-reader, that's fine. However, most writers want their work to be heard and understood. But that desire cuts both ways. Some writers chronically send work out too early. Even when you've learned that writing *The End* is only the beginning, the longing to be heard can drown out the niggling little voice that's still trying to get your attention about that clunky sentence on page four, or the flat chapter which you keep telling yourself is necessary backstory. You press 'Send' half-knowing that you shouldn't.

At the other end of the scale is the writer who wants to have their writing read, but in practice never sends it out at all. They just keep on fiddling and polishing, sometimes for years, to put off the moment when it will be judged and weighed or simply ignored or rejected.

It can be genuinely difficult, especially with novels, to decide when a piece is ready to go, but it helps to be honest with yourself. If your tendency is to jump the gun, then it's worth learning to listen to those niggling voices. If your tendency is to hold fire too long, then polish it to the full, remind yourself that a typo or a slightly saggy sentence is not going to make any difference to its fate, that *you* are not being judged, only the story is, and click 'Send'.

Whenever you send it, however convinced you are that you have found every single flaw, I can guarantee that in a novel-length project there will be four trivial typos, one hilarious typo, and one awful continuity slip that you won't spot until someone else points it out. And it's horribly easy to send a short story out with the title misspelled. But that's just how life is.

Edit: final draft

Revise the story you've just workshopped to incorporate everything that you found in the Workshop 'Think like an editor'. When you would swear that it was perfect, read it aloud as a proof reading exercise, then resist the temptation to fiddle more, and resist the temptation to send it out. Call it finished, and put it away.

Next step

We've explored the processes involved in your story's development, from first imaginings to final polishes. We'll now think about where you might find help and support for you and your writing, and what you might do with the finished stories.

11

What next?: going further, getting published

Once you've learned something about how to write, and got a story as perfect as you can, what do you do next? There are all sorts of places where you might find formal and informal support to develop your writing. Then come the opportunities and challenges of getting your work out into the world, and the possibilities for and misconceptions about writing for a living.

Going further

This book can only be a start. Hemingway said that the way to become a writer was to write a million words; to gain experience you have to write a lot, and learn from what you do. It *is* possible to become a good writer with only a library card and a pile of paper and pens, but you will almost certainly learn faster and better if you seek out informal or formal ways of learning with and from other writers – from bits of one-to-one feedback on an open online forum, to an MA seminar room full of students and well-known lecturer-authors.

When you're thinking about joining a group or a course, think about what aspects of your writing need the most work, and which the group might supply:

- **Learning to read your own work 'like a reader'.** This is best practised by reading others' writing, observing its effect on you, trying to understand why and how it's doing that, and trying to articulate that understanding. So critiquing and giving feedback on other writing is central to improving your own. Earning other writers' feedback on yours is a secondary reason for doing it.

- **Getting feedback from others on your writing.** This is the other side of the same coin: it shows you directly how others experience your work, and that can be salutary, though of course you need to triage the responses into *accept, ignore, adapt* (see Chapter 10).

- **Learning craft and technique,** from finding and developing ideas, to working with viewpoint and psychic distance. This is another way in which you can learn as much from others' efforts on their work as you can from your own, because their work sets them writerly problems which haven't cropped up in yours.

- **Finding support:** writing can be so frustrating, even baffling, and it's easy to feel that you 'ought' to give up and do something more rewarding or lucrative. Never underestimate how much it helps to have someone else around who thinks that it's genuinely worth it, and knows that an 'encouraging rejection' is worth celebrating.

Nicola Morgan

Award-winning writer and past chair of the Society of Authors in Scotland. From *Write to Be Published*:

'You will sometimes find conflicting advice for aspiring writers... Publishing and writing depend to a great extent on individual passions and personal responses to books. Disillusioned writers who have turned to self-publishing vent their disillusion and often misunderstand the reasons why publishers rejected them. Published authors often have a narrow field of knowledge – their own experience – and may wrongly extrapolate generalizations. Some rules apply in the US and not the UK or elsewhere; some practices change over time; situations differ between genres and age-range. Where advice is based on expert opinion, those opinions can differ from each other. Well-meaning experts try to offer concrete answers to the specific questions you ask, when the real answer is usually: "It depends on your book."

'Generally, it's best to avoid taking too much notice of advice from people who have done nothing to prove that they know anything relevant ... Ask yourself how the person knows what she claims to know; whether her experience is up to date and specific to you.'

FINDING INFORMAL WORKSHOPPING

In the right set-up for you, the quality and style of critiquing suits you, you feel safe but stimulated, and the structure and organization (or lack of it) fit your writing habits.

- **A writing buddy or critique partner:** if you have someone who's on your wavelength as a 'beta-reader', then this can be a wonderful long-term relationship.
- **A non-writing super-reader:** one of my sisters doesn't write but is one of my best and most perceptive readers, and I'm not alone in having a super-reader.

- **A writers' circle:** a group which meets regularly to give and receive feedback and provide mutual support. It should feel like a safe space offering respect for everyone's work and personality, while giving honest, detailed and intelligent feedback, not just back-patting.
- **An online writers' circle:** you can use a private group on sites like Facebook to post work as well as chat, or just circulate things by email and mark up with Track Changes.
- **A writing website:** there are plenty of excellent sites, some small and private, some huge and open to all. They can be a goldmine of advice, experience and expertise and can enlarge your readerly and writerly horizons hugely. They're also a good place to find writing buddies and critique partners, and for forming smaller, more intimate groups. But, like all social media, they can equally well (and sometimes simultaneously) be a snake-pit of cliques, flame wars and trolling. That's particularly true of the sites which are competitive, with the prize of, say, having your work read by a publisher's editor: the competition seems to bring out the worst in people, and on the whole if your work's that good then there are better ways of getting it read.

So don't be afraid to walk away from a feedback set-up if you feel that it's not right. Friends or family who want to help can be hard to resist, but they may not be the right readers; there are lots of things to say about a story which are true but don't help the writer; there are phases in your work on a long project where you don't want feedback; your needs may change as your writing develops; and your first duty *is always to your own work*.

Snapshot: find informal help

Go online, drop into your public library, bookshop or arts centre, go to the website of the National Association of Writers' Groups (nawg.co.uk), or hunt down the literature development officer of your local council. You're looking for writers' circles, groups and forums. Try to get a feeling for the different ways these things run: what sort of writers the members are, whether they're focused on (semi-)formal critiques and feedback, or support and writerly discussion. Is there a good fit between how serious you are and the tone of the group? Are there enough members who understand your genre? If people sound very expert, are they justified in their confidence? Is the feedback too bland or too abrasive? Are there rules about how much feedback you must give, in order to get it? Do the bigger sites have smaller groups inside them, to provide a safe space for critiquing? When things get heated, do they simmer down fairly quickly, with all parties trying to mend fences, or does the atmosphere stay sour? Are the moderators too heavy-handed or not firm enough?

It may well take a few tries to find somewhere where you feel really at home, so don't just assume that you're just not a group person. The right group can make all the difference between you stagnating or giving up and you persevering and improving.

WRITING MAGAZINES

Magazines which carry short stories, and occasionally novel extracts, are mostly clustered at the opposite ends of the market: the literary end and the very commercial end. Such magazines are an excellent way to get to know a wider range of good and successful writing, even if you tend to write more towards the middle ground. Even if you're not yourself writing at the super-literary end of things, it's worth exploring the literary magazines, to widen your experience of the art and craft; even if you're not writing women's magazine stories, it's worth looking at how the writers find new and fresh angles on the perennial issues in women's lives, without frightening the horses. Libraries stock them and, as ever, you need to read like a writer, noticing the effect of the story and thinking about how the writer has achieved it, and why the editor decided publishing it would sell copies.

There are also magazines *about* writing which are worth investigating: well-known ones include *Mslexia* and *Writers' News*. These often run their own competitions as well as articles about craft, inspiration and technique, and interviews with writers and sometimes editors. Many have good listings of events, courses, competitions and calls for submission, and carry advertisements for courses, editorial services, self-publishing service companies and even jobs.

COURSES, CLASSES AND CONFERENCES

When you get to the point of spending serious money on your writing, again, put your writing needs first. Don't necessarily assume that a big-name author as a tutor is a good thing: look at their track record. Online teaching suits creative writing, and there are many excellent courses. Try to get a sense of whether the class is mostly about writing prompts and a bit of gentle feedback or something more structured and progressive. If a course is far too simple, far too advanced, or the tutor is incapable of controlling a seminar bully, don't keep going just because you've paid; it's not worth the damage to your confidence and motivation.

- **A regular class,** say at a further education college or arts centre, is great for support and development, but may result in 'writing by committee' if you keep on workshopping the same project.

- **A one-off short course,** most of all a residential one such as Arvon, can be brilliant for immersing yourself in writing, making friends and kick-starting your confidence or your new project, but you do then have to go home and find the same motivation on your own.

- **An examined course** leading to a qualification or degree should be comprehensive and teach you a lot. It can be easier to justify the time and money you spend on a 'proper' qualification like this, but there's still no guarantee of publication. Check how much you'll be able to work on your own project – MAs, in particular, vary a lot – but don't scorn or avoid the poetry or creative non-fiction modules of a course: they can be hugely enriching for your fiction by opening you to all sorts of different techniques and mindsets.

- **Writers' conferences.** Again, the immersion and the contact with authors and the industry can be very energizing, and the workshops, panels and socializing may be very valuable; you can usually book short one-to-one feedback sessions with agents and publishers, although it's a mistake to pin all your hopes on those contacts: useful contacts are as likely to happen in the bar or over lunch.

Key idea: if you find yourself resisting advice

Any feedback on your work, whoever gives it, is only good if it helps your writing to be better or, if that matters to you, to sell better. Bring your *accept, ignore, adapt* scanner to it, hold it up to your experience of your own work and see if it fits, and only then set to work.

On the other hand, humans often resist the thing they need most. Defensive horror every time a certain suggestion comes up may be a clue that it's exactly what you and your writing need: that a natural planner and researcher should relax and learn to fly blind through a first draft; that a natural writer of Victoriana should tackle the harder work of thinking into an ancient Greek mind. Your may feel daunted and your first effort may not be altogether successful, but you will have learned an enormous amount.

MENTORING AND APPRAISALS

Direct, substantial feedback on your work from a professional (sometimes called an editorial consultant) doesn't come cheap, but it can make a huge difference to both your current project and your writing in general. Both writers and editors coming from publishing offer this kind of service and may well say very similar things, but there is a difference. Ex-editors can be very good at assessing product: knowing the market and telling you what yours needs to become saleable. A writer – especially one who also teaches – will probably be better at processes which will help the novel work better.

A one-off appraisal, written or in person, of a full novel or a shorter piece is not a full edit of the sort a publisher will do, but it can be immensely useful to have a coherent, written overview which highlights strengths and weaknesses and gives you a sense of where your work stands, relative to what publishers are looking for and the actual chances of a publisher buying yours.

Mentoring is usually shaped as a series of reasonably regular meetings which will be a mixture of feedback on your work and looking ahead to how the specific piece and your writing in general, might develop. There may well be a life-coaching aspect to the latter, and some mentors will deal less with the specifics of your stories and more with confidence and goal-setting; it's worth making sure you and the mentor are both expecting the same sort of interaction.

Both appraisals and mentoring are available through editorial agencies (not to be confused with literary agencies, which sell books to publishers) or directly with individual writers/editors. Individuals are likely to be cheaper but you need to look at their track record closely, and ask around on forums for personal recommendations: there are some wonderful writer-editors out there, but it's a lot of money to spend. An agency should be trying to match you with a suitable editor, and be willing to sort out problems if they arise, but it will be more expensive and you probably won't get to choose your editor.

The agencies also have links with literary agents, and make much of how they will forward really promising work. This is a great chance, of course, but only a tiny, tiny minority of manuscripts are anywhere near that standard, so don't let the possibility override your judgement about other things. And you *must* check whether you'll be expected to pay anything for this service, either up front or by way of a percentage of any deal.

But, in the end, all any professional can do is show you what work to do: you then have to do it. If you are expecting someone to write your book for you, then that's called ghosting.

Focus point: getting professional appraisals

Anyone can set up as an editorial consultant, and the less reputable in the business may not be entirely honest about how likely it is that you can get your work to the point of being publishable, let alone published. Before you pay a professional to appraise your work, make sure you find out what you can of the following:

- **What experience do they have in helping writers?** Is their background in writing, editing or teaching? What experience do they have in the relevant part of the publishing industry?

If it's an agency, will your appraisal be done by a writer or an editor? Can you see any samples of their reports?

- **Does what they offer suit you?** But don't be **too** narrow about what you're looking for: good, experienced appraisers may know more than you do about the best way to approach it.
- **How much will it cost?** What form will the appraisal and feedback take? Do they offer a choice of forms of feedback? How long will they take? Will you have the opportunity to email questions about what they've said, so that you can make the most of the appraisal?
- **Do they offer links to agents and publishers?** How often do they in fact see a manuscript of that kind of standard? Is there a cost to the writer, or other limitation, and what is it?

COMPETITIONS

In the short fiction world, competitions are a very usual way to get your writing read and sometimes published, and a win or shortlisting on your writerly CV shows that someone other than your mother thinks you can write. It's worth trying to read some previous prizewinners to get an idea of the standard and style, and sometimes you can pay a little extra for a mini-appraisal of your own entry, which can be a useful insight. There are some scam prizes around: use the checklist in the Focus Point below, or ask around on writer's forums for advice.

Competitions for novels are thinner on the ground, and less likely to offer publication as a prize, though they may, but, again, being shortlisted is definitely good for the CV. You will usually only submit a short section: shortlistees may later be asked to send in the full novel, so do make sure it's ready, or very nearly ready.

Focus point: choosing competitions to enter

It can be difficult deciding if a competition is legitimate, let alone worth entering. If you like the look of one, Google the name of the competition and something like 'scam', and see what you get. Try to find the answers to some of these questions:

- **What does it cost to enter,** as a proportion of the value of the prizes? Does that seem reasonable? Must you commit to going to the prize-giving or risk forfeiting your prize?

- **If publication is part of the prize, what does that mean?** What will be published, and in what form? What rights do you grant them for publication or publicity? It is almost never a good idea to give up your copyright, so make sure you retain that. Will you be given a copy, or does it look as if the sole idea is to sell copies to entrants?

- **Who is judging it?** Are there some genuine writers in there? Even writers you've heard of?

- **Who is sponsoring it?** Is the competition well established? Is the organization a charity or an educational body, or perhaps a genuine small publisher with Arts Council funding? If they're a commercial organization, look harder, and ask around the writer's forums.

HISTORICAL ASSOCIATIONS

- The **Historical Novel Society** (historicalnovelsociety.org) has been going for many years on both sides of the Atlantic and in Australia; its membership is a mix of writers and readers, and the website is a goldmine of articles and reviews. The HNS sponsors high-profile novel and short writing competitions, and the HNS Conferences alternate between the UK, the US and now Australia, and attract excellent speakers and workshops.

- The **Historical Writers' Association** (thehwa.co.uk) is made up of professional authors of historical fiction and non-fiction. The HWA's e-zine *Historia* has articles by big-name writers, and regular contributors (including my own 'Dr Darwin's Writing Tips' column). Anyone can join their online forum, which is very useful for advice and chat about research and writing.

- **Re-enactment societies** can be invaluable for research: there are societies for many periods, from ancient Greece to the Second World War. They take pride in the accuracy of their clothes, weapons and battle techniques, but also their cooking pots, footwear, tents, camp followers and so on.

- **Local history societies** often have members who are deeply knowledgeable, and may be fascinated (if occasionally disapproving!) to have a fiction writer in their midst. Some have websites and newsletters which are also sources of information even if you don't live locally.

- **Special interest societies**: some are more enthusiastic and partisan than expert, but they usually have blogs and websites stuffed with images, information and links to further sources, and are delighted that you might be interested in, say, historical postal services, side-saddle riding, vintage airline timetables, costume, Richard III, Rudyard Kipling, railway tickets, knitting, telephone kiosks, or ancient Egyptian food.

- **Heritage organizations** such as English Heritage, Historic Scotland, CADW in Wales and the National Trust often have events which go deeper into their properties and landscapes, while the gift shops often have useful books about the texture of ordinary life which you might not find elsewhere.

- **Learned societies**: the Royal Historical Society, the Historical Association and the Institute of Historical Research, and their equivalents in other countries, are all hubs for professional historical research and teaching. They run events – often podcast – and publish journals and books which give access to the newest research.

Snapshot: finding special interest societies

Think about what historical topics it would help if you knew more about for your current or future projects. Make a list of, say, three such topics. Go online and see what you can find: spend long enough on each site to get a feel for whether it's just peddling the same hand-me-down information as elsewhere, or is genuinely useful and well researched. Don't forget to save any good links: I make a folder for each project's bookmarks.

Getting published

SHORT FICTION

Magazines which take stories divide roughly into three areas: print magazines for the weekly women's magazine ('womag') fiction market, magazines which take literary short stories, and online e-zines which, between them, cover the whole range. You may also come across small publishers asking for submissions for anthologies, often themed. Do your research: every magazine inhabits its own niche, so read sample copies to get a clear sense of the readership and what kind of stories the editor is looking for, and follow their submission guidelines precisely.

Some magazines ask that you don't send anything which you've also sent elsewhere, because it's a problem for an editor if they decide to take on a piece only to find that it's already been published elsewhere. But it causes writers huge problems to have a story tied up for months before you get a response, so you may choose to ignore that rule: just think hard about what you would do in the various possible combinations of acceptance and rejection.

Whether something is accepted by an editor is very chancy and personal, so don't take a rejection as a condemnation of you and your writing, or even a sign that the story is no good. Instead, get back on that horse, rework the story for a different magazine or competition, and send it out again. I have just sold a story I wrote ten years ago, which I've tweaked six times for different competitions and magazines: tweak number seven has worked.

The womag market actually pays, but the competition is fierce and what they're wanting is very specific. In the UK, literary magazines are run on a shoestring and passion and they will pay nothing or a token, although all magazines should send you a copy if they print your story. In the US, the short-fiction market is much better developed, although still very competitive. If you're looking for publication credits, the only e-zines which count are the ones where there is clear editorial policy and stringent sifting, not those where writers upload their own work, or a story is posted every day.

Write: going public

Set yourself the task of finding a print or an online magazine, or a writing competition, that you would like to submit to. Do ensure it has a process of editorial sifting, and don't be afraid to aim high. Your research will need to cover the following:

- What sort of stories the magazine is looking for: genre, theme, subjects, and anything else they say about likes and dislikes
- Their submission requirements *in detail*: not just the lower and upper word limits, but how to format the work, how to submit, whether to enter by post or online, and so on
- Any deadlines, any rules about simultaneous submissions, what the entry fee is for a competition and whether it seems reasonable for the prize on offer.

Look back at the stories you've worked on through this book. Might any of them be suitable? Could you adapt one? Or would you rather write a new one from scratch?

Write or revise a story to fit *exactly* the guidelines of your chosen competition or magazine. If you decide actually to submit it, good luck!

NOVELS

It's no secret that it's very, very difficult to sell a novel to a publisher, which doesn't stop everyone trying. The market has narrowed in recent years for a whole complex of reasons, and publishers are taking even fewer risks on new writers and surprising books. However, historical fiction is having a golden period, and the publishers know it, so we should all thank Hilary Mantel for *Wolf Hall* at one end of the market and the likes of Ben Kane at the other.

A note on novellas: until recently it was a commonplace that they were impossible to sell, and that's still largely true of mainstream publishers large and small, although a few small literary publishers may look at them. However, the rise of the e-book, where it's less obvious how thick a book is, seems to have created a modest interest in novellas and 'pocket novels', which genre- and self-publishers are best placed to exploit.

Most big publishers no longer take submissions from writers direct and unsolicited, but only from literary agents who represent writers, so your first step is to get an agent to take your novel on. That in itself is very competitive (an agent may well receive 40 or 50 unsolicited manuscripts a week, besides all their own authors' work, and only take on a couple of new authors a year), though your odds of being published are fairly high once you have an agent's help. Nicola Morgan's e-book *Dear Agent* is excellent on approaching agents and editors, and the *Writers' & Artists' Yearbook* lists agents to try: it, too, has good basic advice about submissions, and the publishers' and agencies' websites will set out their individual submission guidelines. Follow them, send your work off, and get on with your next project.

Note that no reputable agency asks for a reading fee or an editing fee, or rejects your book with the suggestion that you should spend money on their editorial service. Real agents make their money when they sell your book and not before; they then deal with everything from selling the book and negotiating contracts, to careers advice, selling TV and film options, knowing what the publisher *should* be doing for your book, and being the one to kick up a fuss if they aren't.

Many smaller and independent publishers can be approached directly, but if you intend to approach an agent at any stage it's better to do so at the beginning, as an agent won't be keen to take your book on if you've already exhausted some of the possible places he or she might send the book to. If you're approaching a publisher whose books you've never seen on a bookshop shelf, be careful, since there are plenty of scam and vanity publishers about, as well as hopeful one-man-bands who self-published themselves and have decided to widen their net. You should also approach e-book-only contracts with huge caution, though in very commercial genre publishing there are some perfectly respectable e-only publishers.

If you are offered a deal, the rule is that *money flows to the author*. If you are asked for money, then they are not a publisher. A publisher should offer you an 'advance against royalties': a chunk of money up front which represents your share of the money they expect the book to make. Agents earn commission on the money that comes through from their negotiating your contracts; publishers earn by selling your book. Very small publishers may not offer an advance, although you should look *very* carefully at any deal which doesn't.

If you have been offered a publishing or agency contract, you're eligible to join the Society of Authors (societyofauthors.org) as an Associate Member: their contract-checking service will advise on the contract in detail, and they are the nearest thing that writers have to a trade union. Whether or not you're a member, they have essential information, guides to contracts and all sorts of other advice available to download from their website.

Snapshot: the book market

If you possibly can, go to a good bookshop or your library. Pick up three novels which are clearly appealing to very different readers: say, a literary historical drama, a Cold War thriller and a regency romance. Look at the design of the covers, the blurb (or cover copy) on the back (online blurbs are much longer and so less good for this exercise), and the puffs or quotes on the front if there are any. Look for more examples of each kind, to get a sense of the constants within the genre. How does each genre draw in the right kind of reader, i.e. the reader who is looking for this kind of book? How does it promise them that this is, nonetheless, new, fresh and worth buying?

Harry Bingham

Henry Bingham writes novels and non-fiction, and founded the editorial agency The Writer's Workshop. From *Getting Published*:

'There can be money in writing, but for most people, most of the time, there isn't very much. Authorial careers tend to be short and precarious. There's no sick pay. No health coverage. No unemployment benefit. No pensions. Which, when you think about it, is liberating. You didn't start out writing your book to make money or pay the mortgage or buy that yacht you'd always dreamed of. You started it because of a passion to write, to communicate, to spin dreams and inform others.

'Good. You need to hold on to those motivations, as they're the only ones which can reliably sustain you ... All authors need to find a meeting point between what they want to write, and what the market will buy. You can't neglect the latter, because if you

do you'll remain unpublished. But you mustn't even think of giving up on the former, because that will void your writing of the one purpose that you can entirely rely on: your own passion, the very thing that brought you to writing in the first place.'

SELF-PUBLISHING

Self-publishing no longer means paying for a print run of thousands of books, and then finding somewhere to keep them while you drive round the country persuading shops to take them. Self-publishing a book, in the sense of writing one, pressing a few buttons and having it appear on Amazon, and a few more buttons and having it appear on other e-book platforms, is easy and costs very little. It doesn't cost much more to use one of the print-on-demand companies, such as Lulu, to produce physical books which you only pay for one at a time.

However, the vast, vast majority of self-published books sell to the writer's friends and friends-of-friends, and virtually no one else. Of course, that may be what you want: selling a few copies online from a modest website or through the online distributors such as Smashwords and Amazon; perhaps selling some physical books through your local café, craft market or stately home gift shop. Your local paper may even run a piece, if you can think of an angle which will catch their interest.

But if you want to go beyond that small constituency of readers, it's a completely different game. The difficulty isn't producing the book, it's getting anyone to know it's there and then persuading them to buy it. Publishing companies have had four centuries of learning how to do that, and even they don't get it right quite a lot of the time. The reality is that the self-pub world is filled with several million e-books which are doing well if they sell a few hundred copies, when a publisher would expect to sell 10,000 of a similar title. Nor do self-publishers have access to major markets such as the supermarkets and chain bookshops, or reviews, editorial coverage and literary prizes, and most bookshops won't stock self-published books. You must rely almost entirely on social media, devoting a huge amount of time to self-promotion, sweet-talking review blogs, tweeting, publicity, and manipulating sales rankings with pricing and special offers.

Mark Coker

From the foreword to *The Naked Author: a guide to self-publishing,* by Alison Baverstock. Mark Coker is the founder of the e-publishing platform *smashwords.com.*

'As the power of publishing shifts to you, the writer, so too does the responsibility. The best publishers honor their readers by publishing books worth reading. If you decide to self-publish you must honor your readers by assuming personal responsibility for the same professional publishing duties performed by the best publishers. You're responsible for hiring professionals (or bartering with fellow authors) to help you edit, revise and proof your manuscript. You're responsible for producing a professional quality book cover. You're responsible for book production, marketing and distribution.

'Most self-publishing authors discover effective publishing is much harder than it looks.'

However, if you love writing and want to run a small business, self-publishing is easier to start than most, and Mark Coker is explaining why a self-publisher must learn to think like a publisher. You will need to think like a publisher in other ways too: to produce a steady stream of books which you can sell to a consistent market which you understand and can reach. A couple of novels a year, with a novella in between to keep your name visible, is not uncommon, and you need to be businesslike in paying, as publishers do, for several stages of editorial help, cover design and typography, publicity, marketing, digital formatting for different devices, printing, sales and distribution. *Get Started In Self-publishing*, by Kevin McCann and Tom Green, will also guide you through the necessities.

VANITY AND 'SUBSIDY' PUBLISHING

Paying a good self-publishing service to help you with those aspects of publishing which you don't do yourself is a perfectly good business decision. Real self-publishing services are direct and honest about what things cost and what you will get for your money. Real publishers risk their own money and earn it back by selling lots of your books.

But there are plenty of companies out there who wear the mask of publisher or self-publishing service, and are actually good, old-fashioned vanity publishers, 'subsidy' publishers or outright scams. You can spot a vanity publisher because they will be very plausible in presenting a cleverly distorted picture of how the industry works and quoting satisfied authors. They will explain how wonderfully helpful they are and promise a high royalty rate. If you submit they will probably praise your work to the skies, but they won't offer you an advance, and the contract will be decidedly disadvantageous in all sorts of other ways. They will ask for money, either up front as fees for editing or production, or by you guaranteeing to buy lots of copies, and their production standards will probably be very low.

It can be incredibly painful to realize that the contract you've been offered is actually for a vanity deal but, if you want to spend money on getting your work out there, you're much better off self-publishing: you'll spend less, and keep control. If in doubt, ask the Society of Authors, or google the name of the publisher plus 'scam', and see what you get: the forums at absolutewrite.com and the listings at Preditors and Editors (pred-ed.com) are also good places to check.

 ## Key idea: money flows towards the author

No real publisher or literary agent ever asks you for money for any reason, or compels you to buy copies. If an agent, a publisher or a magazine editor asks for a fee for reading your work or for payment to publish it, or suggests that you should use their editing service, or puts into the contract that you will buy copies of your book, then they are a scam.

Honest self-publishing service companies and editorial agencies don't pretend to be anything other than they are.

Writing as a career

If you're beginning to think that you'd like to write for a living, then I won't say 'Don't' – it's what I do myself – but it's important to understand what you're hoping for. It was never easy to earn a living as a writer – George Gissing's famous novel about just how difficult it is, *New Grub Street*, was published in 1891 – and the big earners and famous names (by no means the same thing) are the exception, not the rule. However, the industry has changed out of all recognition in the last decade, and authors have been among those disadvantaged.

The big-figure advances which create headlines are fewer and farther between than ever: a typical advance for a first novel from a big publisher is perhaps £2,000–7,000, paid in up to four instalments (on signature of contract, on delivery of the manuscript, on hardback or e-book publication, on paperback publication). Many small publishers pay no advance at all. According to the Authors' Licensing and Collecting Society, the median income for professional writers (those spending the majority of their time writing) in 2013 was £11,000 a year. The number of professional writers who get all their income from writing is 11.5 per cent.

Because it's always easier to sell a human a kind of thing that they already know they like, you are at a disadvantage relative to writers who have already found their readers. Many authors who are thought of as established now struggle to get contracts, or have had to change radically what they write. Some events pay their authors a token fee, but many don't even when the audience has paid for tickets. Mainstream publishers should pay your travel expenses, but small publishers may honestly not be able to afford it. Far, far too often, event organizers expect you to do an event for free, and you need to be realistic about whether what they offer in 'exposure' or 'the publicity' (a line in the local paper?) and 'book sales' (10 or 15 copies?) makes economic sense, particularly if you're one of the many authors who don't enjoy doing events.

Essentially, if you want to make your living from writing, there are various possibilities:

- **Making all your living from writing novels** means winning contracts that will ask for a steady book a year which the publisher knows they can sell to the same, large and consistent group of readers. You will need to work hard to develop your brand, and the advances won't be huge but each new book will boost the sales of earlier ones. Add in Public Lending Right from library loans, and it's possible to make a modest if variable living. But if readers change what they will buy and you don't change with them, you may find no publisher will offer you a contract.

- **Making some of your living from writing novels,** and the rest from freelance writing-related work: journalism, teaching, mentoring, or professional editing and writing such as ghosting. You're not quite so dependent on consistently selling to that large market, and you may have a little more flexibility and creative freedom. Virtually all literary writers work this way because their sales and writing speed rarely provide enough income: those starry literary names who teach in universities and review do it because they need the money. And it's still possible to find that everything changes, and you must change too, or give up.

- **Keeping the day job,** or a different freelance career, and writing novels and short fiction in the evenings and at weekends. This can work very well, though it's difficult to manage if you have a third commitment such as a family. Certainly, if you want real creative freedom it's probably the only option – although you still can't entirely ignore what readers want to read, if you want them to read *your* books.

- **Self-publishing your work** makes less difference than you'd think to those basic categories. You may make more money per copy but, as I said earlier, you will in fact be running a small business that has to work to the brute realities of the market just as much as a commercial publisher does. Self-publishing literary fiction in any significant way is almost impossible, since by definition it resists running in the 'known quantity' channel that readers watch.

 ## Focus point: 'hybrid' authors

'Hybrid' authors write for both contracts with publishers and self-publishing, but it's important to look at how those authors first got their 'platform'. An established author, who is a victim of how much the market has narrowed and is now self-publishing their out-of-print backlist and maybe new titles too, is in a very different situation from a new, unknown name who is starting from nothing. Alternatively, the new author may self-publish one or more books, working hard to establish a following on a scale that will interest a mainstream publisher into offering a contract for a new book.

Where will you go next?

So, where will you go next? I hope that by now the dream and practicality of writing historical fiction feels more possible and more exciting; that you've tried new things and got new ideas for the future; that you have more tools in your writerly toolkit and some idea of how and when to use them.

Perhaps this book has slaked your desire to write historical fiction: most writers have at some time liked the idea of a certain form or genre, explored it and decided that, ultimately, it's not where they want to spend their time and energy. That's just as good an outcome, as far as I'm concerned: what matters is that your creative self finds its own best work, and that along the way you learn things worth learning.

Whether your next step is to enter a story about Frederick Douglass in a major competition, research a novel about an imaginary lost tribe of Celts in ancient Galicia (the Spanish or the East European one), or – possibly the bravest step of all – join a small forum and for the first time ever let someone else read your writing, I wish you all the very best of writerly luck!

Key idea: The Society of Authors

The Society of Authors has been the nearest thing that professional writers have to a trade union since 1884. It provides us with detailed legal and professional advice, campaigns for writers' rights at all levels of government and media, acts as the spokesperson for our concerns and interests, administers grants, prizes and literary estates, and arranges seminars and training courses for members. When you realize that the annual subscription represents less than 15 minutes of a specialist lawyer's time, it's easy to see why most authors are members.

There is lots of excellent advice about working as a writer available to everyone on the Society's website, from which you can also download various fact-sheets about everything from contracts and copyright permissions to school visits and literary estates. Anyone who has had a book or several short pieces published, or has sold significant numbers of a self-published book, is eligible to join; writers may apply to be Associate Members if they nearly qualify in this way, for example because they have been offered a contract for representation by an agent, or are self-publishing on a smaller scale.

Appendices

I. TEN REFERENCE BOOKS FOR WRITERS OF HISTORICAL (AND OTHER) FICTION

Books specifically mentioned in the text are listed in the Bibliography.

A Handbook of Dates: for students of British history, revised edition, edited by C. R. Cheney and revised by Michael Jones. Cambridge University Press, 2000. A comprehensive reference for regnal years, Old and New Style calendars, saints' days, etc.

Medieval Underpants and Other Blunders: a writer's (and editor's) guide to keeping historical fiction free of common anachronisms, errors and myths, third edition, by Susanne Alleyn. Spyderwort Press, 2013. Does just what it says on the tin. Also funny.

Brewer's Dictionary of Phrase and Fable, 19th edition, by Ebenezer Cobham Brewer. Chambers, 2013. Endlessly useful for odd historical information: the meanings of sayings and myths, saints' attributes, canonical hours, quarter days (different in Scotland!), the seasons for different game, and so on.

A Dictionary of First Names, 2nd edition, edited by Patrick Hanks, Kate Hardcastle and Flavia Hodges. Oxford University Press, 2006. Covers current and historical names from around the world, their meanings, variations, associations and short and pet forms.

The Penguin Dictionary of British Surnames, by John Titford, Penguin, 2009. Covers the meaning, geographical origin and variations.

The Oxford Companion to Family and Local History, 2nd edition, edited by David Hay. Oxford University Press, 2008. Full of advice and information. The Oxford Companions are usually a good start for research into any topic.

The Penguin Atlas of World History, vols 1 & 2, by Hermann Kinder and Werner Hilgeman. Penguin, 2004. A handy size and lots of maps, as well as a clear chronology of events. Specific atlases for different eras and continents are also available.

Fowler's Dictionary of Modern English Usage, 4th edition, edited by Jeremy Butterfield. Oxford University Press, 2015. The classic guide to usage, including changes over time, and international variations.

Dress and Undress: a history of women's underwear by Elizabeth Ewing. Batsford, 1989. Underwear, along with children's clothes and poor people's clothes, is the hardest costume to find out about, but this book is also standing in for all the reference books for clothes, food, weapons, transport, etc., that I don't have space to list.

A good thesaurus (not the very feeble, free online sites) should help you recall not-familiar, estranging words and other historical vocabulary, but do double-check with a big dictionary that you're using it accurately and idiomatically.

II. TEN BOOKS ABOUT WRITING WORTH READING

Books specifically mentioned in the text are listed in the Bibliography.

Reading Like a Writer: a guide for people who love books and those who want to write them by Francine Prose. Union Books, 2012. The best guide to the sort of close reading which is the foundation of good writing.

The Art of Fiction by David Lodge. Penguin, 1994. Delightful exploration (it started life as a newspaper column) of the techniques that great writers use to tell their story.

Becoming a Writer by Dorothea Brande. Jeremy T. Tarcher, 1981. The classic guide to finding the confidence and energy to write, and then keeping going and growing as a writer.

Zen in the Art of Writing by Ray Bradbury. Non Basic Stock Line, 1994. Fascinating essays on the art and craft by the author of *Fahrenheit 451* and other masterpieces.

Creative Writing: a workbook with readings by Linda Anderson and Derek Neale. Routledge, 2015. The most complete creative writing course you can buy. Highly recommended.

Writing Short Stories by Ailsa Cox. Routledge, 2005. Excellent, thorough guide to the form.

The Joy of Writing Sex by Elizabeth Benedict. Souvenir Press, 2002. *The* book on this notoriously tricky aspect of writing, which many writers find daunting and few other books cover.

Rediscovering Grammar by David Crystal. Longman, 2004. The best guide to how grammar actually works, so you can work with it. The companion volume, *Making Sense of Grammar*, explores the subtleties of usage.

New Hart's Rules: The Oxford Style Guide, 2nd edition. Oxford University Press, 2014. The copy-editor's bible: everything you ever wanted to know about apostrophes, capitalization, abbreviations, etc. The *Penguin Guide to Punctuation* is also good.

Creating a Life Worth Living: a practical course in career design for aspiring writers, artists, filmmakers, musicians and others by Carol Lloyd. HarperCollins, 2007. The best guide to building a career in creative work while staying solvent, happy and reasonably sane.

III. THE PLOTTING GRID

A plotting grid like the one shown below can help you think about the structure of your novel before you start, or bring order to a chaotic first draft. The rows are chapters. The wide, left-hand column 'Onstage' is essential: you need to be able to read what actually happens in the novel straight down.

I've suggested headings for the other columns, but what would be most useful to you? Clues found/clues understood; letters written/ letters read and by whom; standalone elements such as dreams, epigraphs, or real historical newspaper reports? I like to keep track of the word count, mostly just to encourage me, but also to see whether the proportions of the storytelling feel right.

If you have **more than one important viewpoint character**, you could use an initial to show who is the centre of which scene. **If you have a parallel narrative** where the two stories *never* come together, you may want to be able to see each one straight down, so you could have two 'Onstage' and 'Offstage' columns.

Don't feel that you must fill in every square immediately, and if you're working on paper, do it all in pencil. A lot of the point is that you can put in whatever you know at that moment without losing track of what still needs deciding, and then gradually fill things in as you work them out. If you're rebuilding a novel, just fill in what you know you want to keep, and use that to help you work out what the new stuff should be, and where it should go.

An interesting alternative was suggested by a friend rebuilding a 'character-led' novel: she used a wide left-hand column to set out the plot of external, physical obstacles and changes in how characters acted, and a wide right-hand column for the journey of internal, psychological conflicts and growth. Then, in a central column, she started to work out which of the existing scenes might fit, and where she needed to write more or different scenes.

You can download a customizable Excel file for this grid at \This Itch of Writing': emmadarwin.typepad.com/thisitchofwriting/2010/05/help-yourself.html

Act/Part	Chap. & Word count	Day/Date	Onstage	Important offstage	Offstage/ backstory revealed
One	1				
	2				
	3				
	4				
	5				
Two	6				
	7				
	8				

Docs in text	Docs read	Theme(s)	Hist. events	Weather	Misc.

IV. CLUSTERING EXAMPLE

In this example of using clustering as a way of developing an idea, 'Gold' was the starting word. As you can see, some words came up on more than one leg, which is always interesting.

Red Sea — Moses — burning bush — Kate Bush — Kathy — Heathcliff — Laurence Olivier

hot summer — ice cream — Ben & Jerry — Tom & Jerry — Popeye — Olive

cold winter

"once more unto the breach"

go forth

Forth bridge

webbed feet

fen men — sheep — exams — punt

Cambridge

rust

acid

corrode

remould

foretold

"faith, hope & charity & Mathematics

"charity suffereth

"cold as charity — cold — fold — bold — embold

"the greatest of these

GOLD — coins — cash — change — money

hope

bust — City — bank

Hope on an orange

sharp

suit — point

Prince of Orange

bathing suit

pointy hat

Glorious Revolution

French Revolution

witch

best of times

pattern

Hallowe'en

worst of times

knitting

apple bobbing

far better thing

dressing up

Guillotine

— trick or treat

knitting

cold

"a cold coming we had of it

240

V. CONTACTS AND ORGANIZATIONS

National Association of Writers' Groups
c/o 65 Riverside Mead
Peterborough PE2 8JN
www.nawg.co.uk
info@nawg.co.uk

Arvon Foundation
Free Word Centre
60 Farringdon Road
London EC1R 3GA020 7324 2554
national@arvon.org
www.arvon.org
Arvon have three residential centres: Lumb Bank, Totleigh Barton, and The Hurst.

Tŷ Newydd, National Writers' Centre of Wales
Tŷ Newydd, Llanystumdwy
Criccieth
Gwynedd LL52 0LW
01766 522 811
tynewydd@literaturewales.org
www.literaturewales.org/ty-newydd

Moniack Mhor, Scotland's Creative Writing Centre
Moniack Mhor, Teavarran
Kiltarlity, Beauly
Inverness-shire IV4 7HT
info@moniackmhor.org.uk
www.moniackmhor.org.uk

Historical Novel Society
www.historicalnovelsociety.org

Historical Writers' Association
www.thehwa.co.uk

Historia **magazine**
www.historiamag.com

Historical fiction blogs and review websites
www.historicalnovelsociety.org/reviews/
www.historicalfictiononline.com

www.historicalnovels.info
www.thehwa.co.uk/forum/
readingthepast.blogspot.co.uk
the-history-girls.blogspot.co.uk
englishhistoryauthors.blogspot.co.uk

The National Archive
Kew, Richmond
Surrey TW9 4DU
020 8876 3444
www.nationalarchives.gov.uk

Archives Hub
ISC, J Floor
Sackville St Building, Sackville St
Manchester M1 3BB
archiveshub@mimas.ac.uk
www.archiveshub.ac.uk
*(Note that Archives Hub cannot answer questions about the archives
described on the hub, as they do not hold the material; you should
use the link on that archive's entry to contact it directly.)*

The British Library
96 Euston Road
London NW1 2DB
0330 333 1144
Customer-Services@bl.uk
www.bl.uk

The Institute of Historical Research
University of London
Senate House, Malet St
London WC1E 7HU
020 7862 8740
ihr.reception@sas.ac.uk
www.history.ac.uk

History Today
2nd Floor, 9 Staple Inn
London WC1V 7QH
020 3219 7413/14
admin@historytoday.com
www.historytoday.com

The Paris Review
544 West 27th Street
New York, NY 10001
www.theparisreview.org

The Society of Authors
84 Drayton Gardens
London SW10 9SB
020 7373 6642
info@societyofauthors.org
www.societyofauthors.org

National Association of Writers in Education
PO Box 1, Sheriff Hutton
York YO60 7YU
Enquiries: p.johnston@nawe.co.uk
For the Writer's Compass e-bulletin: w.brown@nawe.co.uk
www.nawe.co.uk

Arts Council England
There are five regional offices: London, North, Midlands, South
East, South West
For general enquiries contact: 0161 934 4317 or 0845 300 6200
www.artscouncil.org.uk

Arts Council of Wales
Bute Place
Cardiff CF10 5AL
029 2044 13000
0845 8374 900
information@artscouncilofwales.org.uk
www.artswales.org.uk

Creative Scotland
Waverley Gate
2–3 Waterloo Place
Edinburgh EH1 3EG
0845 603 6000
enquiries@creativescotland.com
www.creativescotland.com

Arts Council of Northern Ireland
MacNeice House
77 Malone Road
Belfast BT9 6AQ
028 9038 5200
info@artscouncil-ni.org
www.artscouncil-ni.org

The Writers' Workshop
The Studio, Sheep St
Charlbury OX7 3RR
0345 459 9560
info@writersworkshop.co.uk
www.writersworkshop.co.uk

The Literary Consultancy
Free Word Centre
60 Farringdon Rd
London EC1R 3G
020 7324 2563
info@literaryconsultancy.co.uk
www.literaryconsultancy.co.uk

Literature and Latte (for Scrivener software)
enquiries@literatureandlatte.com
www.literatureandlatte.com

VI. BIBLIOGRAPHY

Fiction

Ackroyd, Peter, *Hawskmoor*, Abacus, 1985

—— *The House of Doctor Dee*, Hamish Hamilton, 1985

—— *The Plato Papers*, Chatto & Windus, 1999

Aiken, Joan, *The Wolves of Willoughby Chase* and series, Yearling Book, 1962

Atwood, Margaret, *Alias Grace*, Virago, 1996

Austen, Jane, *Northanger Abbey*, Penguin, 2012

Bailey, Martine, *An Appetite for Violets*, Hodder & Stoughton, 2014

Baker, Jo, *Longbourn*, Black Swan, 2013

Barnes, Julian, *Arthur and George*, Jonathan Cape, 2005

Brontë, Charlotte, *Jane Eyre*, Penguin, 2006

Buckley-Archer, *Gideon the Cutpurse*, Simon & Schuster, 2006, and series

Burgess, Anthony, *A Dead Man in Deptford*, Hutchinson, 1993

Byatt, A. S., *Possession*, Chatto & Windus, 1990

—— *Morpho Eugenia* in *Angels and Insects*, Chatto & Windus, 1992

—— *The Conjugial Angel* in *Angels and Insects*, Chatto & Windus, 1992

Carey, Peter, *Parrot & Olivier in America*, Faber, 2010

Carter, Angela, *Nights at the Circus,* Chatto & Windus, 1984

—— *Wise Children*, Chatto & Windus, 1991

Chekhov, Anton, *Letters of Anton Chekhov to His Family and Friends*, trans. Constance Garnett, Project Gutenberg Ebook #6408, 2004

Chekhov, Anton, *The Seagull*, Project Gutenberg Ebook #1754, 2006

Clarke, Susannah, *Jonathan Strange & Mr Norrell*, Bloomsbury, 2004

Cornwell, Bernard, *Sharp's Eagle*, Collins, 1981, and series

Cunningham, Michael, *The Hours*, Fourth Estate, 1999

Darwin, Emma, *A Secret Alchemy*, Headline Review, 2006

—— *The Mathematics of Love*, Headline Review, 2009

de Bernières, Louis, *Captain Corelli's Mandolin*, Secker & Warburg, 1994

de Laclos, Choderlos, *Les Liaisons dangereuses,* trans. Helen Constantine, Penguin, 2007

de Lampedusa, Giuseppe Tomasi, *The Leopard*, trans. David Gilmour, Collins, 1960

deWitt, Patrick, *The Sisters Brothers*, Granta Books, 2011

Dostoevsky, Fyodor, *Crime and Punishment*, trans. Oliver Ready, Penguin, 2014

du Maurier, Daphne, *My Cousin Rachel*, Victor Gollancz, 1951

Duffy, Stella, *The Purple Shroud*, Virago, 2012

—— *Theodora, Actress, Empress, Whore,* Virago, 2010

Dunmore, Helen, *The Siege*, Viking, 2001

Dunne, Suzannah, *The May Bride*, Little, Brown, 2014

Dunnett, Dorothy, *The Game of Kings*, Cassell, 1961, and *Lymond* series

Eco, Umberto, *The Name of the Rose*, trans. William Weaver, Harvest, 1983

Edugyan, Esi, *Half Blood Blues*, Thomas Allen Publishers, 2011

Ellis, Bret Easton, *American Psycho*, Vintage Books, 1991

Faber, Michel, *The Apple*, Canongate, 2006

—— *The Crimson Petal and the White*, Canongate, 2002

Faulkner, William, *Absalom, Absalom!*, Chatto & Windus, 1936

—— *As I Lay Dying*, Chatto & Windus, 1935

Faulks, Sebastian, *Birdsong*, Hutchinson, 1993

Fitzgerald, Penelope, *The Blue Flower*, Flamingo, 1995

Forester, C. S., *The Happy Return*, Michael Joseph, 1937, and Hornblower series

Forster, Margaret, *Lady's Maid*, Chatto & Windus, 1990

Fowles, John, *A Maggot*, Jonathan Cape, 1985

—— *The French Lieutenant's Woman*, Jonathan Cape, 1969

Fox, Essie, *The Somnambulist*, Orion, 2011

Fraser, George MacDonald, *Flashman*, Barrie & Jenkins, 1969, and series

Frazier, Charles, *Cold Mountain*, Atlantic Monthly Press, 1997

Fremantle, Elizabeth, *Sisters of Treason*, Michael Joseph, 2014

George, Margaret, *The Autobiography of Henry VIII*, Macmillan, 1986

Gibson, William and Sterling, Bruce, *The Difference Engine*, VGSF, 1991

Gissing, George, *New Grub Street*, Penguin, 2012

Golding, William, *Rites of Passage*, Faber, 1980, and *To the Ends of the Earth* series

Harris, Robert, *Fatherland*, Arrow, 1993

—— *Pompeii*, Hutchinson, 2003

Heyer, Georgette, *The Grand Sophy*, Pan Books, 1960

Hill, Tobias, *The Love of Stones*, Faber, 2001

Hodgson, Antonia, *The Devil in the Marshalsea*, Hodder & Stoughton, 2014

Holt, Tom, *Alexander at the World's End*, Abacus, 1999

—— *The Walled Orchard*, Macmillan, 1990

Homer, *The Odyssey*, Penguin, 2009

Hugo, Victor, *Les Misérables*, trans. Norman Denny, Penguin, 2012

Ishiguro, Kazuo, *When We Were Orphans*, Faber, 2000

Kaye, M. M., *The Far Pavilions*, Allen Lane, 1978

Keneally, Thomas, *Schindler's Ark*, Hodder & Stoughton, 1982

Kingsnorth, Paul, *The Wake*, Unbound, 2014

Levy, Andrea, *The Long Song*, Headline Review, 2011

MacGregor, Neil, *A History of the World in 100 Objects*, Penguin, 2012

Mantel, Hilary, *A Place of Greater Safety*, Penguin, 1993

—— *Wolf Hall*, Fourth Estate, 2009

—— *Bring Up the Bodies*, Fourth Estate, 2012

McCann, Maria, *As Meat Loves Salt*, Flamingo, 2001

Melville, Herman, *Moby Dick*, Penguin, 2012

Meredith, Christopher, *Griffri*, Seren, 1991

Miller, Andrew, *Casanova*, Sceptre, 1998

—— *Pure*, Sceptre, 2011

Mitchell, David, *Cloud Atlas*, Sceptre, 2004

Morris, R. N., *A Gentle Axe*, Faber, 2007, and series

Morrison, Toni, *Beloved*, Vintage, 1999

Mukherjee, Neel, *The Lives of Others*, Chatto & Windus, 2014

Norman, Marc, and Stoppard, Tom, *Shakespeare in Love: a screenplay*, Hyperion, 1999

Nye, Robert, *The Voyage of the Destiny*, Hamilton, 1982

O'Brian, Patrick, *Master and Commander*, HarperCollins, 1969, and series

O'Connor, Joseph, *Ghost Light*, Vintage, 2011

O'Hagan, Andrew, *The Life and Opinions of Maf the Dog, and of His Friend Marilyn Monroe*, Faber, 2011

O'Reilly, Sally, *Dark Aemilia*, Myriad, 2014

Paton Walsh, Jill, *Knowledge of Angels*, Green Bay, 1994

Pears, Iain, *An Instance of the Fingerpost*, Jonathan Cape, 1997

Phillips, Marie, *The Table of the Less Valued Knights*, Jonathan Cape, 2014

Piercy, Marge, *Gone to Soldiers*, Michael Joseph, 1987

Poe, Edgar Allen, *Collected Tales and Poems*, Wordsworth Editions, 2004,

Renault, Mary, *Fire from Heaven*, Longman, 1970

——*The Persian Boy*, Longman, 1972

Robinson, Marilynne, *Gilead*, Virago, 2004

Rubenhold, Hallie, *Mistress of My Fate*, Doubleday, 2011

Samson, C. J., *Dissolution*, Macmillan, 2003, and series

Scott, M. C., *The Emperor's Spy*, Transworld, 2012

Shakespeare, William, *Hamlet*, Penguin, 2015

—— *Macbeth*, Penguin, 2015

Sheridan, Sara, *Brighton Belle*, Polygon, 2012

Smith, Ali, *How To Be Both*, Penguin, 2015

Smith, Dodie, *I Capture the Castle*, introduction by Valerie Grove, Vintage, 2004

Sontag, Susan, *The Volcano Lover*, Jonathan Cape, 1992

Sterne, Laurence, *Tristram Shandy*, Penguin, 2012

Synge, J. M., *The Playboy of the Western World and Other Plays*, Oxford World's Classics, 2008

Taylor, Andrew, *The Anatomy of Ghosts*, Michael Joseph, 2010

Thynne, Jane, *Black Roses*, Simon & Schuster, 2013, and series

Tóibín, Colm, *The Master*, Picador, 2004

Tolkien, J. R. R., *Lord of the Rings*, George Allen & Unwin, 1954

Tremain, Rose, 'Death of an Advocate' in *The Darkness of Wallis Simpson*, Chatto & Windus, 2005

—— 'The Crossing of Herald Montjoy', in *Evangelista's Fan*, Sinclair-Stevenson, 1994

—— *Restoration*, Hamish Hamilton, 1989

—— *Music and Silence*, Chatto & Windus, 1999

Twain, Mark, *A Connecticut Yankee in King Arthur's Court*, Penguin, 2007

Unsworth, Barry, *Morality Play*, Chivers, 1996

—— *Stone Virgin*, Hamish Hamilton, 1985

Waters, Sarah, *Fingersmith*, Virago, 2002

Young, Robyn, *The Kingdom* series, Hodder & Stoughton, 2010

Yourcenar, Margaret, *Memoirs of Hadrian: and Reflections on the Composition of* Memoirs of Hadrian, trans. Grace Frick, Penguin, 2000

Non-fiction

See also Appendix I: Ten reference books for writers of historical (and other) fiction, and Appendix II: Ten books about writing worth reading.

Aristotle, *Poetics*, Penguin, 1996

Atwood, Margaret, 'In Search of *Alias Grace*', University of Ottawa Press, 1997

Auden, W. H., quoted in *John Cornford: a memoir*, Cape, 1938

Baig, Barbara, *How to Be a Writer: building your creative skills through practice and play*, Writer's Digest Books, 2011

Beauvais, Clémentine, *Complete Writing for Children*, John Murray Learning, 2014

Bingham, Harry, *The WAAYB Guide to Getting Published*, A & C Black, 2010

Byatt, A. S., *On Histories and Stories*, Chatto & Windus, 2000

Cameron, Julia, *The Artist's Way: a spiritual path to higher creativity*, Penguin 1992

Coker, Mark, 'Introduction', in Alison Baverstock, *The Naked Author: a guide to self-publishing*, A & C Black, 2011

de Groot, Jerome, *The Historical Novel*, Routledge, 2010

Eco, Umberto, *Reflections on* The Name of the Rose, trans. William Feaver, Secker & Warburg, 1983

Faber, Michel, 'Introduction', in *All The King's Horses and Other Stories*, Fish Publishing, 2006

Gardiner, Juliet, *Wartime Britain, 1939–1945*, Headline Review, 2004

Gardner, John, *The Art of Fiction: notes on craft for young writers*, Vintage, 2001

Lamott, Ann, *Bird by Bird: instructions on writing and life*, Anchor, 1980

McCann, Kevin and Green, Tom, *Get Started in Self-Publishing*, Teach Yourself, 2013

Morgan, Nicola, *Dear Agent*, Crabbit Publishing, 2013

——*Write to Be Published*, Snowbooks Ltd, 2011

Pascal, Blaise, *Pensées*, trans. as *The Thoughts of Blaise Pascal*, C. Kegan Paul, Project Gutenberg Ebook #46921 2014

Schama, Simon, *Citizens*, Penguin, 1989

Stanton, Andrew, 'Story Telling Is Joke Telling', TED, https://www.youtube.com/watch?v=YtB97uAoR0c, 5 May 2014

The Paston Letters, ed. Norman Davis, Oxford Paperbacks, 2008

The Writers' & Artists' Yearbook 2016, A & C Black, 2015

Tremain, Rose, 'The First Mystery' in *The Agony and the Ego*, Penguin, 1993

Twain, Mark, *How to Tell a Story and Other Essays*, Project Gutenberg Ebook #3250, 2006

Weir, Alison, *Eleanor of Aquitaine*, Jonathan Cape, 1999

Yorke, John, *Into the Woods*, Penguin Books, 2013

Index

Ackroyd, Peter, 71
agents, 220, 226
anachronisms, 76–7
appraisals, 219–21
archives, 62–3
Aristotle, 18
Atwood, Margaret, 55–6, 70–1
Auden, W. H., 40
Austen, Jane, 28

Baig, Barbara, 192–3
Bailey, Martine, 102, 202
Barnes, Julian, 86
Bingham, Harry, 227–8
Burgess, Anthony, 82
Byatt, A. S., 81, 155–6

Cameron, Christian, 61
career in writing, 227–8, 230–2
Carter, Angela, 82
characters, 18–19
    in action, 19–20, 23, 32–3
    development, 26–7
    fictional, 70–1
    immediacy, 7
    journey of change, 102–4
    minor, 20–1
    obstacles, 24–5
    perspectives, 163–4
    readers' interest in, 22–3
    real people, 27–30, 71–2, 74–6
    stakes, 104
    thought processes, 92–4
    viewpoint, 30–6, 129–31
    voices, 89–92
    wants and needs, 21–2
Chekhov, Anton, 135, 146
children's fiction, 182
Clarke, Susannah, 81, 82
clustering, 42–3

Coker, Mark, 229
commercial historical fiction, 177–8, 184–5
competitions, 221–2
conferences, 218
Cornwell, Bernard, 171
counterfactual historical fiction, 180–1
courses in writing, 218

description, 19, 23, 134–7
dialogue, free indirect style, 94–5
documents
    fictional, 160–2
    real, 158–60
drafting, 8–9, 14–15, 46, 193–5, 200–2, 206–7
dual narratives, 154–6

e-books, 228
Eco, Umberto, 172
editing, 196–7, 201–2, 204, 208–10
Edugyan, Esi, 83, 91, 117
Ellis, Bret Easton, 23
endings, 118
experience, senses, 3–4

Fabbri, Robert, 71
Faber, Michel, 150
fantasy fiction, 181–2
Faulkner, William, 153
feedback, 205–6, 215–16, 219–21
fictional elements, 70–1
final draft, 206–7
first drafts, 8–9, 14–15, 46, 193–5
flash fiction, 147–8
form, 146–64, 169
Frazier, Charles, 81, 154–5
free indirect style, 92–5
freewriting, 41–2

Gardner, John, 137–9
genealogical records, 65–6
genre, 168–70
   adventure and thriller, 170–1
   comedy, 174
   crime and mystery, 171–2
   drama and psychological thriller,
     174–5
   mixed, 183–5
   romance, 173
George, Margaret, 108
Golding, William, 158
Google Books, 64
Green, Hilary, 36
Groot, Jerome de, 170

Harris, Robert, 92
historical associations, 222–3
hybrid authors, 232

imagination, 40–8
imagining-on-paper, 191–3
information, conveying, 14
Ishiguro, Kazuo, 54

Keneally, Thomas, 70
Kingsnorth, Paul, 85

Laclos, Choderlos de, 160–1
Lamott, Ann, 8–9
language
   contemporary, 76–7
   grammar and spelling, 203
   historical authenticity, 85–8,
     91
   setting in the past, 9–10
   unfamiliar, 87–8
learning writing skills, 214, 217–19
length of the story, 146–52
letters, 161
libraries, 62–3
literary historical fiction, 176–9,
   184–5

magazines, 217, 224
Mantel, Hilary, 81, 141
mentoring, 219–20
Meredith, Christopher, 85–6
Mitchell, David, 82–3
Morgan, Nicola, 215
Morrison, Toni, 70
motivation to write, 4–5
museums, 63–4
mystery and suspense, 109–10 *see also*
   genre

narrative drive, 108–13
narratives, non-linear, 152–8
narrators
   external, 81–2, 127–31
   free indirect style, 92–5
   internal, 82–3, 124–7
   second person, 84
   viewpoints *see* viewpoints
   voice, 80–5 *see also* voice
non-linear narratives, 152–8
Novalis, 55
novellas, 150, 225
novels, 151–2
   submitting for publication, 225–7

objects, 11
obstacles, 110–12
O'Connor, Joseph, 84, 153
O'Neill, Joseph, 91
online research, 64–5
opening lines, 81–3, 117–18
O'Reilly, Sally, 82

parallel narratives, 155–6
Pascal, Blaise, 182, 191
Pears, Iain, 82
periodicals, 65
perspectives, 163–4 *see also* viewpoints
planning, 188–92
plot, 103–4 *see also* story
point of view *see* viewpoints

process, 188–92
  drafting, 8–9, 14–15, 46, 193–5, 200–2, 206–7
  editing, 196–7, 201–2, 204, 208–10
  research *see* research
Project Gutenberg, 64
prologues, 154
proofreading, 207–8
psychic distance, 137–43
publishers, 207, 225–7
  vanity, 229–30

quasi-historical fiction, 179–82

Rance, Caroline, 91
reported speech, 94–5
reported thought, 92–4
research, 11–12, 67–8, 198–200
  believability, 76–7
  daily life in history, 54–6
  historical facts, 46–7
  knowing when to stop, 69
  online, 64–5
  places to go, 62–6
  reading other historical fiction, 9–10
  sources of information, 56–61
  time for, 73
  treatment of material, 49–50
  for voice, 95–7

Samson, C. J., 172
Scott, M. C., 20, 81, 117
self-publishing, 207, 228–9
sequels, 151–2
setting, 6–7, 44
  location, 68
Shakespeare, William, 143
Sheridan, Sara, 2, 158, 175
short stories, 147–50
  planning, 190–1
  submitting for publication, 224–5
showing and telling, 134–7
Society of Authors, 233–4

sources
  primary, 57–9, 62–6
  secondary, 59–66
Stanton, Andrew, 117
steampunk, 180
story
  characters, 102–4
  historical authenticity, 104–6
  narrative drive, 108–13
  start and finish, 106–8
structure
  five-act, 113–16, 119
  three-act, 112–13
submitting your story, 206–7, 224–7
support, 215–17
suspense and mystery, 109–10 *see also* genre
Swift, Deborah, 13, 50, 116, 155

Taylor, Andrew, 172
tense, 126–7, 131–3
themes, 66–7, 68
Tremain, Rose, 49, 66
trilogies, 151–2
Twain, Mark, 124

vanity publishing, 229–30
verbs, character description, 19, 23
viewpoints, 30–6
  multiple, 128–9, 130–1
  psychic distance, 137–43
  which character to choose, 129–30
  see also perspectives
voice, 80–5
  characters, 89–92
  in documents, 162
  historical authenticity, 85–7, 91, 98
  level of description, 136
  researching for, 95–7

Weir, Alison, 56
Yorke, John, 103, 112
Young, Robyn, 189